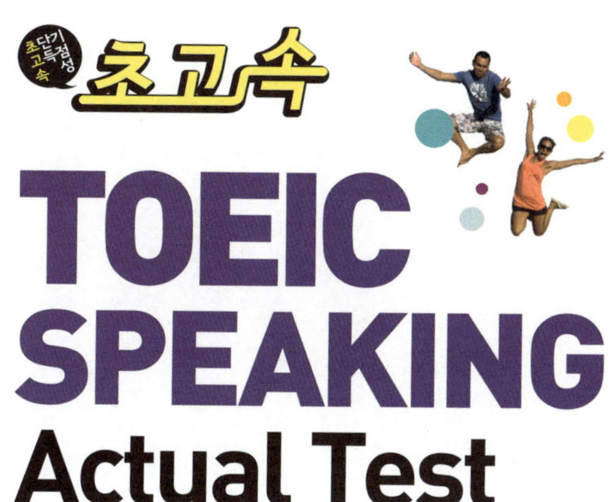

초고속 TOEIC SPEAKING
Actual Test

TOEIC SPEAKING Actual Test

초판 인쇄일 | 2013년 2월 15일
초판 발행일 | 2013년 2월 22일
지은이 | 홍성하, Bob Hildreth
발행인 | 박정모
발행처 | 도서출판
주소 | 서울시 동대문구 장안1동 420-3호
전화 | 02)2212-1227
팩스 | 02)2247-1227
홈페이지 | http://www.hyejiwon.co.kr

편집진행 | 김형진, 이희경
본문디자인 | 이미소
표지디자인 | 이미소
영업마케팅 | 김남권, 황대일, 서지영
ISBN | 978-89-8379-774-2
정가 | 15,800원

초고속

TOEIC SPEAKING
Actual Test

| 홍성하 · Bob Hildreth 공저 |

헤지건

현장에서 학생들과 호흡하면서, 그들의 꿈 이야기를 들으면서 이 후배들의 시행착오를 줄여줄 수 있는 영어 교재를 만들고 싶다는 생각이 점점 커져갔습니다. 영어 실력 향상을 위한 최고의 도서라고 감히 말할 수는 없지만, 지금 여러분이 토익스피킹을 준비하고 있다면, 최적의 도서가 될 수 있다고 자부합니다.

이 책에는 Level 6 혹은 7 이상을 동시에 대비할 수 있도록 수준별 답변을 2개씩 제시했고, 가장 최근 출제 유형을 반영했으며, 그 동안 학생들과 교감하면서 절감한 실전 전략들을 고스란히 담았습니다.

여러분이 조금 더 큰 꿈을 꿀 수 있도록, 혹은 지금 그 꿈을 이루는데 조금 더 속도를 낼 수 있도록 이 책이 작은 힘이 된다면 더 이상의 바람은 없을 것입니다.

집필하면서 함께 일할 때의 큰 즐거움을 안겨준 멋진 친구이자 스승인 Bob, 부족한 제게 무한한 배려와 지원을 해주신 김형진 팀장님 및 도서출판 혜지원의 모든 분들, 마지막으로, 더 멋진 사람이 되어야겠다는 다짐을 매일 하게 해주는 사랑하는 가족들, 내 인생 최고의 행운인 아내 은현이에게 고맙다는 말을 전합니다.

홍성하

I have been very blessed to be surrounded by some amazing people. My wife Catherine is a strong and steady support and the love of my life. In addition to that I have a former student and now a man I am proud to call a terrific colleague Songha Hong!

The book you are holding in your hands is a result of endless hours of encouragement and tireless commitment and effort on the part of these extraordinary people and me. These people hold a common dedication with me that YOU are the most important person because YOU are who we work for! We all get turned on and energized when we see students understanding something better than they did before they met us. It's what we live for and this book drips of that commitment on every single page.

Before a single drop of ink was spilled to create this book both Songha and I signed a paper, an agreement to ourselves and each other that the purpose of this book was YOU!

On behalf of myself and Songha I would like to invite you to start on a journey to a better future and a better life by using this book and connecting completely with the contents inside.

Bob Hildreth

나는 참 축복받은 사람입니다. 주위에 너무도 멋진 사람들이 있기 때문입니다. 내 아내인 Catherine은 강인한 사람이고, 꾸준히 날 지지해주었으며 큰 사랑을 일깨워주었습니다. 또한 예전에 내 학생이었지만 지금은 훌륭하고 자랑스러운 동료인 '성하'에게도 큰 고마움을 전합니다.

지금 여러분이 손에 들고 있는 이 책은 이렇게 훌륭한 이들과 함께 오랜 시간 서로를 격려하며 각고의 노력을 기울여 내놓은 자랑스러운 결과물입니다. 여러분이야말로 우리가 이 책을 집필한 이유이고 가장 중요한 사람이라는 마음으로 함께 헌신적으로 작업했습니다. 여러분이 이 책을 접하면서 더 나은 무언가를 얻을 수 있다면 우리는 큰 보람을 느낄 것입니다. 여러분의 성장이야말로 우리가 선생님으로 사는 이유이며, 이 책의 각 페이지마다 최선을 다해 추구했던 것입니다.

'성하'와 내가 이 책을 집필하기 위한 첫 잉크를 떨어뜨리기 전, 서로에게 그리고 자신에게 했던 약속은 바로 이 책을 집필하는 목적은 '독자'라는 것이었습니다.

여러분이 이 책을 사용하고 그 내용들을 잘 활용하면서 조금이라도 더 나은 미래와 삶으로 나아가는 여정을 시작할 수 있기를 바랍니다.

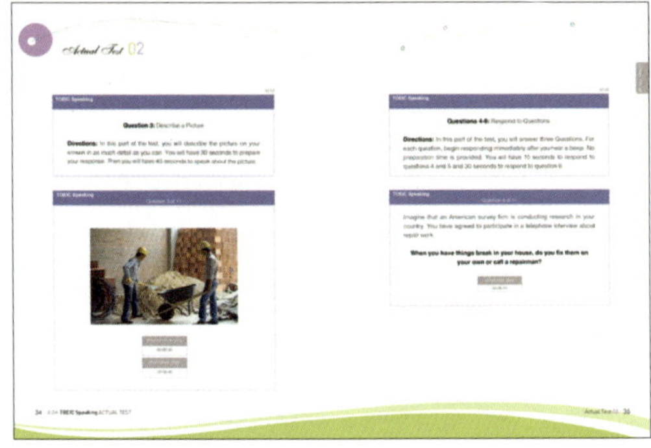

• 문제집

최신 출제경향을 반영한 기출 변형 문제 12세트를
실제 시험과 동일한 형태로 실었습니다.

• 해설집

학습자의 실력과 수준에 맞는 답안을 훈련할 수 있
도록 모든 문제에 초・중급 모범답안과 고급 모범답
안을 함께 수록했습니다. 친절한 해석, 해설, 어휘 및
저자의 노하우를 담은 고득점 TIP을 통해 TOEIC
Speaking을 더 효과적으로 실전 훈련할 수 있습니다.

• 보너스 실전 문제 3세트

3세트의 보너스 실전 문제와 초・중・고급 모범답변
을 부록 CD에 PDF 파일로 수록했습니다.

• 부록 CD

모든 문제와 답변을 원어민의 발음으로 녹음해 MP3 파일로 담았습니다. 실세 시험과
동일한 형태로 구성했기 때문에 실전 시험처럼 사용할 수 있습니다. CD에는 보너스
실전 3세트를 PDF 파일로 담았습니다.

Contents

TOEIC Speaking 시험 소개

★ TOEIC Speaking이란?

TOEIC을 개발한 비영리 시험 개발 기관인 ETS(Educational Testing Service)에서 개발하고 한국 토익 위원회가 주관하는 말하기 능력 측정 시험이다. 인터넷을 이용하여 컴퓨터로 시험을 치르며(iBT-Internet Based Test), 회사나 학교, 일상생활 관련 주제로 말하기 능력을 측정한다.

★ 시험 구성

- **문제 수**   총 6개 Part, 11개 문제로 구성되어 있다.
- **시간**   약 20분 정도 소요된다.
- **평가 방법** 1번~9번 문제는 0~3점, 10번과 11번 문제는 0~5점 범위 내에서 평가된다.
  총점은 0~200점 범위로 환산된다.

★ 접수 방법과 응시료

TOEIC Speaking Test는 인터넷 홈페이지(www.toeicspeaking.co.kr)를 통해서만 접수할 수 있다. 응시료는 77,000원(부가세 10% 포함)이며, Speaking and Writing Tests를 함께 응시하는 경우 104,500원(부가세 10% 포함)이다. 인터넷으로 접수할 때 신용카드나 실시간 계좌이체를 통해 결제 가능하며 접수가 끝나면 시험 일자, 시간 등이 정확하게 입력되었는지 확인해야 한다. 시험 당일 입실 시간을 엄수해야 하며 규정 신분증(주민등록증, 운전면허증, 여권, 공무원증)을 반드시 지참해야 한다.

★ 시험 일정과 실시 방법

TOEIC Speaking 시험은 정기시험 매주 1회, 연간 48회 실시, 1일 총 3~4회 진행된다. 그러나 상황에 따라 추가 시험이 시행되는 경우도 있다. Internet-based test(IBT) 방식으로 이루어지고 ETS 인증 센터 컴퓨터의 인터넷을 매개로 문제가 송신되며, 수험자는 기존의 TOEIC 시험과 같은 지필 방식이 아닌 컴퓨터 상에서 음성을 녹음하는 방식으로 시험을 치른다.

★ 성적 확인

성적 발표	응시일로부터 약 10일 후
성적 확인 방법	www.toeic.co.kr
성적표 수령	온라인 또는 우편
성적표 수령 소요일	온라인: 성적 확인 즉시 성적표 발급 가능 우편: 성적 발표 후 7~10일 이내 성적표 수령

Part별 개요와 고득점 TIP

★ Part 1. Read a text aloud

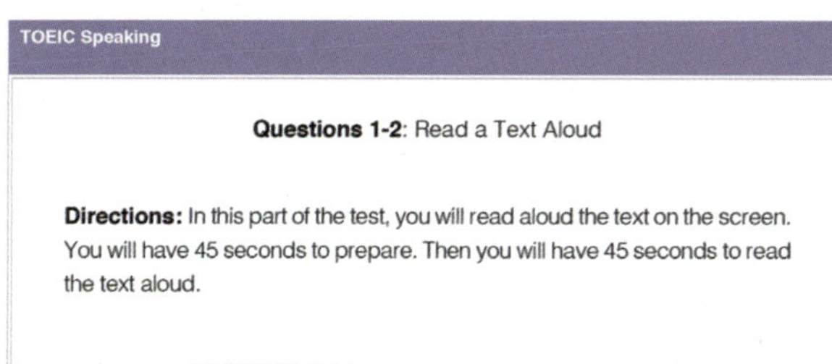

TOEIC Speaking

Questions 1-2: Read a Text Aloud

Directions: In this part of the test, you will read aloud the text on the screen. You will have 45 seconds to prepare. Then you will have 45 seconds to read the text aloud.

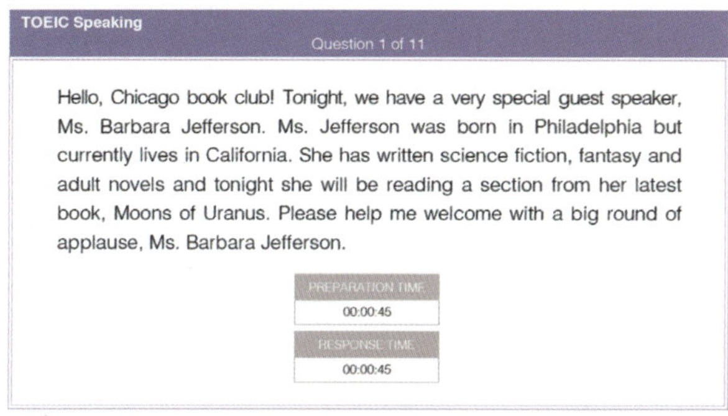

TOEIC Speaking

Question 1 of 11

Hello, Chicago book club! Tonight, we have a very special guest speaker, Ms. Barbara Jefferson. Ms. Jefferson was born in Philadelphia but currently lives in California. She has written science fiction, fantasy and adult novels and tonight she will be reading a section from her latest book, Moons of Uranus. Please help me welcome with a big round of applause, Ms. Barbara Jefferson.

PREPARATION TIME
00:00:45

RESPONSE TIME
00:00:45

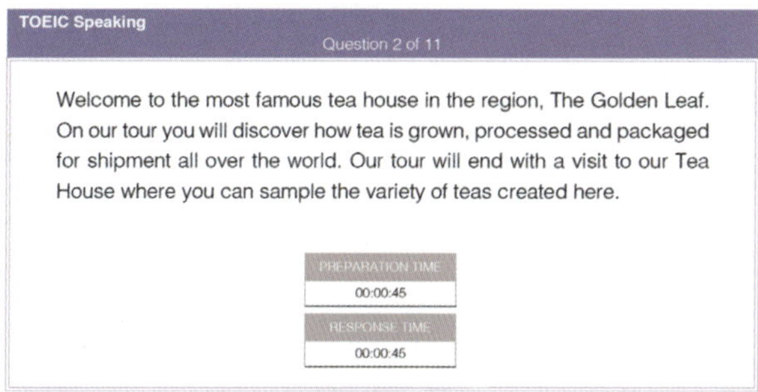

TOEIC Speaking

Question 2 of 11

Welcome to the most famous tea house in the region, The Golden Leaf. On our tour you will discover how tea is grown, processed and packaged for shipment all over the world. Our tour will end with a visit to our Tea House where you can sample the variety of teas created here.

PREPARATION TIME
00:00:45

RESPONSE TIME
00:00:45

- **출제 문항 수 |** 2개 (Q1 & Q2)
- **준비 시간 |** 45초
- **답변 시간 |** 45초
- **시험 방법 |** 지시문에 이어서 지문이 제시되면 각 지문에 대해 45초 동안 준비한 후 45초 동안 읽는다.
- **평가 방법 |** 발음, 억양, 강세

고득점 공략 TIP

⇨ 준비 시간에 최대한 많이 읽어보면서 글의 종류, 내용을 미리 파악하고 실제 상황처럼 읽는다.
⇨ 발음, 억양, 강세, 끊어 읽기 등 유의해야 할 부분을 반복해서 읽고 그 부분의 위치를 미리 파악해둔다.
⇨ 처음부터 끝까지 일정한 속도로 읽는다.
⇨ 실수로 잘못 읽었을 경우 당황하지 말고 그 부분부터 다시 읽는다.

★ Part 2. Describe a picture

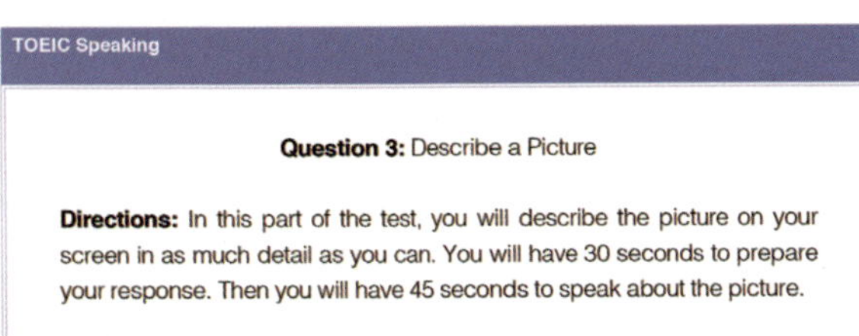

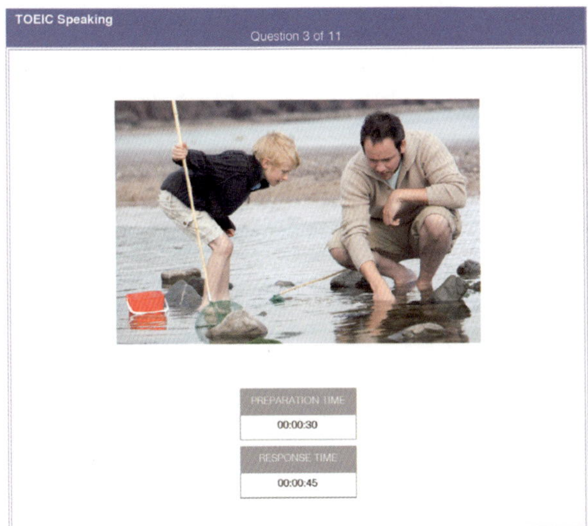

- **출제 문항 수** | 1개 (Q3)
- **준비 시간** | 30초
- **답변 시간** | 45초
- **시험 방법** | 지시문에 이어서 사진이 제시되면 30초 동안 준비한 후 45초 동안 묘사한다.
- **평가 방법** | 발음, 억양, 강세, 어휘, 문법, 연관성

고득점 공략 TIP

↪ 가장 먼저 눈에 띄는 것부터 묘사하고 세밀한 부분으로 묘사를 넓혀나간다.

↪ 사람 묘사를 위주로 하되 동작/의상/머리 순으로 중점을 둔다.

↪ 다수 사람 묘사는 전체 인물들의 공통된 부분을 먼저 말하고(동작, 의상, 성별, 나이 등) 각 인물의 특징을 간단히 묘사한다.

↪ 시제는 현재형이나 현재진행형으로 말한다.

↪ 마지막에 혹은 전체 인물들을 묘사하면서 전반적인 느낌이나 의견 등을 말한다.

★ Part 3. Respond to questions

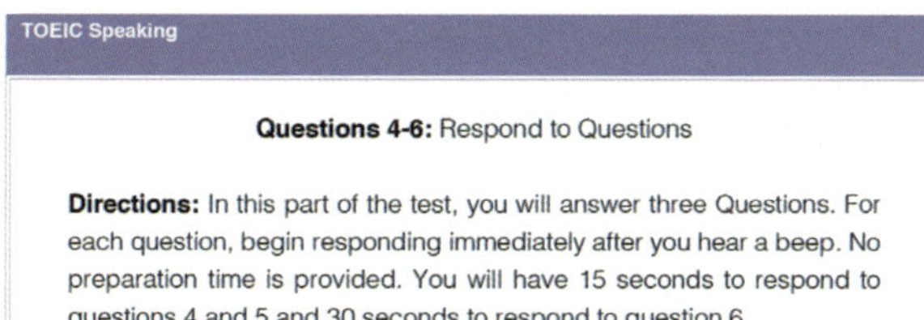

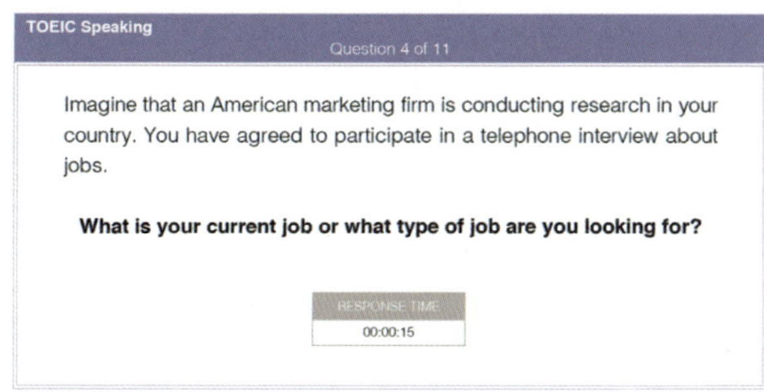

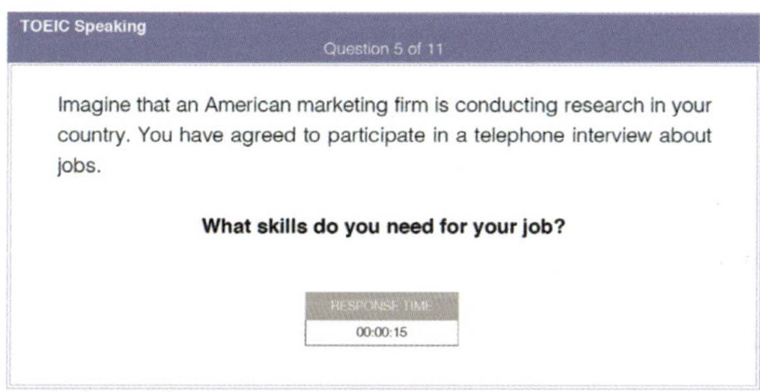

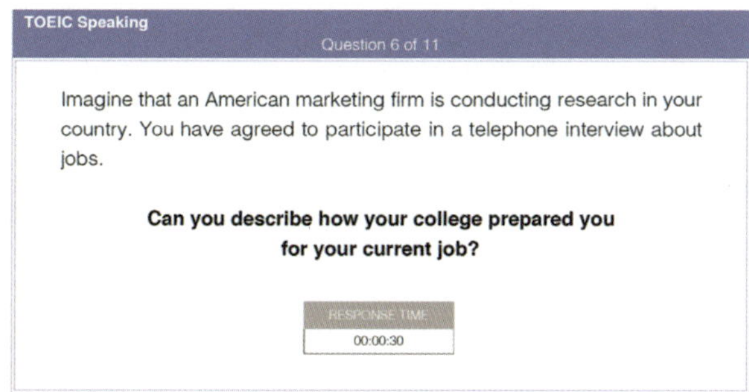

- 출제 문항 수 ┃ 3개 (Q4, Q5, Q6)
- 준비 시간 ┃ 없음
- 답변 시간 ┃ Q4 & Q5 – 15초 / Q6 – 30초
- 시험 방법 ┃ 지시문에 이어서 질문이 제시되면 준비 시간 없이 각 질문에 바로 답변한다.
- 평가 방법 ┃ 발음, 억양, 강세, 어휘, 문법, 내용의 연관성 및 일관성, 유창성

◇ 순발력이 중요하므로 완벽한 문법보다는 자연스럽고 쉽게 말하는데 중점을 둔다.
◇ 답변의 첫 문장은 보통 질문에 나오는 표현을 인용해서 말할 수 있다.
◇ 부연 설명이 빨리 안 떠오르면 최근의 예를 들거나 육하원칙 중에서 설명한다.
◇ 답변은 실제와 다르더라도 상관없으며, 3문제의 답변 내용에 일관성이 있어야 한다.
◇ 주어진 답변 시간을 최대한 활용한다. 답변 후 남는 시간은 3초 이내로 한다.

★ Part 4. Respond to questions using information provided

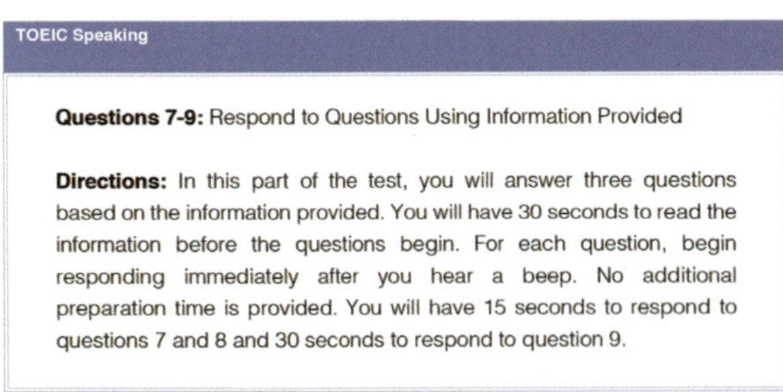

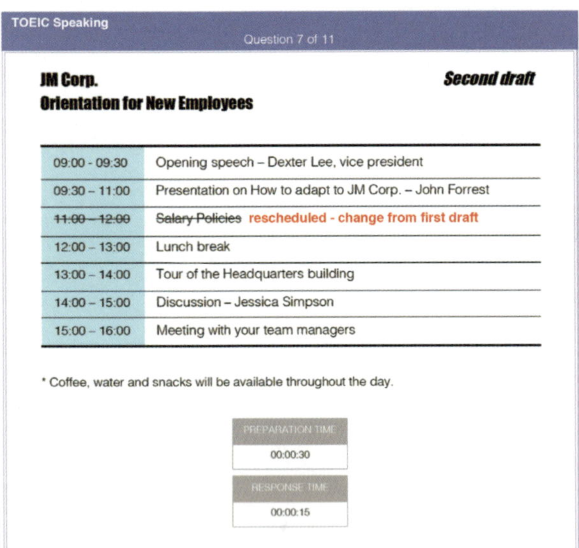

- 출제 문항 수 | 3개 (Q7, Q8, Q9)
- 준비 시간 | 30초
- 답변 시간 | Q7 & Q8 – 15초 / Q9 – 30초
- 시험 방법 | 지시문에 이어서 자료가 제시되면 30초 동안 준비한 후 각 질문을 듣고 바로 답변한다.
- 평가 방법 | 발음, 억양, 강세, 어휘, 문법, 내용의 연관성 및 일관성, 유창성

고득점 공략 TIP

↷ 준비 시간에 출제자의 입장에서 문제를 최대한 예측해본다.

↷ 괄호, 밑줄, 별표 등 특별하게 표시해 놓은 부분이나 이름, 장소 등이 3번 이상 반복될 경우, 그리고 주어진 자료 하단의 추가 내용에 관한 것들은 출제될 확률이 높다.

↷ 7번은 육하원칙, 8번은 잘못된 정보 확인, 9번은 정보들을 열거하는 문제가 자주 출제된다.

↷ 자료를 보면서 문장을 만드는 파트이므로 문법, 디테일이 중요하다. 쉽고 정확하게 말할 수 있도록 노력한다.

↷ 질문에 충분히 답했다면 시간이 남아도 괜찮다. 핵심 답변 이외의 부연 설명은 시간 안에 끝낼 수 있고, 문법 등의 실수가 없이 할 수 있다면 하는 것이 좋다.

★ Part 5. Propose a solution

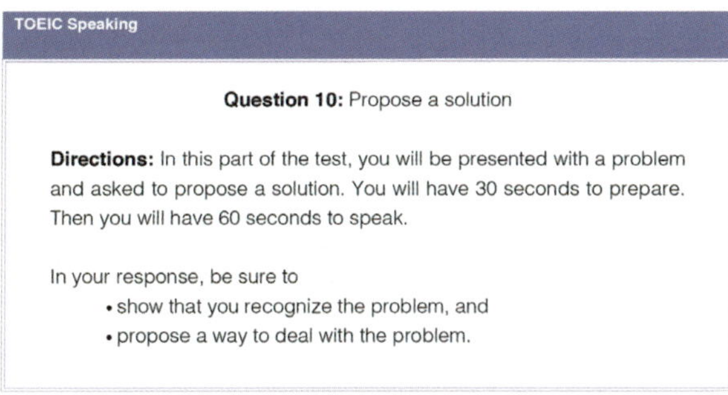

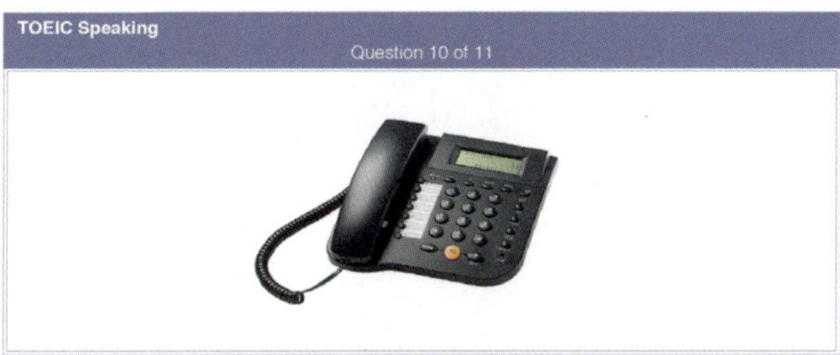

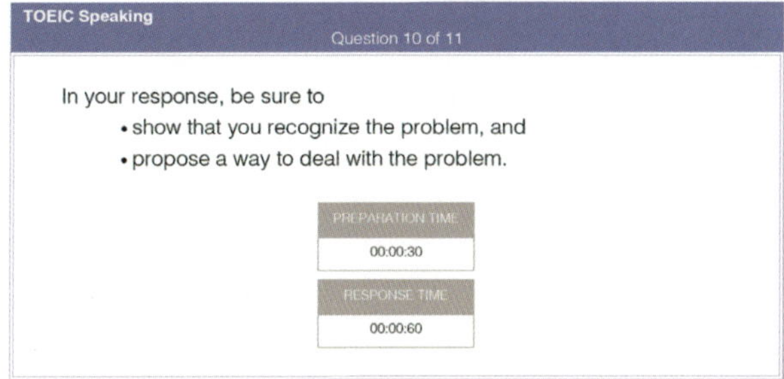

- 출제 문항 수 I 1개 (Q10)
- 준비 시간 I 30초
- 답변 시간 I 60초
- 시험 방법 I 지시문에 이어서 음성으로 제시되는 전화 메시지를 듣고 30초 동안 준비한 후 60초 동안 답변한다.
- 평가 기준 I 발음, 억양, 강세, 어휘, 문법, 내용의 연관성 및 일관성, 유창성

고득점 공략 TIP

- 음성 메시지를 들을 때 사건의 발단과 전화를 건 이유를 파악한다.
- 반복되는 내용, 의문문, 명령문, 필요를 나타내는 표현, 그리고 분위기가 바뀌거나 문제를 요약하는 표현들을 잘 듣는다.
- 나와 상대방이 누구인지 파악하고 그 상황에 알맞게 답변하려고 노력한다.
- 메시지가 끝나기 전에 해결책을 떠올려보고, 준비 시간에 최대한 말을 해본다.
- 인사말, 감사, 사과, 요약과 해결책을 시작하는 표현 등 다수의 문제에 적용할 수 있는 표현을 미리 숙지한다.

★ Part 6. Express an Opinion

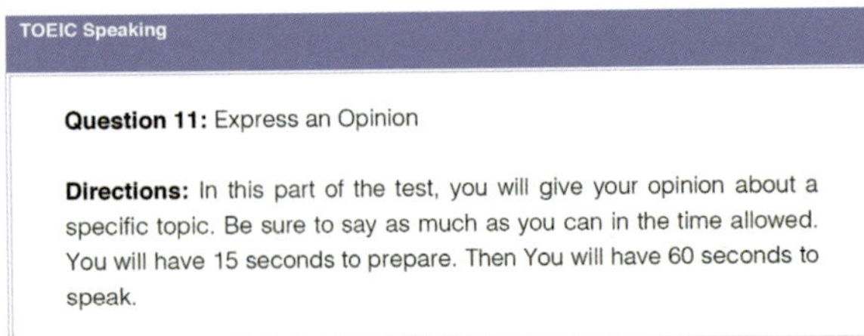

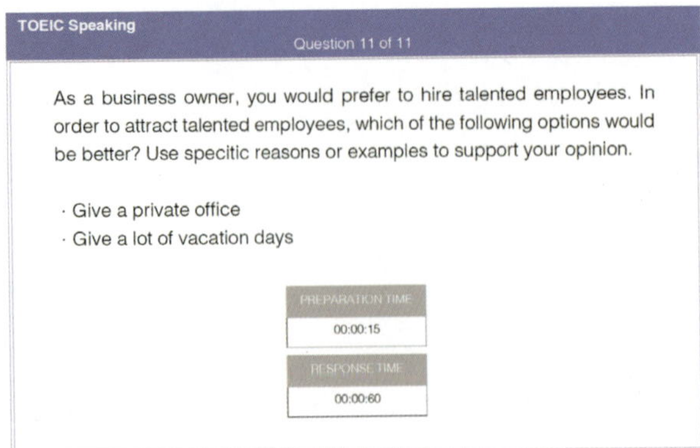

- 출제 문항 수 | 1개 (Q11)
- 준비 시간 | 15초
- 답변 시간 | 60초
- 시험 방법 | 지시문에 이어서 질문이 제시되면 15초 동안 준비한 후 60초 동안 답변한다.
- 평가 기준 | 발음, 억양, 강세, 어휘, 문법, 내용의 연관성 및 일관성, 유창성

고득점 공략 TIP

↪ 질문이 제시되는 동안 의견을 정하고 준비 시간 동안 근거 두 가지를 떠올린다.

↪ 답변의 첫 문장은 보통 질문에 나오는 표현을 인용해서 말할 수 있다.

↪ 부연 설명의 경우 예를 들어 설명하면 수월하다. 자신, 지인 혹은 유명인의 경우를 언급한다.

↪ 발음이나 어휘보다 아이디어가 더 중요하다.

↪ 평소에 내 일상이나 직장인들의 생활, 그리고 사회적으로 굵직한 사안들에 대해서 의견을 정리해본다.

↪ 아이디어가 안 떠오를 경우 '돈, 시간, 사람들 간의 관계'에 대해서 언급하면 많은 문제에 적용이 가능하다.

TOEIC Speaking Test Directions

This is the TOEIC Speaking Test. This test includes eleven questions that measure different aspects of your speaking ability. The test lasts approximately 20 minutes.

Question	TASK DESCRIPTION	EVALUATION CRITERIA
1-2	Read a text aloud	• Pronunciation • Intonation and stress
3	Describe a Picture	All of the above, plus • Grammar • Vocabulary • Cohesion
4-6	Respond to Questions	All of the above, plus • Relevance of content • Completeness of content
7-9	Respond to Questions Using Infomation Provided	All of the above
10	Propose a Solution	All of the above
11	Express an Opinion	All of the above

For each type of question, you will be given specific directions, including the time allowed for preparation and speaking.

It is to your advantage to say as much as you can in the time allowed. It is also important that you speak clearly and that you answer each question according to the directions.

Click on **Continue** to go on.

Actual Test 01

초고속 TOEIC SPEAKING

01-01

TOEIC Speaking

Questions 1-2: Read a Text Aloud

Directions: In this part of the test, you will read aloud the text on the screen. You will have 45 seconds to prepare. Then you will have 45 seconds to read the text aloud.

TOEIC Speaking

Hello, Chicago book club! Tonight, we have a very special guest speaker, Ms. Barbara Jefferson. Ms. Jefferson was born in Philadelphia but currently lives in California. She has written science fiction, fantasy and adult novels and tonight she will be reading a section from her latest book, Moons of Uranus. Please help me welcome with a big round of applause, Ms. Barbara Jefferson.

PREPARATION TIME

00:00:45

RESPONSE TIME

00:00:45

TOEIC Speaking

Welcome to the most famous tea house in the region, The Golden Leaf. On our tour you will discover how tea is grown, processed and packaged for shipment all over the world. Our tour will end with a visit to our Tea House where you can sample the variety of teas created here.

PREPARATION TIME

00:00:45

RESPONSE TIME

00:00:45

01-02

TOEIC Speaking

Question 3: Describe a Picture

Directions: In this part of the test, you will describe the picture on your screen in as much detail as you can. You will have 30 seconds to prepare your response. Then you will have 45 seconds to speak about the picture.

TOEIC Speaking

Question 3 of 11

PREPARATION TIME

00:00:30

RESPONSE TIME

00:00:45

 01-03

TOEIC Speaking

Questions 4-6: Respond to Questions

Directions: In this part of the test, you will answer three Questions. For each question, begin responding immediately after you hear a beep. No preparation time is provided. You will have 15 seconds to respond to questions 4 and 5 and 30 seconds to respond to question 6.

TOEIC Speaking

Question 4 of 11

Imagine that an American marketing firm is conducting research in your country. You have agreed to participate in a telephone interview about jobs.

What is your current job or what type of job are you looking for?

RESPONSE TIME
00:00:15

TOEIC Speaking

Question 5 of 11

Imagine that an American marketing firm is conducting research in your country. You have agreed to participate in a telephone interview about jobs.

What skills do you need for your job?

RESPONSE TIME
00:00:15

TOEIC Speaking

Question 6 of 11

Imagine that an American marketing firm is conducting research in your country. You have agreed to participate in a telephone interview about jobs.

**Can you describe how your college prepared you
for your current job?**

RESPONSE TIME
00:00:30

01-04

TOEIC Speaking

Questions 7-9: Respond to Questions Using Information Provided

Directions: In this part of the test, you will answer three questions based on the information provided. You will have 30 seconds to read the information before the questions begin. For each question, begin responding immediately after you hear a beep. No additional preparation time is provided. You will have 15 seconds to respond to questions 7 and 8 and 30 seconds to respond to question 9.

Hot Springs Arkansas Guided Hiking Tours

From 9 A.M. to 2 P.M. Daily

Hikes leave every hour on the hour

Table Rock Lake to Bear Mountain Hot Springs ▶ Advanced
- Duration: 3 hours
- Cost: $30

Dry Gulch Canyon to The Wishing Pond ▶ Beginner
- Duration: 2 hours
- Cost: $35

---

* Get maps, souvenirs, snacks and more information from the Base Camp store.

PREPARATION TIME
00:00:30

RESPONSE TIME
00:00:15

Hot Springs Arkansas Guided Hiking Tours

From 9 A.M. to 2 P.M. Daily

Hikes leave every hour on the hour

Table Rock Lake to Bear Mountain Hot Springs ▶ Advanced
- Duration: 3 hours
- Cost: $30

Dry Gulch Canyon to The Wishing Pond ▶ Beginner
- Duration: 2 hours
- Cost: $35

---

* Get maps, souvenirs, snacks and more information from the Base Camp store.

PREPARATION TIME
00:00:30

RESPONSE TIME
00:00:15

Hot Springs Arkansas Guided Hiking Tours

From 9 A.M. to 2 P.M. Daily

Hikes leave every hour on the hour

Table Rock Lake to Bear Mountain Hot Springs ▶ Advanced
- Duration: 3 hours
- Cost: $30

Dry Gulch Canyon to The Wishing Pond ▶ Beginner
- Duration: 2 hours
- Cost: $35

---

* Get maps, souvenirs, snacks and more information from the Base Camp store.

PREPARATION TIME
00:00:30

RESPONSE TIME
00:00:30

01-05

Question 10: Propose a solution

Directions: In this part of the test, you will be presented with a problem and asked to propose a solution. You will have 30 seconds to prepare. Then you will have 60 seconds to speak.

In your response, be sure to
- show that you recognize the problem, and
- propose a way to deal with the problem.

<table>
<tr><td>TOEIC Speaking</td></tr>
<tr><td>Question 10 of 11</td></tr>
</table>

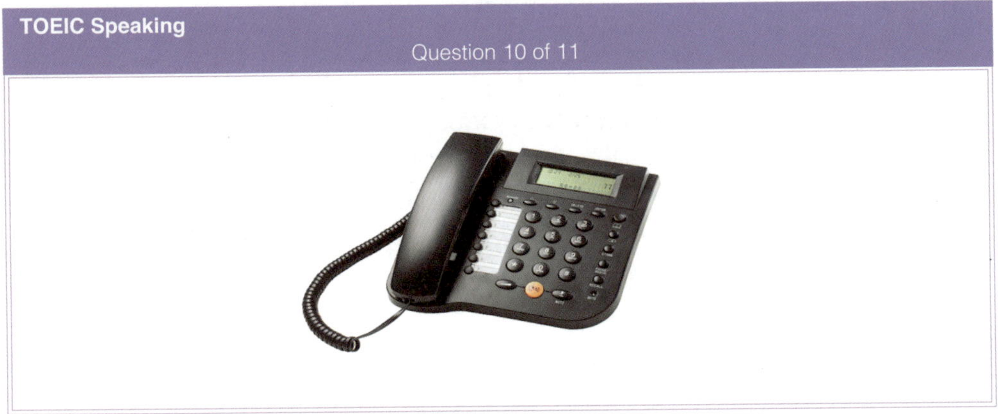

<table>
<tr><td>TOEIC Speaking</td></tr>
<tr><td>Question 10 of 11</td></tr>
</table>

In your response, be sure to
- show that you recognize the problem, and
- propose a way to deal with the problem.

PREPARATION TIME
00:00:30

RESPONSE TIME
00:00:60

01-06

TOEIC Speaking

Question 11: Express an Opinion

Directions: In this part of the test, you will give your opinion about a specific topic. Be sure to say as much as you can in the time allowed. You will have 15 seconds to prepare. Then You will have 60 seconds to speak.

TOEIC Speaking

Question 11 of 11

Do you agree or disagree with the following statement? 'People from large families are more competitive than people from small families.' Use specific reasons or details to support your answer.

PREPARATION TIME
00:00:15

RESPONSE TIME
00:00:60

TOEIC Speaking Test Directions

This is the TOEIC Speaking Test. This test includes eleven questions that measure different aspects of your speaking ability. The test lasts approximately 20 minutes.

Question	TASK DESCRIPTION	EVALUATION CRITERIA
1-2	Read a text aloud	• Pronunciation • Intonation and stress
3	Describe a Picture	All of the above, plus • Grammar • Vocabulary • Cohesion
4-6	Respond to Questions	All of the above, plus • Relevance of content • Completeness of content
7-9	Respond to Questions Using Infomation Provided	All of the above
10	Propose a Solution	All of the above
11	Express an Opinion	All of the above

For each type of question, you will be given specific directions, including the time allowed for preparation and speaking.

It is to your advantage to say as much as you can in the time allowed. It is also important that you speak clearly and that you answer each question according to the directions.

Click on **Continue** to go on.

Actual Test 02

초고속 TOEIC SPEAKING

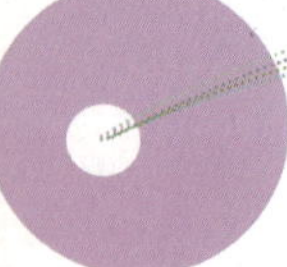

Actual Test 02

TOEIC Speaking

Questions 1-2: Read a Text Aloud

Directions: In this part of the test, you will read aloud the text on the screen. You will have 45 seconds to prepare. Then you will have 45 seconds to read the text aloud.

TOEIC Speaking

Do you enjoy foreign films? The Foreign Film club of Boston Proper Community College would like you to join them for their Thursday evening Foreign Film Academy this semester. We have films from Paris, Munich and Seoul this term. All films will be shown in the recently renovated Avenue Theatre. For more information, call 567-2839.

PREPARATION TIME
00:00:45

RESPONSE TIME
00:00:45

TOEIC Speaking

Hello and welcome to Disneyland's Variety Show Boat Spectacular. Please move all the way to the first available seat on your assigned row. Also, please remember for the courtesy of all our guest that eating, drinking, talking and flash photography are prohibited once the show begins. Once again, welcome and enjoy the show!

PREPARATION TIME
00:00:45

RESPONSE TIME
00:00:45

02-02

TOEIC Speaking

Question 3: Describe a Picture

Directions: In this part of the test, you will describe the picture on your screen in as much detail as you can. You will have 30 seconds to prepare your response. Then you will have 45 seconds to speak about the picture.

TOEIC Speaking

Question 3 of 11

PREPARATION TIME

00:00:30

RESPONSE TIME

00:00:45

02-03

TOEIC Speaking

Questions 4-6: Respond to Questions

Directions: In this part of the test, you will answer three Questions. For each question, begin responding immediately after you hear a beep. No preparation time is provided. You will have 15 seconds to respond to questions 4 and 5 and 30 seconds to respond to question 6.

TOEIC Speaking

Question 4 of 11

Imagine that an American survey firm is conducting research in your country. You have agreed to participate in a telephone interview about repair work.

When you have things break in your house, do you fix them on your own or call a repairman?

RESPONSE TIME

00:00:15

TOEIC Speaking

Question 5 of 11

Imagine that an American survey firm is conducting research in your country. You have agreed to participate in a telephone interview about repair work.

What was the last thing that had to be fixed in your house?

RESPONSE TIME
00:00:15

TOEIC Speaking

Question 6 of 11

Imagine that an American survey firm is conducting research in your country. You have agreed to participate in a telephone interview about repair work.

Why do you think some people do their own repair work as opposed to calling experts?

RESPONSE TIME
00:00:30

 02-04

TOEIC Speaking

Questions 7-9: Respond to Questions Using Information Provided

Directions: In this part of the test, you will answer three questions based on the information provided. You will have 30 seconds to read the information before the questions begin. For each question, begin responding immediately after you hear a beep. No additional preparation time is provided. You will have 15 seconds to respond to questions 7 and 8 and 30 seconds to respond to question 9.

TOEIC Speaking

Question 7 of 11

Storewide Veterans Day Sale

8 A.M.-8 P.M., November 11 ONLY

Department	Items	SALE
Home Furnishings	ALL TVs and freezers	30% off
Jewelry Counter	ALL watches and charm bracelets	25% off
Men's Shoe Department	ALL running shoes and hiking boots	30-40% off
Women's Shoe Department	ALL dress shoes	20% off

PREPARATION TIME
00:00:30

RESPONSE TIME
00:00:15

Storewide Veterans Day Sale

8 A.M.-8 P.M., November 11 ONLY

Department	Items	SALE
Home Furnishings	ALL TVs and freezers	30% off
Jewelry Counter	ALL watches and charm bracelets	25% off
Men's Shoe Department	ALL running shoes and hiking boots	30-40% off
Women's Shoe Department	ALL dress shoes	20% off

PREPARATION TIME

00:00:30

RESPONSE TIME

00:00:15

Storewide Veterans Day Sale

8 A.M.-8 P.M., November 11 ONLY

Department	Items	SALE
Home Furnishings	ALL TVs and freezers	30% off
Jewelry Counter	ALL watches and charm bracelets	25% off
Men's Shoe Department	ALL running shoes and hiking boots	30-40% off
Women's Shoe Department	ALL dress shoes	20% off

PREPARATION TIME

00:00:30

RESPONSE TIME

00:00:30

TOEIC Speaking

Question 10: Propose a solution

Directions: In this part of the test, you will be presented with a problem and asked to propose a solution. You will have 30 seconds to prepare. Then you will have 60 seconds to speak.

In your response, be sure to
- show that you recognize the problem, and
- propose a way to deal with the problem.

TOEIC Speaking

Question 10 of 11

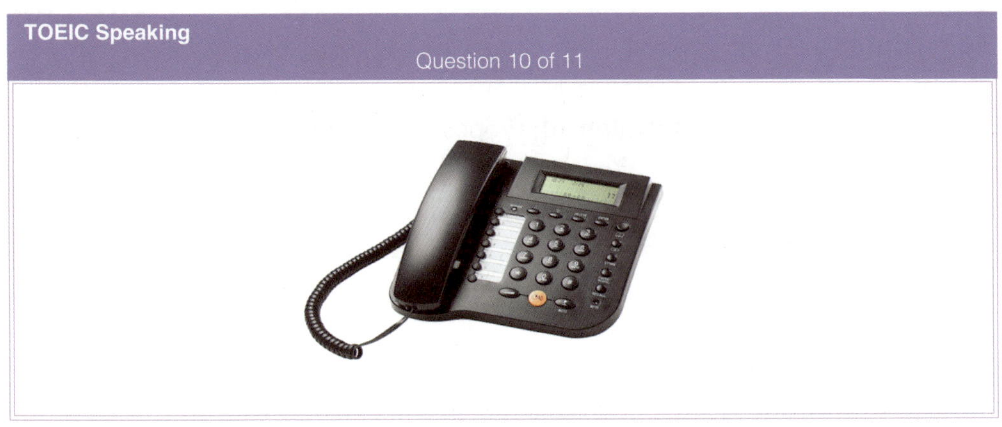

TOEIC Speaking

Question 10 of 11

In your response, be sure to
- show that you recognize the problem, and
- propose a way to deal with the problem.

PREPARATION TIME
00:00:30

RESPONSE TIME
00:00:60

02-06

TOEIC Speaking

Question 11: Express an Opinion

Directions: In this part of the test, you will give your opinion about a specific topic. Be sure to say as much as you can in the time allowed. You will have 15 seconds to prepare. Then You will have 60 seconds to speak.

TOEIC Speaking

Question 11 of 11

Do you think people are more focused on money today than they were in the past? Use specific reasons or examples to support your opinion.

PREPARATION TIME
00:00:15

RESPONSE TIME
00:00:60

TOEIC Speaking Test Directions

This is the TOEIC Speaking Test. This test includes eleven questions that measure different aspects of your speaking ability. The test lasts approximately 20 minutes.

Question	TASK DESCRIPTION	EVALUATION CRITERIA
1-2	Read a text aloud	• Pronunciation • Intonation and stress
3	Describe a Picture	All of the above, plus • Grammar • Vocabulary • Cohesion
4-6	Respond to Questions	All of the above, plus • Relevance of content • Completeness of content
7-9	Respond to Questions Using Infomation Provided	All of the above
10	Propose a Solution	All of the above
11	Express an Opinion	All of the above

For each type of question, you will be given specific directions, including the time allowed for preparation and speaking.

It is to your advantage to say as much as you can in the time allowed. It is also important that you speak clearly and that you answer each question according to the directions.

Click on **Continue** to go on.

Actual Test 03

초고속 TOEIC SPEAKING

Actual Test 03

03-01

TOEIC Speaking

Questions 1-2: Read a Text Aloud

Directions: In this part of the test, you will read aloud the text on the screen. You will have 45 seconds to prepare. Then you will have 45 seconds to read the text aloud.

TOEIC Speaking

Question 1 of 11

BP is proud to announce our Absolutely BP Program results for this year. Our Community Relations Department has distributed over 33 million dollars to organizations working to preserve and protect the oceans of the world through promotion, education and strategic planning.

PREPARATION TIME
00:00:45

RESPONSE TIME
00:00:45

TOEIC Speaking

Question 2 of 11

Here is today's Inside the Beltway Analysis. The Republican Party wants to get tough on waste, fraud and abuse but are they tough enough on their own party members? This is the precise question now being raised by the House Ethics Committee with regard to Senator Bill Parbel. Until further notice, Senator Parbel has been suspended. Stay tuned for updates.

PREPARATION TIME
00:00:45

RESPONSE TIME
00:00:45

 03-02

Question 3: Describe a Picture

Directions: In this part of the test, you will describe the picture on your screen in as much detail as you can. You will have 30 seconds to prepare your response. Then you will have 45 seconds to speak about the picture.

TOEIC Speaking

Question 3 of 11

PREPARATION TIME

00:00:30

RESPONSE TIME

00:00:45

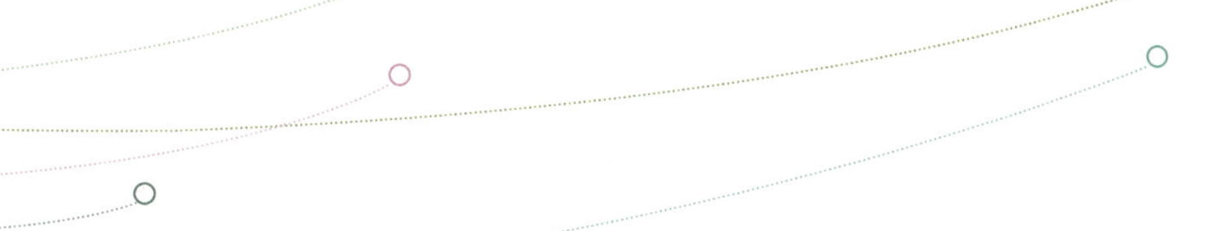

 03-03

TOEIC Speaking

Questions 4-6: Respond to Questions

Directions: In this part of the test, you will answer three Questions. For each question, begin responding immediately after you hear a beep. No preparation time is provided. You will have 15 seconds to respond to questions 4 and 5 and 30 seconds to respond to question 6.

TOEIC Speaking

Question 4 of 11

Imagine that an Australian survey firm is conducting research in your country. You have agreed to participate in a telephone interview about being sick.

How often do you see a doctor?

RESPONSE TIME
00:00:15

TOEIC Speaking

Imagine that an Australian survey firm is conducting research in your country. You have agreed to participate in a telephone interview about being sick.

Do you use home remedies or prescription drugs when you are sick?

RESPONSE TIME

00:00:15

TOEIC Speaking

Imagine that an Australian survey firm is conducting research in your country. You have agreed to participate in a telephone interview about being sick.

What do you think is the worst thing about being sick?

RESPONSE TIME

00:00:30

TOEIC Speaking

Questions 7-9: Respond to Questions Using Information Provided

Directions: In this part of the test, you will answer three questions based on the information provided. You will have 30 seconds to read the information before the questions begin. For each question, begin responding immediately after you hear a beep. No additional preparation time is provided. You will have 15 seconds to respond to questions 7 and 8 and 30 seconds to respond to question 9.

Texas State Dog Show
Texas State Fairgrounds- Dallas Texas

Saturday December 3

9:00 A.M.	Opening Ceremony	Main Hall
10:30 A.M.	First Round Competition	San Antonio Hall
1:30 P.M.	Small Dogs Showing	Austin Hall
3:00 P.M.	Medium Dogs Showing	Houston Hall

Sunday December 4

10:00 A.M.	Second Round Competition	San Antonio Hall
11:00 A.M.	Large Dog Showing	Main Hall
1:30 P.M.	Finals for Best in Show	Main Hall
3:00 P.M.	Awards and Closing Ceremony	Main Hall

PREPARATION TIME

00:00:30

RESPONSE TIME

00:00:15

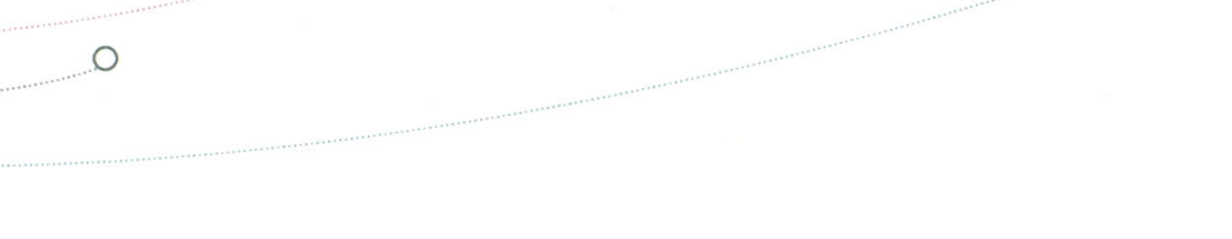

Texas State Dog Show
Texas State Fairgrounds- Dallas Texas

Saturday December 3

9:00 A.M.	Opening Ceremony	Main Hall
10:30 A.M.	First Round Competition	San Antonio Hall
1:30 P.M.	Small Dogs Showing	Austin Hall
3:00 P.M.	Medium Dogs Showing	Houston Hall

Sunday December 4

10:00 A.M.	Second Round Competition	San Antonio Hall
11:00 A.M.	Large Dog Showing	Main Hall
1:30 P.M.	Finals for Best in Show	Main Hall
3:00 P.M.	Awards and Closing Ceremony	Main Hall

PREPARATION TIME
00:00:30

RESPONSE TIME
00:00:15

Texas State Dog Show
Texas State Fairgrounds- Dallas Texas

Saturday December 3

9:00 A.M.	Opening Ceremony	Main Hall
10:30 A.M.	First Round Competition	San Antonio Hall
1:30 P.M.	Small Dogs Showing	Austin Hall
3:00 P.M.	Medium Dogs Showing	Houston Hall

Sunday December 4

10:00 A.M.	Second Round Competition	San Antonio Hall
11:00 A.M.	Large Dog Showing	Main Hall
1:30 P.M.	Finals for Best in Show	Main Hall
3:00 P.M.	Awards and Closing Ceremony	Main Hall

PREPARATION TIME
00:00:30

RESPONSE TIME
00:00:30

 03-05

TOEIC Speaking

Question 10: Propose a solution

Directions: In this part of the test, you will be presented with a problem and asked to propose a solution. You will have 30 seconds to prepare. Then you will have 60 seconds to speak.

In your response, be sure to
- show that you recognize the problem, and
- propose a way to deal with the problem.

TOEIC Speaking

Question 10 of 11

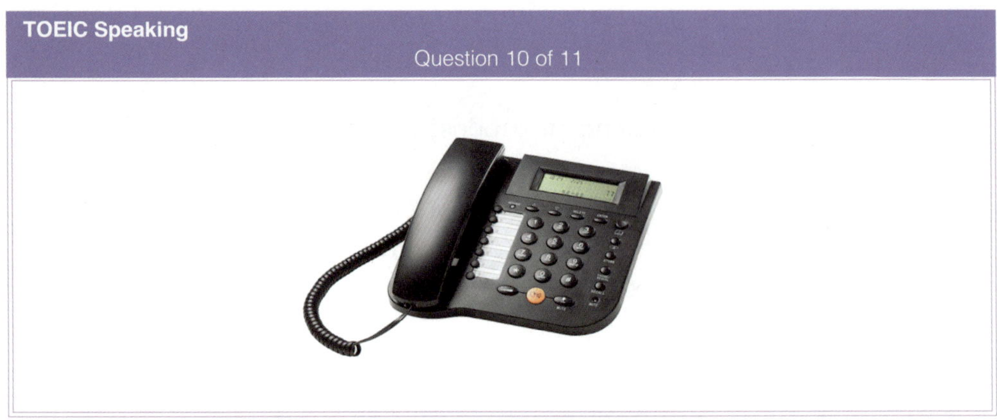

TOEIC Speaking

Question 10 of 11

In your response, be sure to
- show that you recognize the problem, and
- propose a way to deal with the problem.

PREPARATION TIME
00:00:30

RESPONSE TIME
00:00:60

TOEIC Speaking

Question 11: Express an Opinion

Directions: In this part of the test, you will give your opinion about a specific topic. Be sure to say as much as you can in the time allowed. You will have 15 seconds to prepare. Then You will have 60 seconds to speak.

TOEIC Speaking

Question 11 of 11

What do you think of a competitive work environment as opposed to a cooperative work environment? Use specific reasons or examples to support your opinion.

PREPARATION TIME
00:00:15

RESPONSE TIME
00:00:60

TOEIC Speaking Test Directions

This is the TOEIC Speaking Test. This test includes eleven questions that measure different aspects of your speaking ability. The test lasts approximately 20 minutes.

Question	TASK DESCRIPTION	EVALUATION CRITERIA
1-2	Read a text aloud	• Pronunciation • Intonation and stress
3	Describe a Picture	All of the above, plus • Grammar • Vocabulary • Cohesion
4-6	Respond to Questions	All of the above, plus • Relevance of content • Completeness of content
7-9	Respond to Questions Using Infomation Provided	All of the above
10	Propose a Solution	All of the above
11	Express an Opinion	All of the above

For each type of question, you will be given specific directions, including the time allowed for preparation and speaking.

It is to your advantage to say as much as you can in the time allowed. It is also important that you speak clearly and that you answer each question according to the directions.

Click on **Continue** to go on.

Actual Test 04

초고속 TOEIC SPEAKING

Actual Test 04

04-01

Questions 1-2: Read a Text Aloud

Directions: In this part of the test, you will read aloud the text on the screen. You will have 45 seconds to prepare. Then you will have 45 seconds to read the text aloud.

It's time for the Original Organic Chef's Buffet Sale! You will find a smorgasbord of savings on all your organic needs. Everything from organic cocoa, chocolate, butter and margarine are all at once a year reductions. Even our storewide variety of tomatoes, apples, oranges and greens are at drastic discounts. Come by today!

PREPARATION TIME

00:00:45

RESPONSE TIME

00:00:45

Welcome to another edition of Health Opportunity Now! Today we have the opportunity to be taught by one of the leaders in the field, Mr. Ben Penron. He will discuss how to make our diet more precise for our needs and how to create nutritious recipes that will facilitate your optimum balanced life.

PREPARATION TIME

00:00:45

RESPONSE TIME

00:00:45

 04-02

TOEIC Speaking

Question 3: Describe a Picture

Directions: In this part of the test, you will describe the picture on your screen in as much detail as you can. You will have 30 seconds to prepare your response. Then you will have 45 seconds to speak about the picture.

TOEIC Speaking

Question 3 of 11

TOEIC Speaking

Questions 4-6: Respond to Questions

Directions: In this part of the test, you will answer three Questions. For each question, begin responding immediately after you hear a beep. No preparation time is provided. You will have 15 seconds to respond to questions 4 and 5 and 30 seconds to respond to question 6.

TOEIC Speaking

Question 4 of 11

Imagine that a Canadian marketing firm is conducting research in your country. You have agreed to participate in a telephone interview about cultural events.

How often do you go to a cultural event in your area?

RESPONSE TIME

00:00:15

Imagine that a Canadian marketing firm is conducting research in your country. You have agreed to participate in a telephone interview about cultural events.

How do you find out about various events coming up?

RESPONSE TIME
00:00:15

Imagine that a Canadian marketing firm is conducting research in your country. You have agreed to participate in a telephone interview about cultural events.

What was the last special event you went to?
Please describe what it was like.

RESPONSE TIME
00:00:30

TOEIC Speaking

Questions 7-9: Respond to Questions Using Information Provided

Directions: In this part of the test, you will answer three questions based on the information provided. You will have 30 seconds to read the information before the questions begin. For each question, begin responding immediately after you hear a beep. No additional preparation time is provided. You will have 15 seconds to respond to questions 7 and 8 and 30 seconds to respond to question 9.

Lou Phillips School of Film Acting
Classes Offered Fall Term

Day	Time	Class	Instructor
Mondays	5-7 P.M.	Intro to Film Acting	Tom Meeks
Tuesdays	6-9 P.M.	Intermediate Film Acting I	Rick Bell
Tuesdays	9-10 P.M.	Intermediate Film Acting II	Rick Bell
Thursdays	6-10 P.M.	Advanced Film Acting I	Lou Phillips
Fridays	6-10 P.M.	Advanced Film Acting II	Lou Phillips

* Class tuition is $300 for two hour classes, $400 for three hour classes and $500 for four

hour classes.

PREPARATION TIME

00:00:30

RESPONSE TIME

00:00:15

Lou Phillips School of Film Acting
Classes Offered Fall Term

Day	Time	Class	Instructor
Mondays	5-7 P.M.	Intro to Film Acting	Tom Meeks
Tuesdays	6-9 P.M.	Intermediate Film Acting I	Rick Bell
Tuesdays	9-10 P.M.	Intermediate Film Acting II	Rick Bell
Thursdays	6-10 P.M.	Advanced Film Acting I	Lou Phillips
Fridays	6-10 P.M.	Advanced Film Acting II	Lou Phillips

* Class tuition is $300 for two hour classes, $400 for three hour classes and $500 for four hour classes.

PREPARATION TIME
00:00:30

RESPONSE TIME
00:00:15

Lou Phillips School of Film Acting
Classes Offered Fall Term

Day	Time	Class	Instructor
Mondays	5-7 P.M.	Intro to Film Acting	Tom Meeks
Tuesdays	6-9 P.M.	Intermediate Film Acting I	Rick Bell
Tuesdays	9-10 P.M.	Intermediate Film Acting II	Rick Bell
Thursdays	6-10 P.M.	Advanced Film Acting I	Lou Phillips
Fridays	6-10 P.M.	Advanced Film Acting II	Lou Phillips

* Class tuition is $300 for two hour classes, $400 for three hour classes and $500 for four hour classes.

PREPARATION TIME

00:00:30

RESPONSE TIME

00:00:30

 04-05

Question 10: Propose a solution

Directions: In this part of the test, you will be presented with a problem and asked to propose a solution. You will have 30 seconds to prepare. Then you will have 60 seconds to speak.

In your response, be sure to
- show that you recognize the problem, and
- propose a way to deal with the problem.

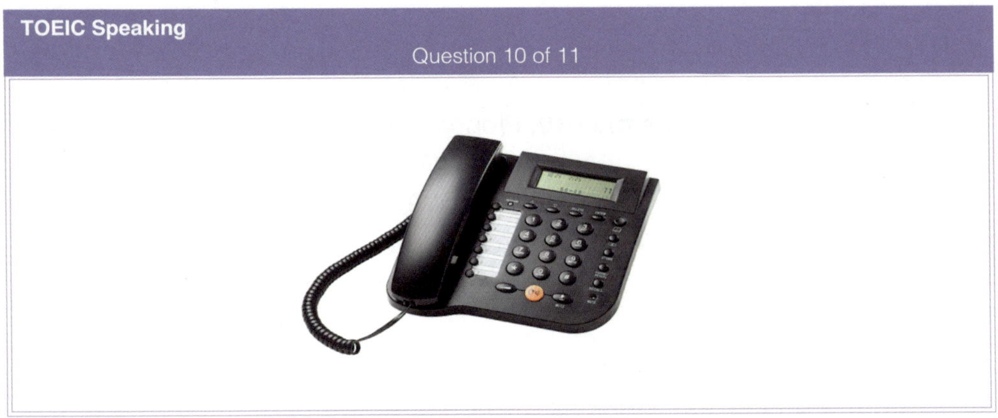

TOEIC Speaking

Question 10 of 11

In your response, be sure to
- show that you recognize the problem, and
- propose a way to deal with the problem.

PREPARATION TIME
00:00:30

RESPONSE TIME
00:00:60

TOEIC Speaking

Question 11: Express an Opinion

Directions: In this part of the test, you will give your opinion about a specific topic. Be sure to say as much as you can in the time allowed. You will have 15 seconds to prepare. Then You will have 60 seconds to speak.

TOEIC Speaking

Question 11 of 11

In your opinion which of the following do you think has the biggest impact on modern society:

a) Smart Phones
b) Social Networking sites
c) Instant Messaging

Give specific reasons or examples to support your opinion.

PREPARATION TIME
00:00:15

RESPONSE TIME
00:00:60

TOEIC Speaking Test Directions

This is the TOEIC Speaking Test. This test includes eleven questions that measure different aspects of your speaking ability. The test lasts approximately 20 minutes.

Question	TASK DESCRIPTION	EVALUATION CRITERIA
1-2	Read a text aloud	• Pronunciation • Intonation and stress
3	Describe a Picture	All of the above, plus • Grammar • Vocabulary • Cohesion
4-6	Respond to Questions	All of the above, plus • Relevance of content • Completeness of content
7-9	Respond to Questions Using Infomation Provided	All of the above
10	Propose a Solution	All of the above
11	Express an Opinion	All of the above

For each type of question, you will be given specific directions, including the time allowed for preparation and speaking.

It is to your advantage to say as much as you can in the time allowed. It is also important that you speak clearly and that you answer each question according to the directions.

Click on **Continue** to go on.

Actual Test 05

초고속 TOEIC SPEAKING

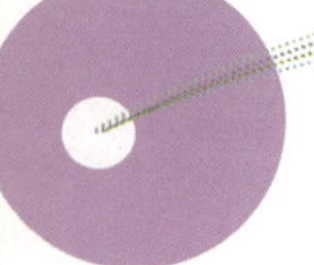

Actual Test 05

TOEIC Speaking

Questions 1-2: Read a Text Aloud

Directions: In this part of the test, you will read aloud the text on the screen. You will have 45 seconds to prepare. Then you will have 45 seconds to read the text aloud.

Hello and thank you for coming to the product launch for this amazing new phone. Motorphona Corp. is proud to launch this precise, well-organized and versatile line of phones called the Tiger Line. As you can see, this sleek, stylish and sexy phone looks great, but wait till you see what it can do! For individual product demonstrations see our Associates up front now.

PREPARATION TIME

00:00:45

RESPONSE TIME

00:00:45

KHOO FM100 is your station for the latest news, sports, weather and hits from the 70s, 80s and 90s. In addition, don't forget about our variety of talk shows available on Sunday including our recently added Dr. Tom's wisdom on what to eliminate from your life for the health of It. All this and so much more only here at KHOO.

PREPARATION TIME

00:00:45

RESPONSE TIME

00:00:45

TOEIC Speaking

Question 3: Describe a Picture

Directions: In this part of the test, you will describe the picture on your screen in as much detail as you can. You will have 30 seconds to prepare your response. Then you will have 45 seconds to speak about the picture.

TOEIC Speaking

Question 3 of 11

PREPARATION TIME
00:00:30

RESPONSE TIME
00:00:45

TOEIC Speaking

Questions 4-6: Respond to Questions

Directions: In this part of the test, you will answer three Questions. For each question, begin responding immediately after you hear a beep. No preparation time is provided. You will have 15 seconds to respond to questions 4 and 5 and 30 seconds to respond to question 6.

TOEIC Speaking

Question 4 of 11

Imagine that a Canadian marketing firm is conducting research in your country. You have agreed to participate in a telephone interview about sunglasses.

When was the last time you bought sunglasses and where did you go to shop for them?

RESPONSE TIME

00:00:15

TOEIC Speaking

Question 5 of 11

Imagine that a Canadian marketing firm is conducting research in your country. You have agreed to participate in a telephone interview about sunglasses.

How long did it take to choose the sunglasses that you bought?

RESPONSE TIME

00:00:15

TOEIC Speaking

Question 6 of 11

Imagine that a Canadian marketing firm is conducting research in your country. You have agreed to participate in a telephone interview about sunglasses.

Can you describe your decision making process when you buy sunglasses?

RESPONSE TIME

00:00:30

Questions 7-9: Respond to Questions Using Information Provided

Directions: In this part of the test, you will answer three questions based on the information provided. You will have 30 seconds to read the information before the questions begin. For each question, begin responding immediately after you hear a beep. No additional preparation time is provided. You will have 15 seconds to respond to questions 7 and 8 and 30 seconds to respond to question 9.

Smokey Mountain Resort and Conference Center
Restaurant Availability

New Year's Weekend Dec.31-Jan.2

Date	Restaurant	Seating availability - Total/Available
December 31	Mountain View	250 / 9
	Creek Café	175 / 22
	Boulder Bistro	150 / 15
January 1	Mountain View	250 / 12
	Creek Café	175 / 8
	Boulder Bistro	150 / 10
January 2	Mountain View	250 / 55
	Creek Café	175 / 80
	Boulder Bistro	150 / 50

* All restaurants will close by 9 P.M. on December 31st to prepare for the New Year's Eve party.

PREPARATION TIME

00:00:30

RESPONSE TIME

00:00:15

Smokey Mountain Resort and Conference Center
Restaurant Availability

New Year's Weekend Dec.31-Jan.2

Date	Restaurant	Seating availability - Total/Available
December 31	Mountain View	250 / 9
	Creek Café	175 / 22
	Boulder Bistro	150 / 15
January 1	Mountain View	250 / 12
	Creek Café	175 / 8
	Boulder Bistro	150 / 10
January 2	Mountain View	250 / 55
	Creek Café	175 / 80
	Boulder Bistro	150 / 50

* All restaurants will close by 9 P.M. on December 31st to prepare for the New Year's Eve party.

PREPARATION TIME
00:00:30

RESPONSE TIME
00:00:15

Smokey Mountain Resort and Conference Center
Restaurant Availability

New Year's Weekend Dec.31-Jan.2

Date	Restaurant	Seating availability - Total/Available
December 31	Mountain View	250 / 9
	Creek Café	175 / 22
	Boulder Bistro	150 / 15
January 1	Mountain View	250 / 12
	Creek Café	175 / 8
	Boulder Bistro	150 / 10
January 2	Mountain View	250 / 55
	Creek Café	175 / 80
	Boulder Bistro	150 / 50

* All restaurants will close by 9 P.M. on December 31st to prepare for the New Year's Eve party.

PREPARATION TIME
00:00:30

RESPONSE TIME
00:00:30

 05-05

Question 10: Propose a solution

Directions: In this part of the test, you will be presented with a problem and asked to propose a solution. You will have 30 seconds to prepare. Then you will have 60 seconds to speak.

In your response, be sure to
- show that you recognize the problem, and
- propose a way to deal with the problem.

TOEIC Speaking

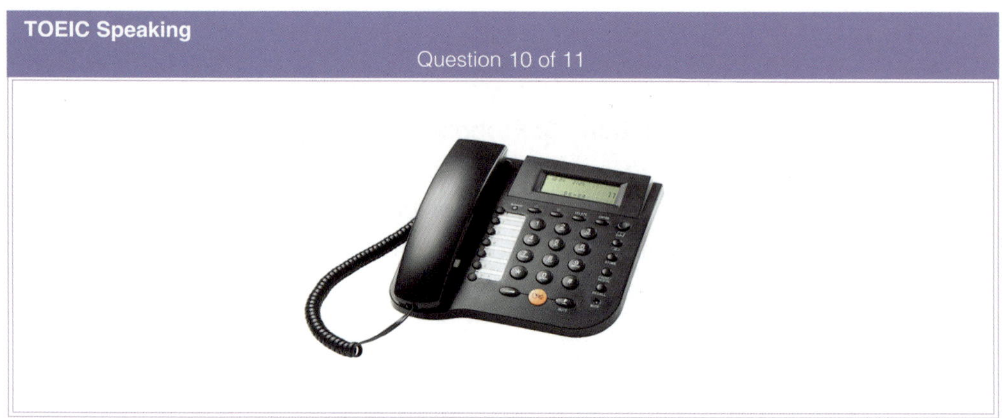

TOEIC Speaking

In your response, be sure to
- show that you recognize the problem, and
- propose a way to deal with the problem.

PREPARATION TIME
00:00:30

RESPONSE TIME
00:00:60

TOEIC Speaking

Question 11: Express an Opinion

Directions: In this part of the test, you will give your opinion about a specific topic. Be sure to say as much as you can in the time allowed. You will have 15 seconds to prepare. Then You will have 60 seconds to speak.

TOEIC Speaking

Question 11 of 11

Some people think that it is better to stay in the same workplace while other people prefer to work at various workplaces. What are your thoughts and why? Use specific reasons or examples to support your opinion.

PREPARATION TIME
00:00:15

RESPONSE TIME
00:00:60

TOEIC Speaking Test Directions

This is the TOEIC Speaking Test. This test includes eleven questions that measure different aspects of your speaking ability. The test lasts approximately 20 minutes.

Question	TASK DESCRIPTION	EVALUATION CRITERIA
1-2	Read a text aloud	• Pronunciation • Intonation and stress
3	Describe a Picture	All of the above, plus • Grammar • Vocabulary • Cohesion
4-6	Respond to Questions	All of the above, plus • Relevance of content • Completeness of content
7-9	Respond to Questions Using Infomation Provided	All of the above
10	Propose a Solution	All of the above
11	Express an Opinion	All of the above

For each type of question, you will be given specific directions, including the time allowed for preparation and speaking.

It is to your advantage to say as much as you can in the time allowed. It is also important that you speak clearly and that you answer each question according to the directions.

Click on **Continue** to go on.

Actual Test 06

초고속 TOEIC SPEAKING

 06-01

TOEIC Speaking

Questions 1-2: Read a Text Aloud

Directions: In this part of the test, you will read aloud the text on the screen. You will have 45 seconds to prepare. Then you will have 45 seconds to read the text aloud.

Good Morning and welcome to the New York Public Library. Please listen to this message before proceeding. You are currently in front of the Sawyer Lion sculpture. Your options are fiction, non-fiction, periodicals and information desk. For fiction and nonfiction, proceed to the 3rd floor. For periodicals, proceed to the second floor and for all other information please see the information desk behind this sculpture. Thank you and we hope you enjoy your visit.

PREPARATION TIME
00:00:45

RESPONSE TIME
00:00:45

Good evening. On this edition of Teacher's Tip's, we will hear the latest from Tom Rippen. Tom is the man who is getting students excited about math analysis functions. Today he is going to share with us his precise methodology on how to help students analyze, calculate, draw a graph and keep smiling through it all.

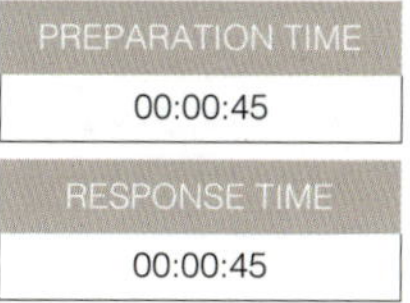

PREPARATION TIME
00:00:45

RESPONSE TIME
00:00:45

06-02

TOEIC Speaking

Question 3: Describe a Picture

Directions: In this part of the test, you will describe the picture on your screen in as much detail as you can. You will have 30 seconds to prepare your response. Then you will have 45 seconds to speak about the picture.

TOEIC Speaking

Question 3 of 11

PREPARATION TIME

00:00:30

RESPONSE TIME

00:00:45

TOEIC Speaking

Questions 4-6: Respond to Questions

Directions: In this part of the test, you will answer three Questions. For each question, begin responding immediately after you hear a beep. No preparation time is provided. You will have 15 seconds to respond to questions 4 and 5 and 30 seconds to respond to question 6.

TOEIC Speaking

Question 4 of 11

Imagine that a British marketing firm is conducting research in your country. You have agreed to participate in a telephone interview about sports.

What sport was the most popular in your high school?

RESPONSE TIME
00:00:15

TOEIC Speaking

Question 5 of 11

Imagine that a British marketing firm is conducting research in your country. You have agreed to participate in a telephone interview about sports.

Did you play sports? Which ones? What positions?

RESPONSE TIME

00:00:15

TOEIC Speaking

Question 6 of 11

Imagine that a British marketing firm is conducting research in your country. You have agreed to participate in a telephone interview about sports.

If you had to describe the perfect coach what would they be like?

RESPONSE TIME

00:00:30

Questions 7-9: Respond to Questions Using Information Provided

Directions: In this part of the test, you will answer three questions based on the information provided. You will have 30 seconds to read the information before the questions begin. For each question, begin responding immediately after you hear a beep. No additional preparation time is provided. You will have 15 seconds to respond to questions 7 and 8 and 30 seconds to respond to question 9.

Museum of Natural History
National Teachers Appreciation Day

Date: May 8
Admission: Free to all teachers and their families
Location: Central Park West at 79th Street, New York, NY, 10024-5192

09:00 - 10:30	Real Science - Larry Gould (CBS "Science Guy")
10:30 - 12:00	Film - Mysteries of the Deep
12:00 - 13:00	Free Lunch sponsored by NYC Teachers Credit Union
13:00 - 15:30	Browse the museum at your leisure
15:30 - 16:30	Teacher Appreciation Awards - Mayor of NYC

* All scheduled events will happen in the Main Auditorium

PREPARATION TIME
00:00:30

RESPONSE TIME
00:00:15

Museum of Natural History
National Teachers Appreciation Day

Date: May 8
Admission: Free to all teachers and their families
Location: Central Park West at 79th Street, New York, NY, 10024-5192

09:00 - 10:30	Real Science - Larry Gould (CBS "Science Guy")
10:30 - 12:00	Film - Mysteries of the Deep
12:00 - 13:00	Free Lunch sponsored by NYC Teachers Credit Union
13:00 - 15:30	Browse the museum at your leisure
15:30 - 16:30	Teacher Appreciation Awards - Mayor of NYC

* All scheduled events will happen in the Main Auditorium

PREPARATION TIME
00:00:30

RESPONSE TIME
00:00:15

Museum of Natural History
National Teachers Appreciation Day

Date: May 8
Admission: Free to all teachers and their families
Location: Central Park West at 79th Street, New York, NY, 10024-5192

09:00 - 10:30	Real Science - Larry Gould (CBS "Science Guy")
10:30 - 12:00	Film - Mysteries of the Deep
12:00 - 13:00	Free Lunch sponsored by NYC Teachers Credit Union
13:00 - 15:30	Browse the museum at your leisure
15:30 - 16:30	Teacher Appreciation Awards - Mayor of NYC

* All scheduled events will happen in the Main Auditorium

PREPARATION TIME

00:00:30

RESPONSE TIME

00:00:30

 06-05

Question 10: Propose a solution

Directions: In this part of the test, you will be presented with a problem and asked to propose a solution. You will have 30 seconds to prepare. Then you will have 60 seconds to speak.

In your response, be sure to
- show that you recognize the problem, and
- propose a way to deal with the problem.

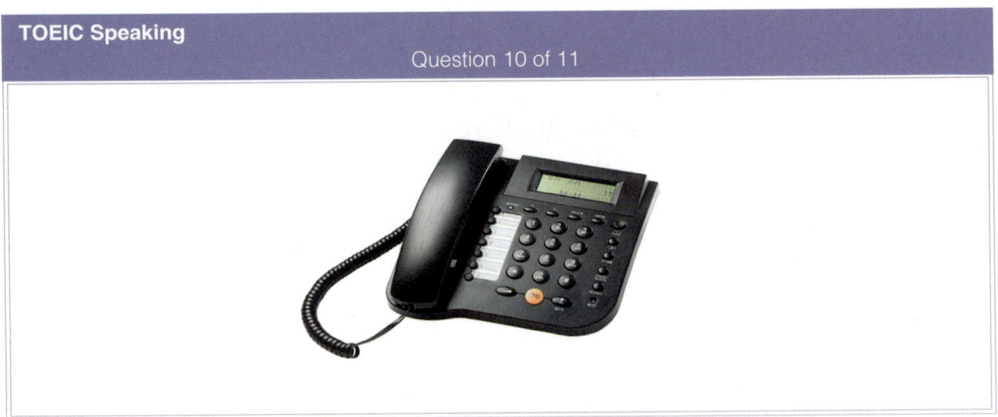

TOEIC Speaking

Question 10 of 11

In your response, be sure to
- show that you recognize the problem, and
- propose a way to deal with the problem.

PREPARATION TIME
00:00:30

RESPONSE TIME
00:00:60

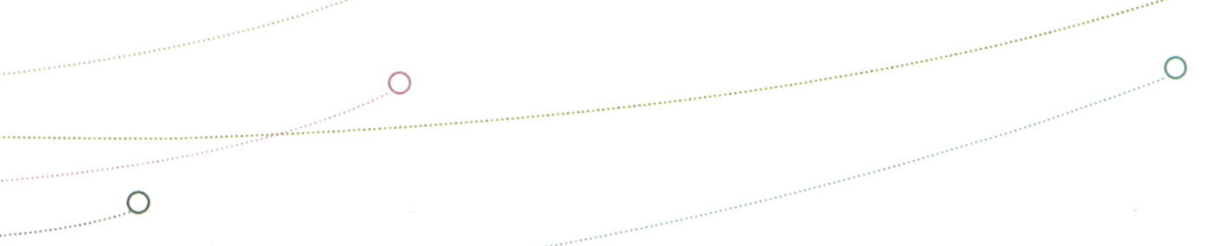

TOEIC Speaking

Question 11: Express an Opinion

Directions: In this part of the test, you will give your opinion about a specific topic. Be sure to say as much as you can in the time allowed. You will have 15 seconds to prepare. Then You will have 60 seconds to speak.

TOEIC Speaking

Question 11 of 11

Do you agree or disagree that new employees should have to work a certain period before being considered for a promotion? Give specific reasons or examples to support your opinion.

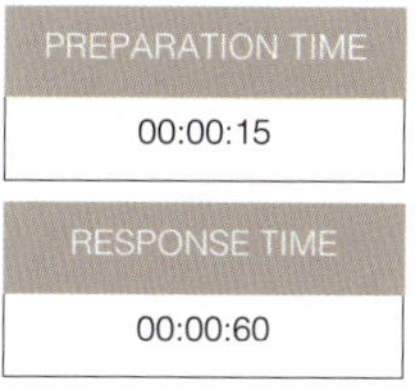

PREPARATION TIME
00:00:15

RESPONSE TIME
00:00:60

TOEIC Speaking Test Directions

This is the TOEIC Speaking Test. This test includes eleven questions that measure different aspects of your speaking ability. The test lasts approximately 20 minutes.

Question	TASK DESCRIPTION	EVALUATION CRITERIA
1-2	Read a text aloud	• Pronunciation • Intonation and stress
3	Describe a Picture	All of the above, plus • Grammar • Vocabulary • Cohesion
4-6	Respond to Questions	All of the above, plus • Relevance of content • Completeness of content
7-9	Respond to Questions Using Infomation Provided	All of the above
10	Propose a Solution	All of the above
11	Express an Opinion	All of the above

For each type of question, you will be given specific directions, including the time allowed for preparation and speaking.

It is to your advantage to say as much as you can in the time allowed. It is also important that you speak clearly and that you answer each question according to the directions.

Click on **Continue** to go on.

Actual Test 07

초고속 TOEIC SPEAKING

Actual Test 07

 07-01

Questions 1-2: Read a Text Aloud

Directions: In this part of the test, you will read aloud the text on the screen. You will have 45 seconds to prepare. Then you will have 45 seconds to read the text aloud.

Attention Edwin Mart shoppers. We have a red light sale going on right now in the sporting goods department. Get an automatic 25% off of bats, balls and bases as long as the red light is flashing. Additionally, don't forget our Daily Hot Item in our Bed and Bath department. See any Sales Associate around you for more information.

PREPARATION TIME
00:00:45

RESPONSE TIME
00:00:45

Attention passengers, this is your Captain speaking one more time. I wanted to update you on some gates for transfers. The flights that I have are for Vicksburg, Pittsburg and Baltimore. Flight 101 for Vicksburg will be out of gate 7, Pittsburgh flight 345 will leave from gate 9 and the Baltimore flight 478 will be out of gate 3. We will be arriving at gate 1, and if you need further information, a screen for departing flights is on your right as you exit the gate.

PREPARATION TIME
00:00:45

RESPONSE TIME
00:00:45

TOEIC Speaking

Question 3: Describe a Picture

Directions: In this part of the test, you will describe the picture on your screen in as much detail as you can. You will have 30 seconds to prepare your response. Then you will have 45 seconds to speak about the picture.

TOEIC Speaking

Question 3 of 11

PREPARATION TIME

00:00:30

RESPONSE TIME

00:00:45

TOEIC Speaking

Questions 4-6: Respond to Questions

Directions: In this part of the test, you will answer three Questions. For each question, begin responding immediately after you hear a beep. No preparation time is provided. You will have 15 seconds to respond to questions 4 and 5 and 30 seconds to respond to question 6.

TOEIC Speaking

Question 4 of 11

Imagine that an Australian marketing firm is conducting research in your country. You have agreed to participate in a telephone interview about visiting museums.

How often do you visit a museum?

RESPONSE TIME
00:00:15

TOEIC Speaking

Question 5 of 11

Imagine that an Australian marketing firm is conducting research in your country. You have agreed to participate in a telephone interview about visiting museums.

**When was the last time you visited a museum,
and what did you see there?**

RESPONSE TIME
00:00:15

TOEIC Speaking

Question 6 of 11

Imagine that an Australian marketing firm is conducting research in your country. You have agreed to participate in a telephone interview about visiting museums.

**Are you more likely to tour a museum by yourself
or with a tour group? Why?**

RESPONSE TIME
00:00:30

TOEIC Speaking

Questions 7-9: Respond to Questions Using Information Provided

Directions: In this part of the test, you will answer three questions based on the information provided. You will have 30 seconds to read the information before the questions begin. For each question, begin responding immediately after you hear a beep. No additional preparation time is provided. You will have 15 seconds to respond to questions 7 and 8 and 30 seconds to respond to question 9.

TOEIC Speaking

Question 7 of 11

Sarah Jameson

sjisawinner@hatmail.com
382 Main Apt. A Idyllwild CA. 68945
Phone: 294-398-4718

Desired Position: Intern or entry level position, Marketing Department for YG

Experience: (2007-2010) Marketing and Campus Sales Rep. for Zale's Jewelry on

University of Texas Campus

Education: BBA (University of Texas 2008), MBA (UT 2010)

Certifications: Social Media Management Certification-2009, Microsoft Suite Certification-

2010

PREPARATION TIME

00:00:30

RESPONSE TIME

00:00:15

Sarah Jameson

sjisawinner@hatmail.com
382 Main Apt. A Idyllwild CA. 68945
Phone: 294-398-4718

Desired Position: Intern or entry level position, Marketing Department for YG

Experience: (2007-2010) Marketing and Campus Sales Rep. for Zale's Jewelry on

University of Texas Campus

Education: BBA (University of Texas 2008), MBA (UT 2010)

Certifications: Social Media Management Certification-2009, Microsoft Suite Certification-

2010

PREPARATION TIME

00:00:30

RESPONSE TIME

00:00:15

Sarah Jameson

sjisawinner@hatmail.com
382 Main Apt. A Idyllwild CA. 68945
Phone: 294-398-4718

Desired Position: Intern or entry level position, Marketing Department for YG

Experience: (2007-2010) Marketing and Campus Sales Rep. for Zale's Jewelry on

University of Texas Campus

Education: BBA (University of Texas 2008), MBA (UT 2010)

Certifications: Social Media Management Certification-2009, Microsoft Suite Certification-

2010

PREPARATION TIME

00:00:30

RESPONSE TIME

00:00:30

TOEIC Speaking

Question 10: Propose a solution

Directions: In this part of the test, you will be presented with a problem and asked to propose a solution. You will have 30 seconds to prepare. Then you will have 60 seconds to speak.

In your response, be sure to
- show that you recognize the problem, and
- propose a way to deal with the problem.

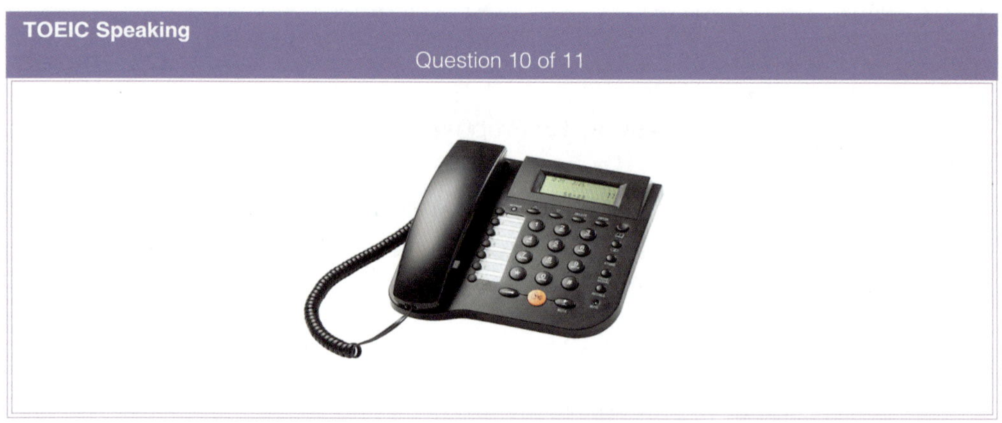

TOEIC Speaking

Question 10 of 11

In your response, be sure to
- show that you recognize the problem, and
- propose a way to deal with the problem.

PREPARATION TIME
00:00:30

RESPONSE TIME
00:00:60

TOEIC Speaking

Question 11: Express an Opinion

Directions: In this part of the test, you will give your opinion about a specific topic. Be sure to say as much as you can in the time allowed. You will have 15 seconds to prepare. Then You will have 60 seconds to speak.

TOEIC Speaking

Question 11 of 11

What do you think is the most important thing for parents to educate their children about? Choose one of the options provided below and give some specific reasons or examples to support your idea.

- how to achieve goals
- how to learn from mistakes
- how to socialize with others

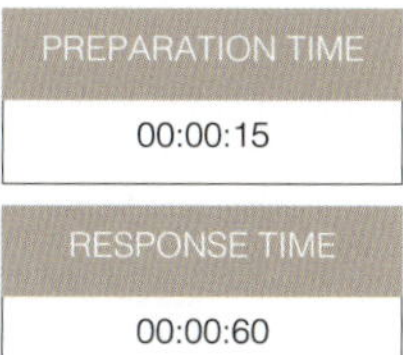

TOEIC Speaking Test Directions

This is the TOEIC Speaking Test. This test includes eleven questions that measure different aspects of your speaking ability. The test lasts approximately 20 minutes.

Question	TASK DESCRIPTION	EVALUATION CRITERIA
1-2	Read a text aloud	• Pronunciation • Intonation and stress
3	Describe a Picture	All of the above, plus • Grammar • Vocabulary • Cohesion
4-6	Respond to Questions	All of the above, plus • Relevance of content • Completeness of content
7-9	Respond to Questions Using Infomation Provided	All of the above
10	Propose a Solution	All of the above
11	Express an Opinion	All of the above

For each type of question, you will be given specific directions, including the time allowed for preparation and speaking.

It is to your advantage to say as much as you can in the time allowed. It is also important that you speak clearly and that you answer each question according to the directions.

Click on **Continue** to go on.

Actual Test 08

초고속 TOEIC SPEAKING

08-01

Questions 1-2: Read a Text Aloud

Directions: In this part of the test, you will read aloud the text on the screen. You will have 45 seconds to prepare. Then you will have 45 seconds to read the text aloud.

The Sports Academy is happy to announce the Grand Opening of another store in Seattle. This means huge savings on all men's, women's and children's sporting apparel. Everything from our famous retro jerseys to our Bell's basketball and baseball equipment has been drastically reduced and is marked down even further this weekend only. Come to the Sports Academy today!

PREPARATION TIME
00:00:45

RESPONSE TIME
00:00:45

Hello, Mr. Jackson. This is Belinda Packard from Tim's Terrific Temps. I am calling to let you know that based on your resume and experience we might have a long term temp position for you. It's for a company that is solid, with a relaxed work environment and seems to be growing. Please call me at 898-3425 if this is something you might be interested in.

PREPARATION TIME
00:00:45

RESPONSE TIME
00:00:45

08-02

Question 3: Describe a Picture

Directions: In this part of the test, you will describe the picture on your screen in as much detail as you can. You will have 30 seconds to prepare your response. Then you will have 45 seconds to speak about the picture.

Question 3 of 11

PREPARATION TIME

00:00:30

RESPONSE TIME

00:00:45

TOEIC Speaking

Questions 4-6: Respond to Questions

Directions: In this part of the test, you will answer three Questions. For each question, begin responding immediately after you hear a beep. No preparation time is provided. You will have 15 seconds to respond to questions 4 and 5 and 30 seconds to respond to question 6.

TOEIC Speaking

Imagine that a British marketing firm is conducting research in your country. You have agreed to participate in a telephone interview about drinking beverages.

What kind of beverages do you like to drink the most often and when do you usually drink them?

RESPONSE TIME

00:00:15

TOEIC Speaking

Question 5 of 11

Imagine that a British marketing firm is conducting research in your country. You have agreed to participate in a telephone interview about drinking beverages.

Where do you usually buy the beverages that you like?

RESPONSE TIME

00:00:15

TOEIC Speaking

Question 6 of 11

Imagine that a British marketing firm is conducting research in your country. You have agreed to participate in a telephone interview about drinking beverages.

**What is the most important thing to consider
when you drink beverages?**

RESPONSE TIME

00:00:30

Questions 7-9: Respond to Questions Using Information Provided

Directions: In this part of the test, you will answer three questions based on the information provided. You will have 30 seconds to read the information before the questions begin. For each question, begin responding immediately after you hear a beep. No additional preparation time is provided. You will have 15 seconds to respond to questions 7 and 8 and 30 seconds to respond to question 9.

Hero Fitness Center

289 Main Street
Sacramento, California
207-1764
Hours: Monday to Saturday 6 A.M. – 11 P.M.

★ **June Specials:**
New members – first month free
3 classes of Aerobic & Jazz dance free (Group Exercise)

★ **July Specials:**
Early class free (6 A.M. – 8 A.M.)
All beverages and snacks at The Health Bar 10% off

★ **August Specials:**
Club dance 5% off
Personal training 10% off

* "Club Dance" is our unique class of high intensity, fast paced club music that makes a great workout and a lot of fun with other group members!

Start Being a Hero Today!!

PREPARATION TIME
00:00:30

RESPONSE TIME
00:00:15

Hero Fitness Center

289 Main Street
Sacramento, California
207-1764
Hours: Monday to Saturday 6 A.M. – 11 P.M.

★ **June Specials:**
New members – first month free
3 classes of Aerobic & Jazz dance free (Group Exercise)

★ **July Specials:**
Early class free (6 A.M. – 8 A.M.)
All beverages and snacks at The Health Bar 10% off

★ **August Specials:**
Club dance 5% off
Personal training 10% off

* "Club Dance" is our unique class of high intensity, fast paced club music that makes a great workout and a lot of fun with other group members!

Start Being a Hero Today!!

PREPARATION TIME
00:00:30

RESPONSE TIME
00:00:15

Hero Fitness Center

289 Main Street
Sacramento, California
207-1764
Hours: Monday to Saturday 6 A.M. – 11 P.M.

★ **June Specials:**
New members – first month free
3 classes of Aerobic & Jazz dance free (Group Exercise)

★ **July Specials:**
Early class free (6 A.M. – 8 A.M.)
All beverages and snacks at The Health Bar 10% off

★ **August Specials:**
Club dance 5% off
Personal training 10% off

* "Club Dance" is our unique class of high intensity, fast paced club music that makes a great workout and a lot of fun with other group members!

Start Being a Hero Today!!

PREPARATION TIME
00:00:30

RESPONSE TIME
00:00:30

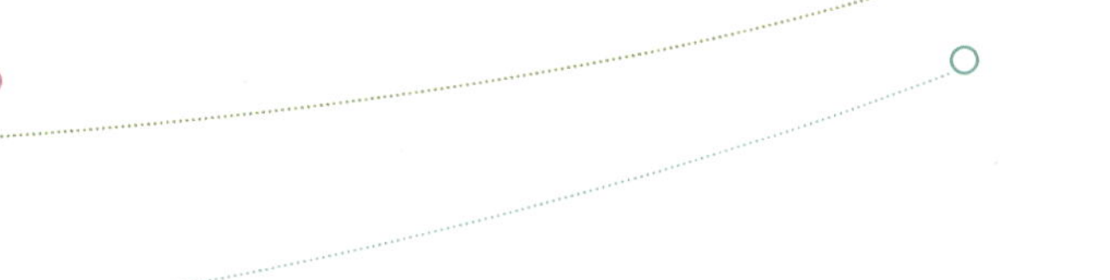

Question 10: Propose a solution

Directions: In this part of the test, you will be presented with a problem and asked to propose a solution. You will have 30 seconds to prepare. Then you will have 60 seconds to speak.

In your response, be sure to
- show that you recognize the problem, and
- propose a way to deal with the problem.

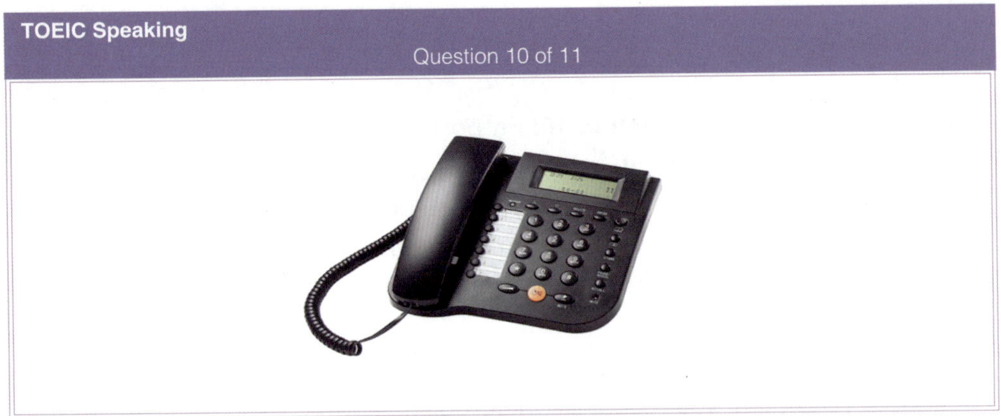

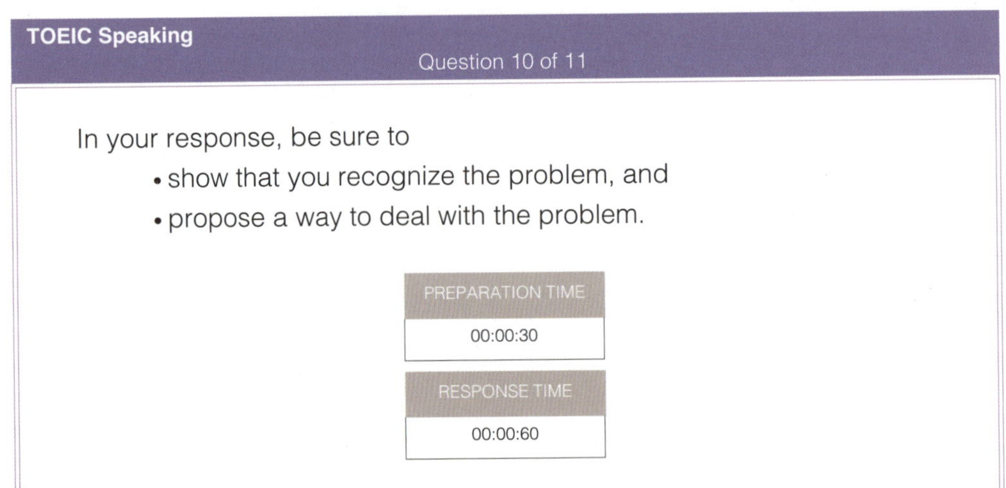

In your response, be sure to
- show that you recognize the problem, and
- propose a way to deal with the problem.

PREPARATION TIME
00:00:30

RESPONSE TIME
00:00:60

TOEIC Speaking

Questions 11: Express an Opinion

Directions: In this part of the test, you will give your opinion about a specific topic. Be sure to say as much as you can in the time allowed. You will have 15 seconds to prepare. Then You will have 60 seconds to speak.

TOEIC Speaking

Question 11 of 11

Do you agree or disagree with the following statement?
'Young people today are more interested in helping others than they have been in the past.'
Use specific reasons or examples to support your opinion.

PREPARATION TIME
00:00:15

RESPONSE TIME
00:00:60

TOEIC Speaking Test Directions

This is the TOEIC Speaking Test. This test includes eleven questions that measure different aspects of your speaking ability. The test lasts approximately 20 minutes.

Question	TASK DESCRIPTION	EVALUATION CRITERIA
1-2	Read a text aloud	• Pronunciation • Intonation and stress
3	Describe a Picture	All of the above, plus • Grammar • Vocabulary • Cohesion
4-6	Respond to Questions	All of the above, plus • Relevance of content • Completeness of content
7-9	Respond to Questions Using Infomation Provided	All of the above
10	Propose a Solution	All of the above
11	Express an Opinion	All of the above

For each type of question, you will be given specific directions, including the time allowed for preparation and speaking.

It is to your advantage to say as much as you can in the time allowed. It is also important that you speak clearly and that you answer each question according to the directions.

Click on **Continue** to go on.

Actual Test 09

초고속 TOEIC SPEAKING

Actual Test 09

09-01

<table>
<tr><td>**TOEIC Speaking**</td></tr>
</table>

Questions 1-2: Read a Text Aloud

Directions: In this part of the test, you will read aloud the text on the screen. You will have 45 seconds to prepare. Then you will have 45 seconds to read the text aloud.

Are you up for a challenge? Do you crave a new adventure? Check out Beach Boys Power Scuba! We have professional instructors who can take anyone from an absolute amateur to the seasoned vet and get them to the next level. Our well organized staff and immaculate facilities will give you the opportunity to experience an amazing world. Call now at 982-8364!

PREPARATION TIME

00:00:45

RESPONSE TIME

00:00:45

Hello, Mr. Prichard. This is Bob Sheffield with Exhibition Auto parts. I recently met you at the Dallas Auto Exhibit. We manufacture quality antennas, batteries, horns and rear-view mirrors for all sorts of vehicles. We talked for a while about your diesel truck repair shops and if possible I would like to get back in touch with you. Please feel free to contact me at 975-2310.

PREPARATION TIME

00:00:45

RESPONSE TIME

00:00:45

09-02

Question 3: Describe a Picture

Directions: In this part of the test, you will describe the picture on your screen in as much detail as you can. You will have 30 seconds to prepare your response. Then you will have 45 seconds to speak about the picture.

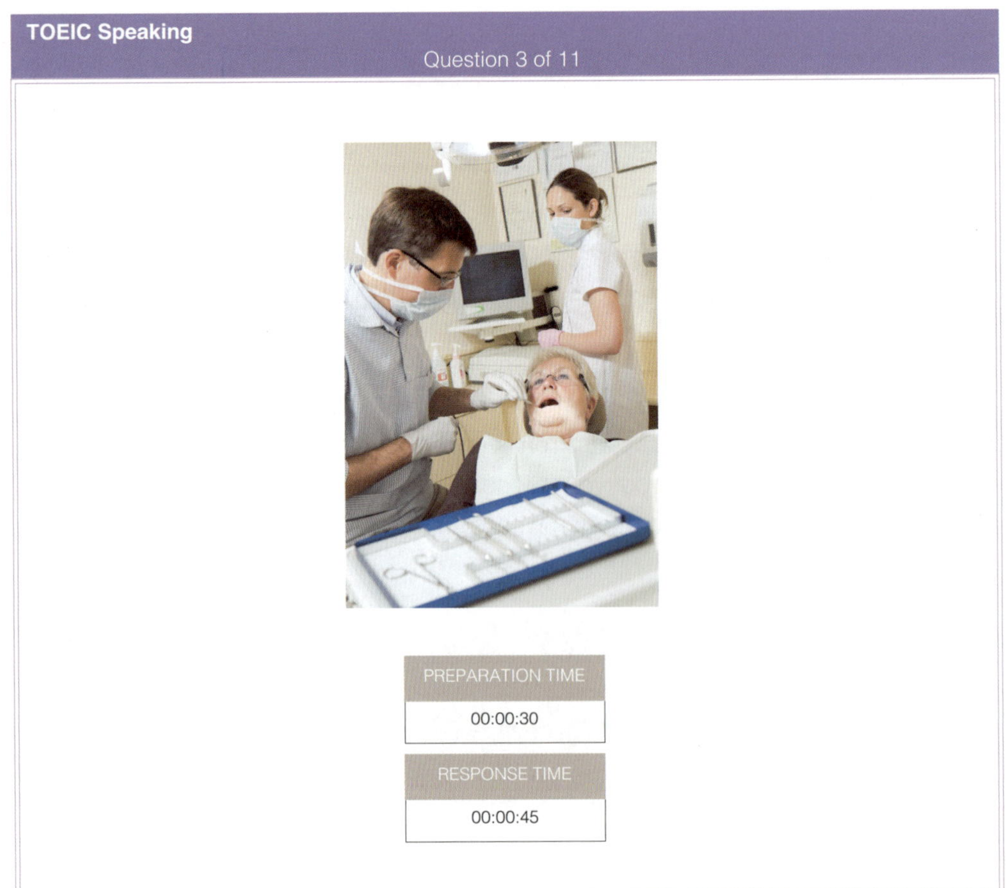

PREPARATION TIME

00:00:30

RESPONSE TIME

00:00:45

TOEIC Speaking

Questions 4-6: Respond to Questions

Directions: In this part of the test, you will answer three Questions. For each question, begin responding immediately after you hear a beep. No preparation time is provided. You will have 15 seconds to respond to questions 4 and 5 and 30 seconds to respond to question 6.

TOEIC Speaking

Question 4 of 11

Imagine that an Australian marketing firm is conducting research in your country. You have agreed to participate in a telephone interview about sharing a ride with other people.

How often do you share a ride to work or school with other people?

RESPONSE TIME

00:00:15

Imagine that an Australian marketing firm is conducting research in your country. You have agreed to participate in a telephone interview about sharing a ride with other people.

Besides commuting to work or school, when would you consider sharing a ride with other people?

RESPONSE TIME

00:00:15

TOEIC Speaking

Question 6 of 11

Imagine that an Australian marketing firm is conducting research in your country. You have agreed to participate in a telephone interview about sharing a ride with other people.

Which of the following is the most beneficial when sharing a ride?
- **Convenience**
- **Saving money**
- **Protecting the environment**

RESPONSE TIME

00:00:30

TOEIC Speaking

Questions 7-9: Respond to Questions Using Information Provided

Directions: In this part of the test, you will answer three questions based on the information provided. You will have 30 seconds to read the information before the questions begin. For each question, begin responding immediately after you hear a beep. No additional preparation time is provided. You will have 15 seconds to respond to questions 7 and 8 and 30 seconds to respond to question 9.

Trinity Lake Festival

10th Anniversary
Sat. Aug. 14

Noon – 1 P.M.	Lunch on the beach: · $10 plate - hamburger, two vegetable rolls and two of our famous biscuits! · $5 plate - hotdog, one vegetable roll and one biscuit! · Plus - salads, fruits, drinks available separately!
1 P.M. – 3 P.M.	Boat show on Trinity Lake ($10 per person to ride)
3 P.M. – 5 P.M.	Horseback riding ($10 per person - 2 hour ride)
4 P.M. – 6 P.M.	Trinity Nature Walk / Petting Zoo ($2 per person for guided tour). Check out our unique plants and feed animals!

PREPARATION TIME

00:00:30

RESPONSE TIME

00:00:15

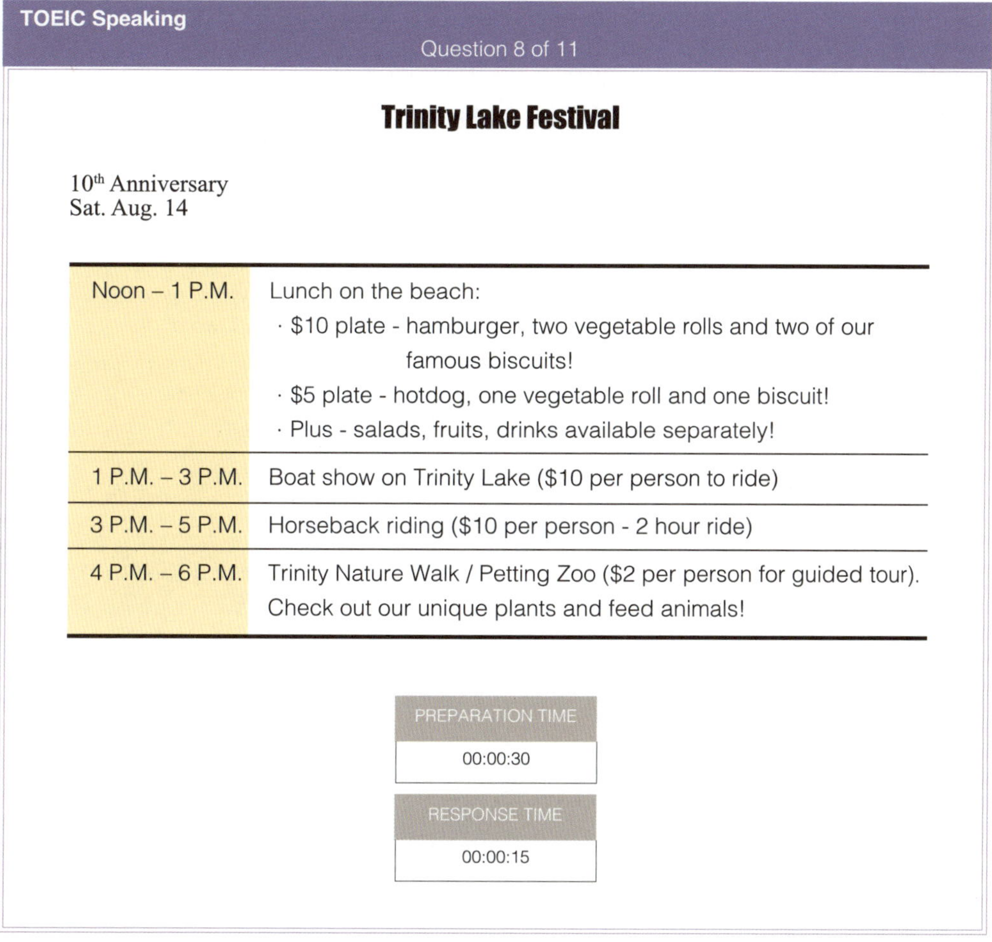

Trinity Lake Festival

10th Anniversary
Sat. Aug. 14

Noon – 1 P.M.
Lunch on the beach:
· $10 plate - hamburger, two vegetable rolls and two of our famous biscuits!
· $5 plate - hotdog, one vegetable roll and one biscuit!
· Plus - salads, fruits, drinks available separately!

1 P.M. – 3 P.M.
Boat show on Trinity Lake ($10 per person to ride)

3 P.M. – 5 P.M.
Horseback riding ($10 per person - 2 hour ride)

4 P.M. – 6 P.M.
Trinity Nature Walk / Petting Zoo ($2 per person for guided tour). Check out our unique plants and feed animals!

PREPARATION TIME
00:00:30

RESPONSE TIME
00:00:15

Trinity Lake Festival

10th Anniversary
Sat. Aug. 14

Noon – 1 P.M.	Lunch on the beach: · $10 plate - hamburger, two vegetable rolls and two of our famous biscuits! · $5 plate - hotdog, one vegetable roll and one biscuit! · Plus - salads, fruits, drinks available separately!
1 P.M. – 3 P.M.	Boat show on Trinity Lake ($10 per person to ride)
3 P.M. – 5 P.M.	Horseback riding ($10 per person - 2 hour ride)
4 P.M. – 6 P.M.	Trinity Nature Walk / Petting Zoo ($2 per person for guided tour). Check out our unique plants and feed animals!

PREPARATION TIME

00:00:30

RESPONSE TIME

00:00:30

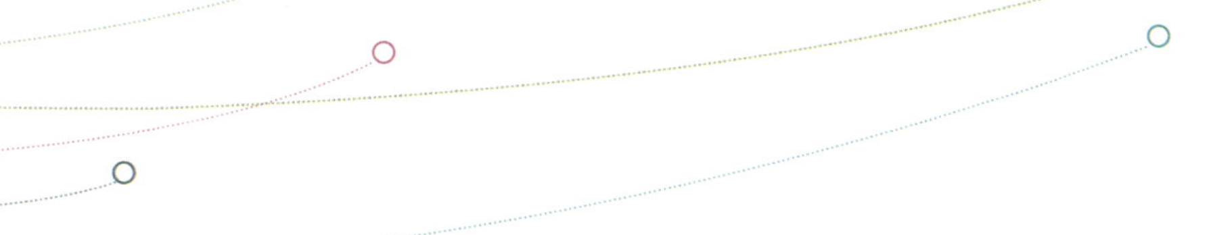

TOEIC Speaking

Question 10: Propose a solution

Directions: In this part of the test, you will be presented with a problem and asked to propose a solution. You will have 30 seconds to prepare. Then you will have 60 seconds to speak.

In your response, be sure to
- show that you recognize the problem, and
- propose a way to deal with the problem.

TOEIC Speaking

Question 10 of 11

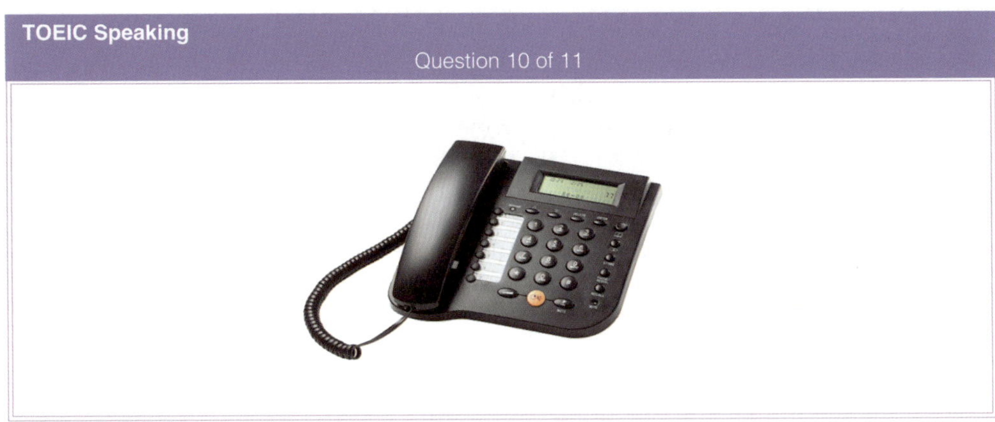

TOEIC Speaking

Question 10 of 11

In your response, be sure to
- show that you recognize the problem, and
- propose a way to deal with the problem.

PREPARATION TIME
00:00:30

RESPONSE TIME
00:00:60

TOEIC Speaking

Question 11: Express an Opinion

Directions: In this part of the test, you will give your opinion about a specific topic. Be sure to say as much as you can in the time allowed. You will have 15 seconds to prepare. Then You will have 60 seconds to speak.

TOEIC Speaking

Question 11 of 11

As a business owner, you would prefer to hire talented employees. In order to attract talented employees, which of the following options would be better? Use specitic reasons or examples to support your opinion.

· Give a private office
· Give a lot of vacation days

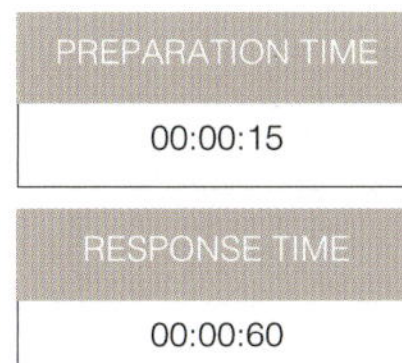

TOEIC Speaking Test Directions

This is the TOEIC Speaking Test. This test includes eleven questions that measure different aspects of your speaking ability. The test lasts approximately 20 minutes.

Question	TASK DESCRIPTION	EVALUATION CRITERIA
1-2	Read a text aloud	• Pronunciation • Intonation and stress
3	Describe a Picture	All of the above, plus • Grammar • Vocabulary • Cohesion
4-6	Respond to Questions	All of the above, plus • Relevance of content • Completeness of content
7-9	Respond to Questions Using Infomation Provided	All of the above
10	Propose a Solution	All of the above
11	Express an Opinion	All of the above

For each type of question, you will be given specific directions, including the time allowed for preparation and speaking.

It is to your advantage to say as much as you can in the time allowed. It is also important that you speak clearly and that you answer each question according to the directions.

Click on **Continue** to go on.

Actual Test 10

초고속 TOEIC SPEAKING

10-01

TOEIC Speaking

Questions 1-2: Read a Text Aloud

Directions: In this part of the test, you will read aloud the text on the screen. You will have 45 seconds to prepare. Then you will have 45 seconds to read the text aloud.

May I have your attention please? Will all priority passengers for Royal Line flight 1901 please proceed to gate 58. Royal Line flight 1901 will begin general boarding in 10 minutes. Priority passengers are those who will require extra time and assistance, those traveling with small children, active duty service members or members of the Royal Air Alliance.

PREPARATION TIME

00:00:45

RESPONSE TIME

00:00:45

If you are thinking about Rome, think no further than the Coliseum Bed and Breakfast. Located just behind Termini Station, we are central to everything you would want to see and enjoy while you are here. Termini Station has all the bus, train and tourist transportation right at the front door. In addition, our rooms are near all the best night life. Check us out online at ColiseumB&B.com.

PREPARATION TIME

00:00:45

RESPONSE TIME

00:00:45

 10-02

TOEIC Speaking

Question 3: Describe a Picture

Directions: In this part of the test, you will describe the picture on your screen in as much detail as you can. You will have 30 seconds to prepare your response. Then you will have 45 seconds to speak about the picture.

TOEIC Speaking

Question 3 of 11

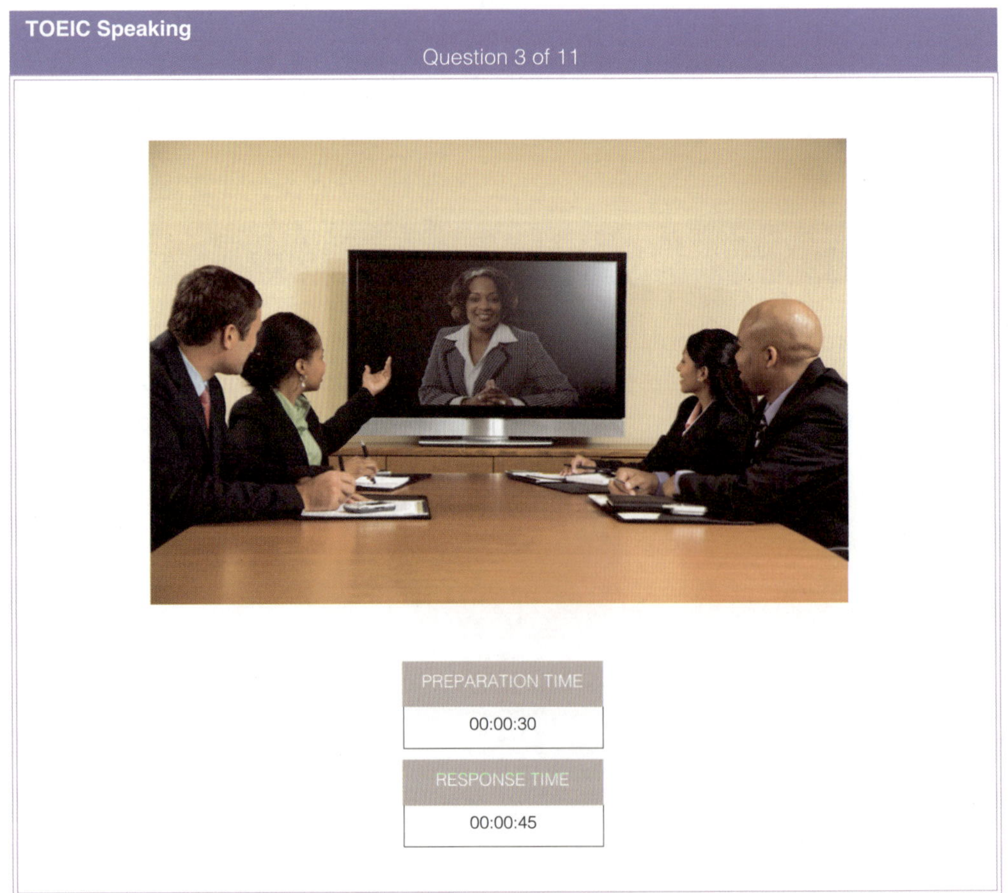

PREPARATION TIME

00:00:30

RESPONSE TIME

00:00:45

Questions 4-6: Respond to Questions

Directions: In this part of the test, you will answer three Questions. For each question, begin responding immediately after you hear a beep. No preparation time is provided. You will have 15 seconds to respond to questions 4 and 5 and 30 seconds to respond to question 6.

Imagine that an American marketing firm is conducting research in your country. You have agreed to participate in a telephone interview about libraries.

What services do you use when you go to a library?

RESPONSE TIME

00:00:15

TOEIC Speaking

Question 5 of 11

Imagine that an American marketing firm is conducting research in your country. You have agreed to participate in a telephone interview about libraries.

What services could the library offer to be more helpful?

RESPONSE TIME

00:00:15

TOEIC Speaking

Question 6 of 11

Imagine that an American marketing firm is conducting research in your country. You have agreed to participate in a telephone interview about libraries.

Which of the following three things do you think is the most in need of change with regard to the library?

- **hours of operation**
- **computer systems**
- **materials available**

RESPONSE TIME

00:00:30

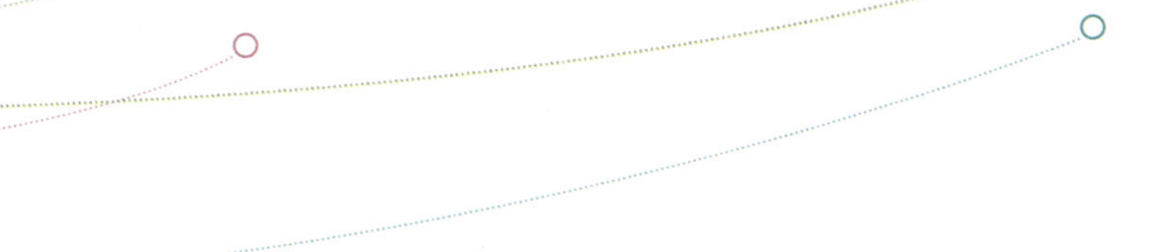

Questions 7-9: Respond to Questions Using Information Provided

Directions: In this part of the test, you will answer three questions based on the information provided. You will have 30 seconds to read the information before the questions begin. For each question, begin responding immediately after you hear a beep. No additional preparation time is provided. You will have 15 seconds to respond to questions 7 and 8 and 30 seconds to respond to question 9.

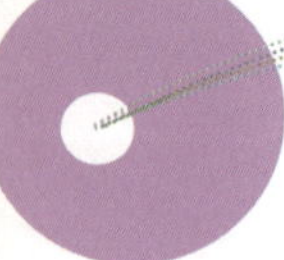

Actual Test 10

JM Corp.
Orientation for New Employees

Second draft

09:00 - 09:30	Opening speech – Dexter Lee, vice president
09:30 – 11:00	Presentation on How to adapt to JM Corp. – John Forrest
~~11:00 – 12:00~~	~~Salary Policies~~ **rescheduled - change from first draft**
12:00 – 13:00	Lunch break
13:00 – 14:00	Tour of the Headquarters building
14:00 – 15:00	Discussion – Jessica Simpson
15:00 – 16:00	Meeting with your team managers

* Coffee, water and snacks will be available throughout the day.

PREPARATION TIME

00:00:30

RESPONSE TIME

00:00:15

JM Corp.
Orientation for New Employees

Second draft

09:00 - 09:30	Opening speech – Dexter Lee, vice president
09:30 – 11:00	Presentation on How to adapt to JM Corp. – John Forrest
11:00 – 12:00	~~Salary Policies~~ **rescheduled - change from first draft**
12:00 – 13:00	Lunch break
13:00 – 14:00	Tour of the Headquarters building
14:00 – 15:00	Discussion – Jessica Simpson
15:00 – 16:00	Meeting with your team managers

* Coffee, water and snacks will be available throughout the day.

PREPARATION TIME
00:00:30

RESPONSE TIME
00:00:15

JM Corp.
Orientation for New Employees

Second draft

09:00 - 09:30	Opening speech – Dexter Lee, vice president
09:30 – 11:00	Presentation on How to adapt to JM Corp. – John Forrest
~~11:00 – 12:00~~	~~Salary Policies~~ **rescheduled - change from first draft**
12:00 – 13:00	Lunch break
13:00 – 14:00	Tour of the Headquarters building
14:00 – 15:00	Discussion – Jessica Simpson
15:00 – 16:00	Meeting with your team managers

* Coffee, water and snacks will be available throughout the day.

PREPARATION TIME

00:00:30

RESPONSE TIME

00:00:30

 10-05

Question 10: Propose a solution

Directions: In this part of the test, you will be presented with a problem and asked to propose a solution. You will have 30 seconds to prepare. Then you will have 60 seconds to speak.

In your response, be sure to
- show that you recognize the problem, and
- propose a way to deal with the problem.

TOEIC Speaking

Question 10 of 11

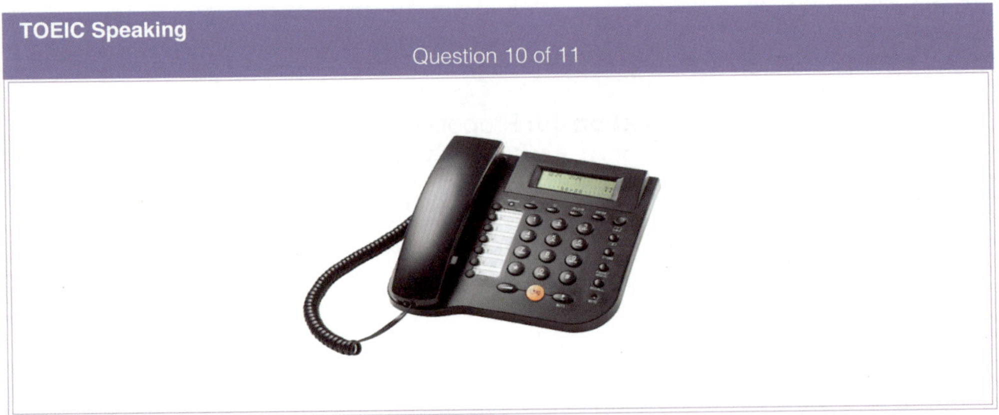

TOEIC Speaking

Question 10 of 11

In your response, be sure to
- show that you recognize the problem, and
- propose a way to deal with the problem.

PREPARATION TIME
00:00:30

RESPONSE TIME
00:00:60

10-06

TOEIC Speaking

Question 11: Express an Opinion

Directions: In this part of the test, you will give your opinion about a specific topic. Be sure to say as much as you can in the time allowed. You will have 15 seconds to prepare. Then You will have 60 seconds to speak.

TOEIC Speaking

Question 11 of 11

Which of the following jobs contributed to the world the most? Give specific reasons or examples to support your opinion.

· lawyer
· doctor
· farmer

PREPARATION TIME
00:00:15

RESPONSE TIME
00:00:60

TOEIC Speaking Test Directions

This is the TOEIC Speaking Test. This test includes eleven questions that measure different aspects of your speaking ability. The test lasts approximately 20 minutes.

Question	TASK DESCRIPTION	EVALUATION CRITERIA
1-2	Read a text aloud	• Pronunciation • Intonation and stress
3	Describe a Picture	All of the above, plus • Grammar • Vocabulary • Cohesion
4-6	Respond to Questions	All of the above, plus • Relevance of content • Completeness of content
7-9	Respond to Questions Using Infomation Provided	All of the above
10	Propose a Solution	All of the above
11	Express an Opinion	All of the above

For each type of question, you will be given specific directions, including the time allowed for preparation and speaking.

It is to your advantage to say as much as you can in the time allowed. It is also important that you speak clearly and that you answer each question according to the directions.

Click on **Continue** to go on.

Actual Test 11

초고속 TOEIC SPEAKING

Actual Test 11

11-01

Questions 1-2: Read a Text Aloud

Directions: In this part of the test, you will read aloud the text on the screen. You will have 45 seconds to prepare. Then you will have 45 seconds to read the text aloud.

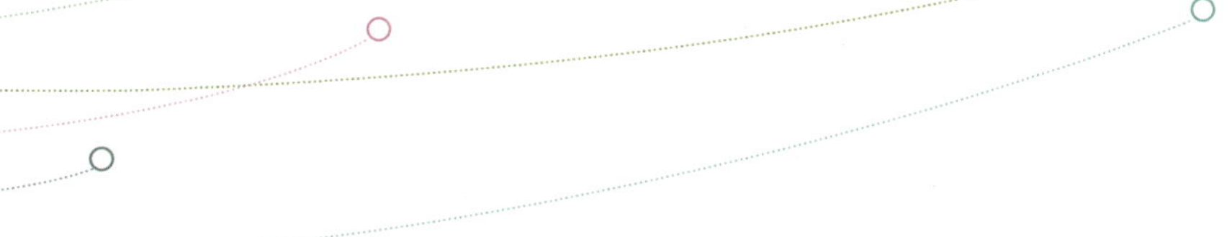

Atlanta's Museum of Photography is proud to announce a new exhibition of World War 2 photographs. This exhibit contains photos from French, Spanish, Italian and Polish photographers who risked life and limb in order to document this amazing time in history. For more information call 789-2745.

PREPARATION TIME

00:00:45

RESPONSE TIME

00:00:45

Hello and welcome to the KPBP hourly traffic update. The new asphalt on 635 is causing a delay all the way to the 36 kilometer mark east bound. In addition, we have the regular backup on the toll way. That's at the Jupiter on ramp where Iron Corp. and TWR Inc. all leave work to head home at the same time. Other than that it looks like the problems on 183 have been eliminated so enjoy the ride home.

PREPARATION TIME

00:00:45

RESPONSE TIME

00:00:45

11-02

TOEIC Speaking

Question 3: Describe a Picture

Directions: In this part of the test, you will describe the picture on your screen in as much detail as you can. You will have 30 seconds to prepare your response. Then you will have 45 seconds to speak about the picture.

TOEIC Speaking

Question 3 of 11

PREPARATION TIME

00:00:30

RESPONSE TIME

00:00:45

TOEIC Speaking

Questions 4-6: Respond to Questions

Directions: In this part of the test, you will answer three Questions. For each question, begin responding immediately after you hear a beep. No preparation time is provided. You will have 15 seconds to respond to questions 4 and 5 and 30 seconds to respond to question 6.

TOEIC Speaking

Question 4 of 11

Imagine that a Canadian marketing firm is conducting research in your country. You have agreed to participate in a telephone interview about traditions around gift giving.

When was the last time you gave a gift to any of your friends or family?

RESPONSE TIME

00:00:15

Imagine that a Canadian marketing firm is conducting research in your country. You have agreed to participate in a telephone interview about traditions around gift giving.

Are there special days when you are more apt to give a gift to your friends or perhaps a family member?

RESPONSE TIME

00:00:15

Imagine that a Canadian marketing firm is conducting research in your country. You have agreed to participate in a telephone interview about traditions around gift giving.

What are some key deciding factors for you when considering what gift you will give your friends and family members?

RESPONSE TIME

00:00:30

TOEIC Speaking

Questions 7-9: Respond to Questions Using Information Provided

Directions: In this part of the test, you will answer three questions based on the information provided. You will have 30 seconds to read the information before the questions begin. For each question, begin responding immediately after you hear a beep. No additional preparation time is provided. You will have 15 seconds to respond to questions 7 and 8 and 30 seconds to respond to question 9.

Food & Style Magazine

Rough draft meeting – Monday Dec. 3

Topic	Author	Status
"'All In' Annual Chili Cook Off - Chance to win a new F-150!"	Jack Bowers	In progress - need photos and rules
"10 Foods for Good Luck"	Crystal Smith	To be edited - too long Interview on Tues. Dec. 4
"Soused mackerel with pickled vegetables"	Jackie Pans	Need more photos Taking photos on Wed. Dec. 5
"The Best Red Wines from Johnson Mountain Winery"	Rob Teaman	To be edited - too long

Final Deadline – Fri. Dec. 7

PREPARATION TIME
00:00:30

RESPONSE TIME
00:00:15

Food & Style Magazine

Rough draft meeting – Monday Dec. 3

Topic	Author	Status
"'All In' Annual Chili Cook Off - Chance to win a new F-150!"	Jack Bowers	In progress - need photos and rules
"10 Foods for Good Luck"	Crystal Smith	To be edited - too long Interview on Tues. Dec. 4
"Soused mackerel with pickled vegetables"	Jackie Pans	Need more photos Taking photos on Wed. Dec. 5
"The Best Red Wines from Johnson Mountain Winery"	Rob Teaman	To be edited - too long

Final Deadline – Fri. Dec. 7

PREPARATION TIME
00:00:30

RESPONSE TIME
00:00:15

Food & Style Magazine

Rough draft meeting – Monday Dec. 3

Topic	Author	Status
"'All In' Annual Chili Cook Off - Chance to win a new F-150!"	Jack Bowers	In progress - need photos and rules
"10 Foods for Good Luck"	Crystal Smith	To be edited - too long Interview on Tues. Dec. 4
"Soused mackerel with pickled vegetables"	Jackie Pans	Need more photos Taking photos on Wed. Dec. 5
"The Best Red Wines from Johnson Mountain Winery"	Rob Teaman	To be edited - too long

Final Deadline – Fri. Dec. 7

PREPARATION TIME
00:00:30

RESPONSE TIME
00:00:30

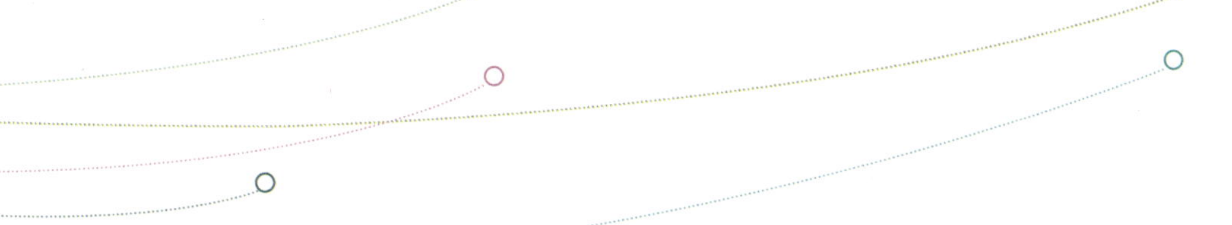

TOEIC Speaking

Question 10: Propose a solution

Directions: In this part of the test, you will be presented with a problem and asked to propose a solution. You will have 30 seconds to prepare. Then you will have 60 seconds to speak.

In your response, be sure to
- show that you recognize the problem, and
- propose a way to deal with the problem.

TOEIC Speaking

Question 10 of 11

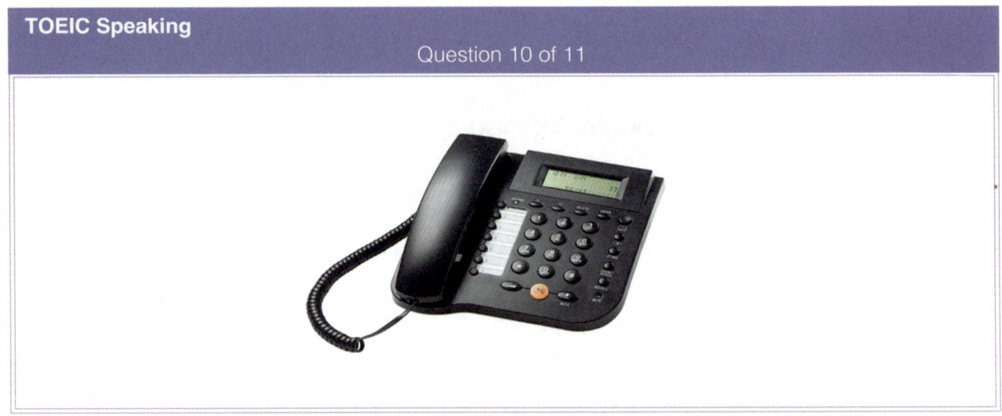

TOEIC Speaking

Question 10 of 11

In your response, be sure to
- show that you recognize the problem, and
- propose a way to deal with the problem.

PREPARATION TIME

00:00:30

RESPONSE TIME

00:00:60

TOEIC Speaking

Question 11: Express an Opinion

Directions: In this part of the test, you will give your opinion about a specific topic. Be sure to say as much as you can in the time allowed. You will have 15 seconds to prepare. Then You will have 60 seconds to speak.

TOEIC Speaking

Question 11 of 11

Do you prefer to work in a big company or in a small company? Why? Use specific reasons or examples to support your opinion.

PREPARATION TIME

00:00:15

RESPONSE TIME

00:00:60

TOEIC Speaking Test Directions

This is the TOEIC Speaking Test. This test includes eleven questions that measure different aspects of your speaking ability. The test lasts approximately 20 minutes.

Question	TASK DESCRIPTION	EVALUATION CRITERIA
1-2	Read a text aloud	• Pronunciation • Intonation and stress
3	Describe a Picture	All of the above, plus • Grammar • Vocabulary • Cohesion
4-6	Respond to Questions	All of the above, plus • Relevance of content • Completeness of content
7-9	Respond to Questions Using Infomation Provided	All of the above
10	Propose a Solution	All of the above
11	Express an Opinion	All of the above

For each type of question, you will be given specific directions, including the time allowed for preparation and speaking.

It is to your advantage to say as much as you can in the time allowed. It is also important that you speak clearly and that you answer each question according to the directions.

Click on **Continue** to go on.

Actual Test 12

초고속 TOEIC SPEAKING

 12-01

Questions 1-2: Read a Text Aloud

Directions: In this part of the test, you will read aloud the text on the screen. You will have 45 seconds to prepare. Then you will have 45 seconds to read the text aloud.

Question 1 of 11

Attention, Bed and Bath Avenue Shoppers. We would like to remind you that until further notice all Pebo Laru bathmats have an additional 35% off. That's right all the colorful, soft and stylish bathmats by Pebo Laru that you love are now 35% off! Your discount will be applied at the cash register for a limited time only!

PREPARATION TIME
00:00:45

RESPONSE TIME
00:00:45

Question 2 of 11

Hello and thank you for coming to the product launch of this exciting new innovative battery. This battery can be recharged by solar, wind and hydro power. The light on the right of the battery gives a constant indication for what is needed and the light will exhibit a progressively brighter red light to show the need to be recharged.

PREPARATION TIME
00:00:45

RESPONSE TIME
00:00:45

 12-02

TOEIC Speaking

Question 3: Describe a Picture

Directions: In this part of the test, you will describe the picture on your screen in as much detail as you can. You will have 30 seconds to prepare your response. Then you will have 45 seconds to speak about the picture.

TOEIC Speaking

Question 3 of 11

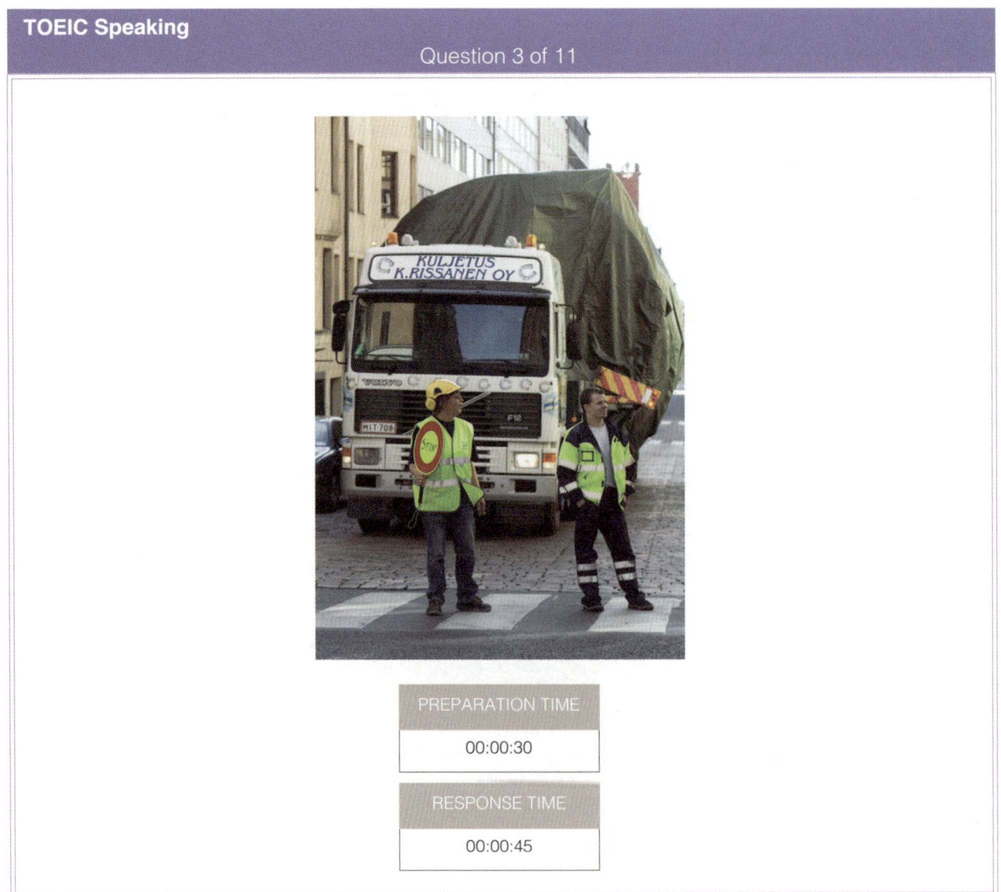

PREPARATION TIME
00:00:30

RESPONSE TIME
00:00:45

TOEIC Speaking

Questions 4-6: Respond to Questions

Directions: In this part of the test, you will answer three Questions. For each question, begin responding immediately after you hear a beep. No preparation time is provided. You will have 15 seconds to respond to questions 4 and 5 and 30 seconds to respond to question 6.

TOEIC Speaking

Question 4 of 11

Imagine that an American marketing firm is conducting research in your country. You have agreed to participate in a telephone interview about American food.

How often do you cook at home and have you ever cooked American food?

RESPONSE TIME

00:00:15

TOEIC Speaking

Question 5 of 11

Imagine that an American marketing firm is conducting research in your country. You have agreed to participate in a telephone interview about American food.

What kinds of American food do you think are better to eat at a restaurant than to cook at home?

RESPONSE TIME

00:00:15

TOEIC Speaking

Question 6 of 11

Imagine that an American marketing firm is conducting research in your country. You have agreed to participate in a telephone interview about American food.

Do you think you are a good cook with American food? Why? Would cooking classes help?

RESPONSE TIME

00:00:30

TOEIC Speaking

Questions 7-9: Respond to Questions Using Information Provided

Directions: In this part of the test, you will answer three questions based on the information provided. You will have 30 seconds to read the information before the questions begin. For each question, begin responding immediately after you hear a beep. No additional preparation time is provided. You will have 15 seconds to respond to questions 7 and 8 and 30 seconds to respond to question 9.

Travel Itinerary – Keith Grace

The annual conference for IT Professionals
Marriot Conference Center, Main Hall
Marriot Hotel
100 Marriot Drive
Boston, MA

	▸ **Friday May 13**
11 A.M.-3:30 P.M.	Delta Flight 156 Atlanta to Boston Change planes in Memphis (Shuttle bus to the Hotel)
6:30 P.M.	Welcome dinner @ The Marriot Restaurant and social mixer to follow
	▸ **Saturday May 14**
9 A.M.-3 P.M.	Conference and meetings
5:00 P.M.	Dinner with sub-committee
	▸ **Sunday May 15**
9 A.M.-11 A.M.	Delta Flight 155 Boston to Atlanta (Direct flight)

PREPARATION TIME
00:00:30

RESPONSE TIME
00:00:15

Travel Itinerary – Keith Grace

The annual conference for IT Professionals
Marriot Conference Center, Main Hall
Marriot Hotel
100 Marriot Drive
Boston, MA

▸ Friday May 13	
11 A.M.-3:30 P.M.	Delta Flight 156 Atlanta to Boston Change planes in Memphis (Shuttle bus to the Hotel)
6:30 P.M.	Welcome dinner @ The Marriot Restaurant and social mixer to follow
▸ Saturday May 14	
9 A.M.-3 P.M.	Conference and meetings
5:00 P.M.	Dinner with sub-committee
▸ Sunday May 15	
9 A.M.-11 A.M.	Delta Flight 155 Boston to Atlanta (Direct flight)

PREPARATION TIME

00:00:30

RESPONSE TIME

00:00:15

Travel Itinerary – Keith Grace

The annual conference for IT Professionals
Marriot Conference Center, Main Hall
Marriot Hotel
100 Marriot Drive
Boston, MA

▸ Friday May 13	
11 A.M.-3:30 P.M.	Delta Flight 156 Atlanta to Boston Change planes in Memphis (Shuttle bus to the Hotel)
6:30 P.M.	Welcome dinner @ The Marriot Restaurant and social mixer to follow
▸ Saturday May 14	
9 A.M.-3 P.M.	Conference and meetings
5:00 P.M.	Dinner with sub-committee
▸ Sunday May 15	
9 A.M.-11 A.M.	Delta Flight 155 Boston to Atlanta (Direct flight)

PREPARATION TIME

00:00:30

RESPONSE TIME

00:00:30

TOEIC Speaking

Question 10: Propose a solution

Directions: In this part of the test, you will be presented with a problem and asked to propose a solution. You will have 30 seconds to prepare. Then you will have 60 seconds to speak.

In your response, be sure to

- show that you recognize the problem, and
- propose a way to deal with the problem.

TOEIC Speaking

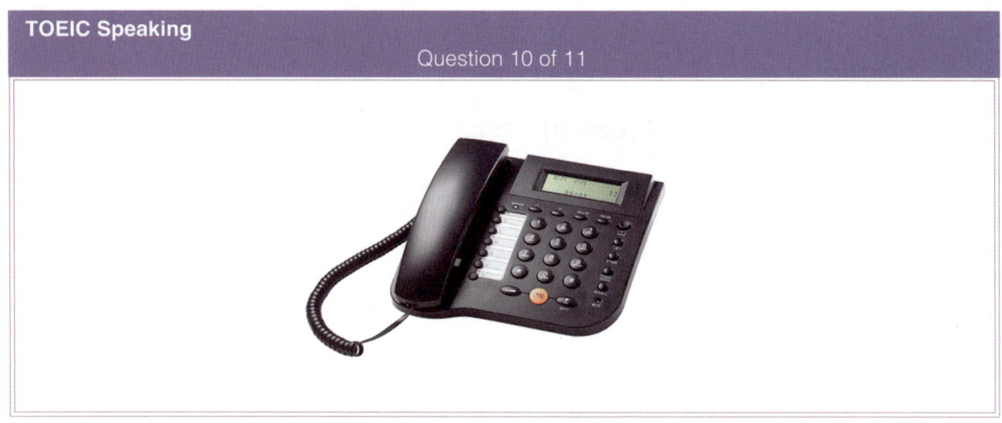

TOEIC Speaking

Question 10 of 11

In your response, be sure to

- show that you recognize the problem, and
- propose a way to deal with the problem.

PREPARATION TIME
00:00:30

RESPONSE TIME
00:00:60

TOEIC Speaking

Question 11: Express an Opinion

Directions: In this part of the test, you will give your opinion about a specific topic. Be sure to say as much as you can in the time allowed. You will have 15 seconds to prepare. Then You will have 60 seconds to speak.

TOEIC Speaking

Question 11 of 11

Do you agree with this statement?
'In order for a business to succeed it needs to have a continual flow of new customers as well as dedicated regular customers.'
Give specific reasons or examples to support your opinion.

PREPARATION TIME
00:00:15

RESPONSE TIME
00:00:60

TOEIC SPEAKING
Actual Test

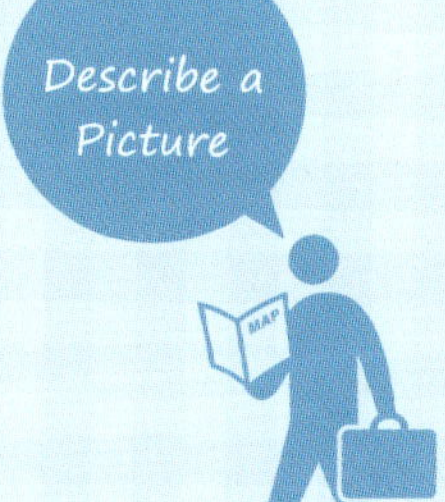
Read a
text aloud
Describe a
Picture

Respond to
Questions

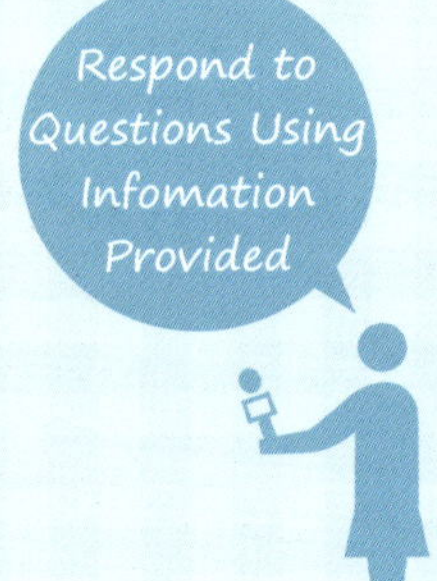
Respond to
Questions Using
Infomation
Provided

Propose a
Solution

Express an
Opinion

초고속 TOEIC SPEAKING Actual Test

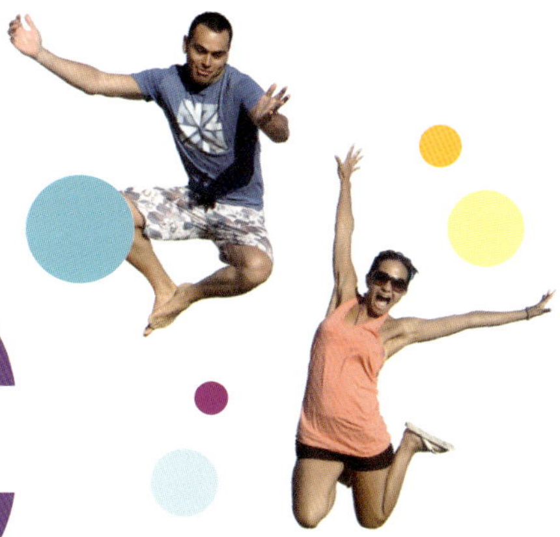

초고속

| 홍성하 · Bob Hildreth 공저 |

Actual Test

모범답안 · 해설

혜지연

초고속 TOEIC SPEAKING Actual Test

초단기 고속 특점성

| 홍성하 · Bob Hildreth 공저 |

모범답안 · 해설

혜지원

About This Book

모범답안의 한글 해석입니다.

MP3 파일명입니다.

문제별 저자의 노하우를 설명하는 '고득점 TIP' 입니다.

문제와 모범답안에 사용된 필수어휘입니다.

학습자의 실력에 맞게 선택하여 훈련할 수 있도록 모든 문제의 모범답안은 초 · 중급 답변 1개, 고급 답변 1개, 총 2개씩 실었습니다. MP3 파일을 듣고 따라하며 훈련하세요.

★ 그 밖에 Question 1, 2는 강조 어휘, 빈출 어휘, 발음과 강세에 수의해야 힐 어휘, 연음, 끊어읽기, 올려읽기, 내려읽기가 표시되어 있습니다.

Contents

목차

초고속
TOEIC
Speaking

Actual Test 01~12

정답 및 해설

Actual Test 01

Questions 1-2 Read a Text Aloud

Question 1

🎧 01-01-01

Hello, / **Chicago book club!** ↘ // **Tonight,** ↗ we have a very **special guest speaker,** ↗ / **Ms. Barbara Jefferson.** ↘ // **Ms.** Jefferson was born in **Philadelphia** ↗ / but **currently** lives in **California.** ↘ // She has written **science fiction,** ↗ / **fantasy** ↗ / and **adult novels** / and tonight / she will be **reading** a section / from her **latest book,** ↗ / **Moons of Uranus.** ↘ // Please help me **welcome** / with a **big round of applause,** ↗ **Ms. Barbara Jefferson.** ↘

안녕하세요, Chicago book club 여러분! 오늘 저희는 아주 특별한 손님을 한 분 모셨습니다. 바로, Barbara Jefferson 씨 입니다. Jefferson 씨는 Philadelphia에서 태어나셨고 지금은 California에서 살고 계십니다. 그녀는 그 동안 SF, 판타지 그리고 성인 소설을 써 오셨는데, 오늘밤 그녀의 가장 최근 작품인 'Moons of Uranus'를 직접 읽어주실 것입니다. 큰 박수와 함께 Barbara Jefferson 씨를 모셔보겠습니다.

| 고득점 TIP | 소개 지문이므로 소개되는 사람의 **이름, 출생지, 사는 곳, 업적(저서 종류 및 제목)** 등을 강조해서 읽는다. |

| 어 휘 | **currently** 현재   **moon** 달, 위성   **Uranus** 천왕성   **applause** 박수 |

Question 2

🎧 01-01-02

Welcome to the **most famous tea house** in the **region,** ↗ / **The Golden Leaf.** ↘ // On our tour / you will **discover** / how tea is grown, ↗ / **processed** ↗ / and **packaged** for shipment / **all over** the world. ↘ // Our tour will **end with a visit** / to our **Tea House** ↗ where you can **sample** the **variety** of **teas** / **created** here. ↘

이 지역에서 가장 유명한 찻집인 'The Golden Leaf'에 오신 것을 환영합니다. 저희 투어에서 여러분은 어떻게 찻잎이 자라고 가공 처리되며, 전 세계로 수송되기 위해 포장되는지에 대한 과정을 살펴보게 될 것입니다. 저희 투어는 여러분이 이 곳에서 직접 생산된 다양한 차들을 시음하는 프로그램을 마지막으로 끝을 맺게 됩니다.

| 고득점 TIP | 가이드가 관광객들에게 전하는 공지이다. 현재 도착지(The Golden Leaf), 앞으로 하게 될 일들을 강조해서 읽는다. |

| 어 휘 | **tea house** 찻집   **process** 가공(처리)하다   **package** 포장하다   **shipment** 수송(품)   **sample** 시식(시음)하다   **a(the) variety of** 다양한 |

Question 3 Describe a Picture

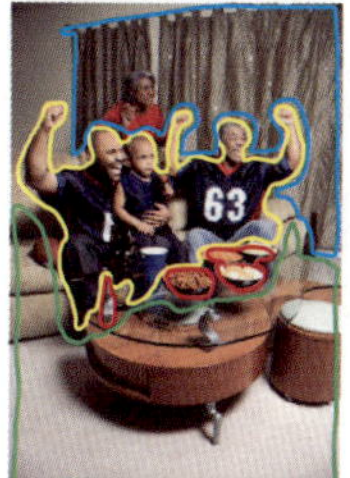

— 도입　— 중심　— 주변　— 마무리

고득점 TIP '**장소** ⇨ **전반적인 구도** ⇨ **위치 별 세부묘사** ⇨ **느낌**' 순으로 묘사한다. 인원 수는 2~4명이 가장 자주 출제되는데, 우선 사람들의 **공통된 행동이나 의상을 최대한 많이 묘사**하고 그 후에 특징적인 것들을 덧붙인다. 그래야 짧은 묘사 시간을 잘 활용할 수 있다.

Question 3　🎧 01-01-03

초·중급 Model Answer

This picture appears to be in a living room. The first thing I notice is a family cheering for something. On the left, a man is raising up his right hand and holding a child with his left hand. Next to him, an elderly man with glasses is also holding his hands up. These three people are wearing sportswear and sitting on the sofa. In front of them, there are some snacks and beer bottles on the table. Behind the sofa, I can see an elderly woman in red clothes and a light brown curtain. It seems that they are watching a sports game on TV.

이 사진은 거실에서 찍힌 것 같습니다. 가장 먼저 보이는 것은 무언가에 환호하는 한 가족입니다. 왼쪽에는 한 남성이 그의 오른손을 올리고 있고, 왼손으로는 한 아이를 안고 있습니다. 그 남성의 옆에는 안경을 쓴 중년 남성이 또한 그의 두 손을 올리고 있습니다. 이 세 사람은 운동복을 입고 소파에 앉아 있습니다. 이들 앞에는 테이블 위에 간식과 맥주병들이 있습니다. 소파 뒤에는 붉은색 옷을 입은 한 중년 여성과 밝은 갈색 톤의 커튼을 볼 수 있습니다. 이 사람들은 TV를 통해 스포츠 게임을 보고 있는 것 같습니다.

고급 Model Answer

This picture appears to be of a family in their living room. The first thing I notice is that the whole family is cheering for a sports event they are watching. On the left, a man is raising up his right hand and holding a child on his knee with his left hand. Next to him on his left, an elderly man with glasses wearing a jersey with number 63 is holding up both hands. Both of the men are sitting on a sofa along with the child on the man's knee while behind them is a woman leaning on the back of the sofa. In front of the sofa the men are sitting on is a table with snacks and beers. My guess is that something good just happened and they are celebrating.

이 사진은 거실에서 찍힌 한 가족의 사진인 것 같습니다. 가장 먼저 보이는 것은 한 가족이 그들이 보고 있는 스포츠 경기에 환호하고 있는 모습입니다. 왼쪽에는 한 남성이 그의 오른손을 들고 있고, 왼손으로 한 아이를 그의 무릎에 앉혀 놓고 있습니다. 그의 왼쪽 옆에는 한 중년 남성이 안경을 쓰고 63이라고 적혀있는 저지 셔츠를 입고, 그의 두 손을 올리고 있습니다. 이 두 남성은 한 남성의 무릎에 앉아 있는 아이와 함께 소파에 앉아 있습니다. 그리고 그들 뒤에는 소파 뒤쪽에 기대어 있는 한 여성이 있습니다. 남성들이 앉아 있는 소파 앞에는 간식과 맥주들이 놓여 있는 테이블이 있습니다. 제 생각에 어떤 좋은 일이 생겨서 이 사람들이 그것을 축하하고 있는 것 같습니다.

|어 휘| **cheer** 환호하다 (**cheer for** 응원하다)　**elderly man** 노인　**jersey** (운동 경기용) 셔츠
along with ~와 함께　**celebrate** 축하하다

Actual Test 01

Questions 4-6 Respond to Questions

Imagine that an American marketing firm is conducting research in your country. You have agreed to participate in a telephone interview about jobs.

미국의 한 마케팅 회사가 당신의 나라에서 설문조사를 하고 있다고 가정해 보세요. 당신은 '직업'에 관한 전화 인터뷰에 응하기로 동의했습니다.

Question 4
01-01-04

Q. What is your current job or what type of job are you looking for?

당신의 현재 직업은 무엇이며, 혹은 찾고 있는 직업은 무엇입니까?

초·중급 Model Answer

A. I'm an office worker. I work for a construction company 5 days a week but I am off on weekends.

저는 사무직 근로자입니다. 건설회사에서 일을 하는데, 일주일에 5일 일하고 주말에는 쉽니다.

고급 Model Answer

A. Currently I work in a restaurant for my uncle but I'm looking for a job with a large firm like Samsung or LG in the Marketing department.

현재 저는 삼촌께서 운영하시는 식당에서 일을 하고 있습니다. 하지만 삼성, LG같은 대기업의 마케팅부서에서 일을 하고 싶습니다.

고득점 TIP 4, 5번의 답변은 2~3 문장이면 된다. 첫 문장은 문제에 대한 짧고 직접적인 답변을 하고, 두 번째 문장은 그에 대한 간단한 부연설명을 한다.

Question 5
01-01-05

Q. What skills do you need for your job? 당신의 직업을 위해 어떠한 능력이 필요합니까?

초·중급 Model Answer

A. Computer skills are important such as managing a spread sheet or word processing program. Also, I should be able to get along with others well.

스프레드시트나 문서작성 프로그램을 다루는 것과 같은 컴퓨터 활용 능력이 중요합니다. 또한 다른 사람들과 원만하게 어울릴 줄 알아야 합니다.

고급 Model Answer

A. The skills I need for my job involve interporsonal skills like getting along with coworkers even in stressful situations. Additionally, some job skills are task related like kitchen clean up at the end of the night.

제 직업에 필요한 능력 중에는 스트레스가 쌓이는 상황에서도 다른 직원들과 원만하게 잘 어울릴 줄 아는 대인관계 능력이 포함됩니다. 또한 일과 후에 주방을 청소하는 등의 직무와 관계된 능력들도 있습니다.

Question 6

01-01-06

Q. Can you describe how your college prepared you for your current job?

당신의 대학 생활이 현재 직업을 준비하는 데 있어 어떠한 영향을 끼쳤나요?

초·중급 Model Answer

A. In college, I majored in construction. I use some of the theories that I learned in school at my work place now. The most important skills I learned from college were interpersonal skills or how to get along with a wide variety of people. Thanks to these experiences, I can work well as a part of my team.

대학교 때 전공은 건축이었습니다. 그 때 배운 이론들 중 일부를 지금 일하면서 활용하고 있습니다. 대학 시절에 체득한 능력들 중에서 가장 중요한 것은 대인관계 능력, 혹은 다양한 사람들과 잘 어울릴 줄 아는 방법들입니다. 이러한 경험들 덕분에 저는 팀의 일원으로서 업무를 잘 수행할 수 있게 되었습니다.

고급 Model Answer

A. In my opinion, my college study taught me many facts and figures. While at college, I learned a lot of theories and ideas that have worked in my field. I feel like many of the ideas had merit and I have used them already but perhaps the best education from my college days was with interpersonal interaction. College taught me how to get along with a wide variety of people with different ways of thinking. The people skills I learned in college I use continuously.

제 생각에 저는 대학시절에 많은 자세한 정보들을 배웠습니다. 대학 시절에 저는 많은 이론과 생각들을 배웠는데 지금 제가 일하는 분야에도 적용이 됩니다. 그들 중 많은 것들이 가치가 있고 이미 활용해오고 있지만, 아마도 대학 때 배운 가장 중요한 교훈은 바로 대인관계에 관한 것입니다. 대학교 때 저는 다양한 생각을 가진 많은 사람들과 잘 어울릴 수 있는 방법을 터득할 수 있었습니다. 이렇게 대학시절 배운 대인관계 능력을 현재 계속해서 활용하고 있습니다.

| 고득점 TIP | 6번 문제의 경우, **아이디어가 안 떠오르면 한 가지만 이야기하고 그에 대한 예를 들면서 총 5문장 정도** 만들면 된다. 이 문제의 경우에는 본인의 전공과 관련해 전공과목을 이야기할 수도 있고, 더 좋은 방법은 능력과 소양을 묻는 문제이므로 위의 5번처럼 **대인관계(interpersonal skill)**에 대해 이야기하고 동아리 활동 등 본인의 예를 들어 부연설명한다.

| 어 휘 | **look for** ~을 찾다   **office worker** 사무직 근로자   **construction company** 건설 회사
get along with ~와 잘 지내다   **interpersonal skill** 대인관계 능력   **coworker** 직장 동료
facts and figures 자세한 정보   **merit** 가치   **interaction** 상호작용   **continuously** 지속적으로

Hot Springs Arkansas Guided Hiking Tours

From 9 A.M. to 2 P.M. Daily

Hikes leave every hour on the hour

Table Rock Lake to Bear Mountain Hot Springs ▶ Advanced
- Duration: 3 hours
- Cost: $30

Dry Gulch Canyon to The Wishing Pond ▶ Beginner
- Duration: 2 hours
- Cost: $35

---

* Get maps, souvenirs, snacks and more information from the Base Camp store.

가이드가 안내하는 Arkansas 온천 하이킹 투어

매일 오전 9시~오후 2시
매시 정각 출발

Table Rock Lake부터 Bear Mountain Hot Springs까지 ▶ 상급
- 소요 시간: 3시간
- 비용: 30달러

Dry Gulch Canyon부터 Wishing Pond까지 ▶ 초급
- 소요 시간: 2시간
- 비용: 35달러

---

* 지도, 기념품, 간식 및 추가 정보들을 Base Camp 매장에서 구할 수 있습니다.

Hello, my name is Sonny James and I would like to plan a hiking trip with you but I need more information. Are you the person I need to talk to?

안녕하세요, 저는 Sonny James라고 합니다. 귀사에서 진행하는 도보 여행에 관심이 있는데요, 더 많은 정보가 필요합니다. 궁금한 사항들을 여쭤어봐도 될까요?

Question 7

 01-01-07

Q. What times do the hikes start? 하이킹의 시작 시간이 어떻게 되나요?

 **초·중급 Model Answer**

A. Our hiking tours are from 9 A.M. to 2 P.M. daily. The hikes leave every hour on the hour.

저희 도보 여행은 매일 오전 9시부터 오후 2시까지입니다. 매시 정각에 출발합니다.

고급 Model Answer

A. Our hiking tours start at 9 A.M. daily. They leave every hour on the hour and the last hike starts at 2 P.M.

저희 도보 여행은 매일 오전 9시부터 출발합니다. 매시 정각에 출발하며 마지막 출발 시간은 2시입니다.

고득점 TIP **의문사의문문**은 어떤 의문사인지를 잘 파악해야 한다. **What time~**으로 시작했으므로 시간 관련 정보를 언급한다.

Question 8

 01-01-08

Q. Do I need to bring my own food? 음식을 직접 따로 준비해 올 필요가 있습니까?

 **초·중급 Model Answer**

A. No, you don't have to bring your own food. We have some snacks at our Base Camp store.

아닙니다. 음식을 따로 가져오실 필요는 없습니다. 저희 Base Camp 상점에서 간식 종류를 취급합니다.

고급 Model Answer

A. No, you don't have to bring your own food. We have some snacks at the Base Camp store but if you want more than that you need to bring it yourself.

아닙니다. 음식을 따로 가져오실 필요는 없습니다. 저희 Base Camp 상점에서 간식 종류를 취급합니다. 하지만 그 이상의 음식이 필요하시다면 따로 준비하셔도 됩니다.

고득점 TIP **Do/Have/Be동사** 등으로 시작하는 의문문일 경우, 첫 대답은 **Yes/No**로 시작한다.

Question 9

01-01-09

Q. I am a beginner at hiking. What do you have that I could do?

저는 하이킹 초보입니다. 제가 이용할 만한 코스가 있을까요?

초·중급 **Model Answer**

A. There is a hiking trail for beginners. It's from Dry Gulch Canyon to The Wishing Pond. It takes about 2 hours and it costs $35 per person.

초보자용 하이킹 코스가 있습니다. Dry Gulch Canyon부터 The Wishing Pond까지 입니다. 2시간 정도 소요되며 비용은 개인당 35달러입니다.

고급 **Model Answer**

A. Hot Springs Arkansas Guided Hiking Tours has a great hike for beginners. We have a beautiful trail from Dry Gulch Canyon to The Wishing Pond. It takes about 2 hours from start to finish and the cost is $35 per person.

저희 '가이드가 안내하는 Arkansas 온천 하이킹 투어'에는 초보자들을 위한 멋진 하이킹 코스가 있습니다. Dry Gulch 부터 The Wishing Pond까지의 아름다운 코스입니다. 시작부터 끝까지 2시간 정도 소요되며 비용은 개인당 35달러입니다.

고득점 **TIP** | key word인 **beginner**를 잘 들어야 한다. 그 후에 표에 있는 정보들을 바탕으로 완전한 문장을 만든다.

|어 휘| **guided** 가이드가 안내하는　　**daily** 매일　　**on the hour** 정시에　　**advanced** 고급의　　**intermediate** 중급의　**beginner** 초보자　　**duration** 지속, 기간　　**souvenir** 기념품

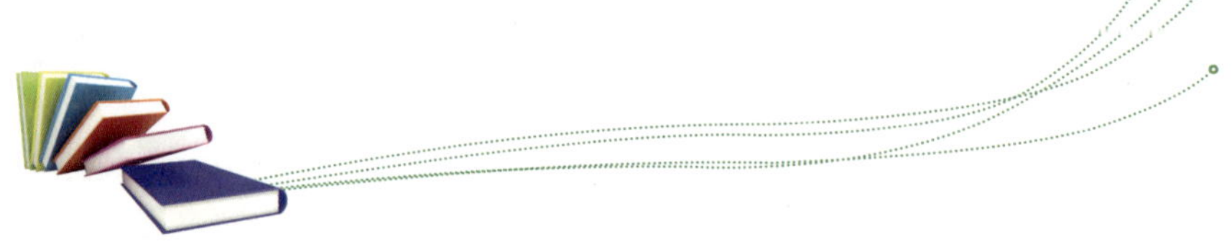

Question 10 Propose a solution

Hi, this is William. I would like you to work on getting more information on the new facility that the company just opened up - the staff lounge. I'm very satisfied with the staff lounge but in my opinion we need to try to set a tone for this area very early. This should be a place where employees can share ideas comfortably with each other and hopefully with us as well. How do we go about collecting ideas from employees to make this staff lounge a better place? I would like to get your thoughts on this and see what ideas you have. As the person in charge of HR, I will consider your suggestions, add mine and bring them up at the board meeting next week.

안녕하세요, William입니다. 회사가 최근에 문을 연 새 시설물 직원휴게실에 대해서 더 많은 정보를 얻어주셨으면 합니다. 저는 그 휴게실에 대해 아주 만족하고 있는데요, 제 생각에는 이 장소에 대한 공론의 분위기를 아주 일찍 조성해야 할 것 같습니다. 이곳은 직원들이 서로의 생각을 편안하게 공유할 수 있는 장소가 되어야 합니다. 물론 저희 부서하고도 말이죠. 이 휴게실을 더 훌륭한 장소로 만들기 위해서 직원들의 아이디어를 어떻게 모으는 것이 좋을까요? 이 문제에 대해 당신이 어떠한 의견을 갖고 있는지 듣고 싶습니다. 인사 팀의 팀장으로서, 당신의 제안들을 고려해 본 후 제 의견을 더해서 다음 주에 있을 임원회의 때 제안하려고 합니다.

Question 10

 01-01-10

초·중급 Model Answer

Hello, Sir. This is Bob. I'm returning your call about your request. I got your message saying that you're satisfied with the new staff lounge and you are asking me how to collect ideas from employees for this place. Why don't we run an idea contest for the entire staff? As far as I know, we have some brand new computers in stock. We can give them out to the winners who suggest the best ideas. I hope this helps. If you have any other questions, please feel free to contact me anytime. Bye.

안녕하십니까, 팀장님. Bob입니다. 요청하셨던 사안에 대해서 답변 드리고자 합니다. 팀장님께서는 새 직원 휴게실에 대해 만족하시고, 이 장소를 위해 직원들의 생각들을 어떻게 모을지에 대해서 제게 물어보셨습니다. 전 직원을 상대로 아이디어를 공모하는 것은 어떻습니까? 제가 알기로는, 재고로 새 컴퓨터가 조금 남았을 겁니다. 최고의 아이디어를 낸 직원들에게 그 컴퓨터들을 포상으로 지급할 수 있습니다. 이 의견이 도움이 되길 바랍니다. 다른 궁금하신 사항이 있으면 언제든 연락주십시오. 감사합니다.

고급 Model Answer

Hello, William. This is Bob. I'm returning your call regarding the new staff lounge. I got your message and I understand that you're very satisfied with the new staff lounge and you think it should be a comfortable place for employees to share ideas each other. Additionally, you would like to know how we could gather good ideas from employees to make this staff lounge a better place. Here is an idea off the top of my head, why don't we run an idea contest for the entire staff? As far as I know, we have some brand new computers in stock for the customer appreciation events. We could give some out to the staff winners who suggest the best ideas. I hope this helps. Please think about my idea and if you have any other questions or concerns, feel free to contact me anytime. Bye.

안녕하십니까, William 팀장님. 저는 Bob입니다. 새 직원 휴게실과 관련해서 답신 드립니다. 팀장님께서는 새 직원 휴게실에 대해 만족하시고, 이 장소가 직원들이 서로의 생각들을 편안하게 공유할 수 있는 곳이 되어야 한다고 말씀하셨습니다. 또한, 이 휴게실을 더 훌륭한 장소로 만들기 위해서 직원들의 아이디어를 어떻게 모을지에 대해 생각해보라고 하셨습니다. 문득 떠오른 아이디어가 있는데요, 전 직원을 대상으로 아이디어를 공모하는 것은 어떻습니까? 제가 알기로는 고객 사은행사 때 사용하고 재고로 남은 새 컴퓨터들이 있을 것입니다. 최고의 아이디어를 낸 직원들에게 그 컴퓨터들을 포상으로 지급할 수 있을 것입니다. 이 의견이 도움이 되길 바랍니다. 제 아이디어를 한 번 고려해주시길 부탁 드리며, 혹시 다른 궁금하신 사항이나 우려되시는 부분이 있으면 언제든 연락 주십시오. 감사합니다.

고득점 TIP | 회사에서 **이슈가 무엇이 되었든지** (ex. 신제품 반응이 좋지 않음, 고객 불만이 많음, 직원 사기 진작 등) **해결책을 제시해야 하는 경우**, 혹은 이 문제와 같이 직접적으로 어떠한 현안에 대해 아이디어를 어떻게 모아야 하는가 하는 질문에는 **'아이디어 콘테스트를 해서 좋은 의견을 낸 직원들에게 포상을 한다'**는 식으로 답변할 수 있다.

어휘 | **facility** 시설 **staff lounge** 직원 휴게실 **be satisfied with** ~에 만족하다 **set a tone** 분위기를 조성하다 **in charge of** ~를 담당하고 있는 **board meeting** 이사회 **why don't we** ~하는 게 어떨까요? **run an idea contest** 아이디어를 공모하다 **entire** 전체의 **brand new** 아주 새로운 **in stock** 비축되어, 재고로 **off the top of my head** 문득 떠오른 **appreciation** 감사, 공감

Question 11 Express an Opinion

Do you agree or disagree with the following statement? 'People from large families are more competitive than people from small families.' Use specific reasons or details to support your answer.

당신은 다음 의견에 동의합니까, 반대합니까? '대가족 출신의 사람들이 소가족 출신 사람들보다 더 경쟁력이 있다(경쟁심이 강하다).' 당신의 답변을 뒷받침할 구체적인 근거 혹은 예를 제시하십시오.

Question 11   01-01-11

초·중급 Model Answer

I agree that people from large families are more competitive than people from small families for the following reasons. First of all, they always compete with brothers or sisters for limited resources. In my case, when I was young I used to try to get more food than my brother got. Secondly, they can learn how to get along with others. Social skills are very important these days especially at work. For these reasons, I go along with this opinion.

저는 다음과 같은 이유로 대가족 출신의 사람들이 소가족 출신의 사람들보다 더 경쟁력이 있다(경쟁심이 강하다)라는 의견에 동의합니다. 첫째로, 그들은 한정된 자원을 두고 형제자매들과 항상 경쟁합니다. 제 경우에는, 어렸을 때 형보다 더 많은 음식을 먹으려고 애쓰던 기억이 있습니다. 두 번째로, 그들은 다른 사람들과 어울리는 법을 배울 수 있습니다. 대인 관계 기술은 이 시대에 특히 직장에서 아주 중요합니다. 이러한 이유들 때문에, 저는 이 의견에 찬성합니다.

고급 Model Answer

I agree that people from large families are more competitive than people from small families. Here are some reasons to support my opinion. First of all, people from larger families had to be more competitive because they constantly had more people around them competing for the same limited resources such as the same amount of food, love and home support. As a result, they had to work harder, be smarter and show that they deserved more than their siblings. Secondly, they can learn how to get along better with others. In other words, because they had to keep communicating with their siblings, they have better social skills. People's social skills are very important in modern society especially at work. That's why I see eye to eye with this statement.

저는 대가족 출신의 사람들이 소가족 출신 사람들보다 더 경쟁력이 있다(경쟁심이 강하다)라는 의견에 동의합니다. 제 의견을 뒷받침할 몇 가지 이유가 있습니다. 첫째로, 대가족 출신의 사람들은 더 경쟁심이 강해야 합니다. 왜냐하면 그들 주위에는 음식, 가족들의 사랑과 지원 같은 한정된 자원을 놓고 경쟁을 해야 하는 누군가가 항상 곁에 있기 때문입니다. 그 결과 그들은 더 열심히 일해야 하고, 더 뛰어난 사람이 되어야 하며, 그들의 형제자매들에 비해 더 누릴 자격이 있다는 것을 증명해내야 합니다. 둘째, 그들은 다른 사람들과 더 잘 어울리는 방법을 배울 수 있습니다. 다시 말해서, 그들은 형제자매들과 계속해서 소통해야 했기 때문에 사회성을 더 많이 개발할 수 있습니다. 사람들의 사회성은 현대 사회에서, 특히 직장생활을 함에 있어 매우 중요합니다. 이러한 이유들 때문에 저는 이 의견에 동의합니다.

고득점 TIP 성우가 문제를 읽는 동안 먼저 눈으로 문제를 빨리 읽고 동의할 것인가 반대할 것인가 결정한다. 그리고 **준비시간 15초 동안 근거 2개를 떠올린다. 시간이 빠듯하므로 구체적인 설명이 아닌 아이디어 2개를 생각해보려고 노력한다.** Model Answer에서는 주어진 진술에 동의하는 입장을 취했다. 일반적으로 말을 하기 쉬운 쪽으로 의견을 정하는 것이 좋다.

어휘 **competitive** 경쟁력 있는, 경쟁심이 강한 **compete** 경쟁하다 **limited** 제한된 **used to** ~하곤 했다 **get along with** ~와 어울리다 **social skills** 대인 관계 기술 **go along with** ~에 동의하다 **deserve** ~할 자격이 있다 **sibling** 형제자매 **modern society** 현대 사회 **see eye to eye** 동의하다

Questions 1-2 Read a Text Aloud

> ★ **Bold** ⇨ 강조 어휘   ★ 녹색 ⇨ 빈출 어휘, 발음과 강세에 주의해야 할 어휘
> ★ 밑줄 ⇨ 연음   ★ / ⇨ 끊어읽기   ★ ↗ ↘ ⇨ 올려읽기, 내려읽기

Question 1

01-02-01

Do you **enjoy foreign films**? ↗ // The **Foreign Film club** / of **Boston Proper Community College** / would <u>like</u> **you** ↗ / to **join** them / for their **Thursday evening Foreign Film Academy** / <u>this semester</u>. ↘ // We have **films** from **Paris**, ↗ / **Munich** ↗ / and **Seoul** this term. ↘ // **All films** will be **shown** / in the **recently renovated** / **Avenue Theatre**. ↘ // For **more** information, ↗ / **call 567-2839**. ↘

당신은 외국 영화를 좋아합니까? 저희 Boston Proper 전문대학의 외국 영화 클럽에서 이번 학기 목요일 저녁에 있는 외국 영화 아카데미에 당신을 초대합니다. 저희는 이번 학기에 파리와 뮌헨, 그리고 서울 등지에서 수집한 영화들을 선보입니다. 모든 영화들은 최근에 재건축을 마친 Avenue 극장에서 상영될 예정입니다. 궁금한 사항이 있으면 567-2839로 연락 바랍니다.

| 고득점 TIP | 영화 아카데미에 대한 **공지문**이므로 **주요 정보(주최, 일시, 장소, 내용 등)를 강조**해서 읽는다. **열거하는 부분은 억양에 주의**해서 읽고, **전화번호는 숫자 한 자리씩 끊어서** 읽는다.

| 어 휘 | **community college** 지역 전문대학   **semester** 학기   **Munich** 뮌헨   **renovate** 개조(보수)하다
theatre(= theater) 극장, 공연장

Question 2

01-02-02

Hello / and **welcome** / to **Disneyland's Variety Show Boat Spectacular**. ↘ // Please <u>move</u> **all** the way ↗ / to the <u>**first available**</u> seat / on your <u>**assigned row**</u>. ↘ // **Also,** / please **remember** / for the <u>**courtesy**</u> of <u>**all**</u> our **guest** / that **eating**, ↗ / **drinking**, ↗ / **talking** / and **flash photography** / are **prohibited** ↗ / **once** the **show begins**. ↘ // <u>**Once**</u> again, ↗ / **welcome** / and **enjoy** the **show**! ↘

안녕하세요, 저희 디즈니랜드의 다양한 쇼 공연 행사에 오신 여러분을 환영합니다. 지정된 열의 맨 앞줄부터 채워 앉아주시길 부탁 드립니다. 또한 일단 쇼가 시작된 이후에는 음식 및 음료 섭취나 잡담, 그리고 사진 촬영이 금지된다는 점에 대해 관객 여러분의 협조바랍니다. 다시 한 번 여러분을 환영합니다. 즐거운 관람되시길 바랍니다!

| 고득점 TIP | 공연 직전 관객들의 협조를 구하는 공지문이다. **문장의 호흡이 길기 때문에 끊어 읽기에 주의**하고, 실제 관객이 앞에 있다고 생각하면서 느낌을 살려 읽는다.

| 어 휘 | **variety** 각양각색   **spectacular** 화려한 공연   **available** 이용할 수 있는   **assigned** 할당된
courtesy of ~의 호의로(허가로)   **prohibit** 금지하다

Question 3 Describe a Picture

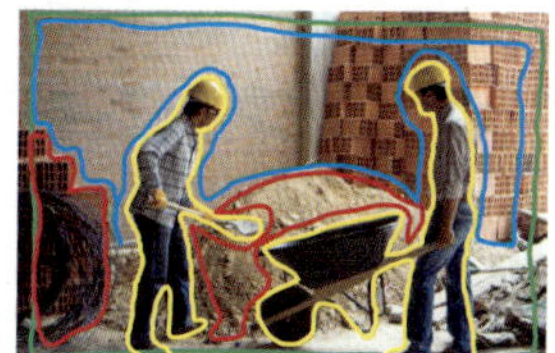

고득점 TIP 두 사람의 공통점(행동 및 의상)을 먼저 묘사하고, 한 명씩 차례로 추가 내용을 묘사한다. 사람 묘사가 끝나면 그 주위 사물들에 대해 말한다.

Question 3

01-02-03

초·중급 Model Answer

This picture appears to be at a construction site. The first thing I notice is two people working together. They are wearing yellow safety helmets, checkered shirts and jeans. The man on the left is using a shovel and the man on the right is holding a wheelbarrow. It seems that they are very busy. In front of them there is a pile of dirt. On the left, I can see some wire and stacks of bricks. In the background, I can also see a wall and other bricks stacked up pretty high.

이 사진은 공사 현장에서 찍힌 것 같습니다. 가장 먼저 보이는 것은 함께 일하고 있는 두 사람입니다. 그들은 노란색 안전모를 쓰고, 체크무늬 셔츠와 청바지를 입고 있습니다. 왼쪽에 있는 남성은 삽을 사용하고 있으며 오른쪽 남성은 손수레를 들고 있습니다. 그들은 매우 바쁜 것처럼 보입니다. 그들 앞에는 흙더미가 있습니다. 왼쪽에는 철사 뭉치와 벽돌 더미가 보입니다. 배경에는 벽과 높게 쌓아 올린 벽돌들도 볼 수 있습니다.

고급 Model Answer

This picture appears to be at a construction site. The first thing I notice is two construction workers in the middle of the picture. They are wearing yellow hardhats, jeans and work boots. The man on the right side is holding the handles of a wheelbarrow. He is wearing a brown plaid shirt with a brown belt. The man on the left appears to be using a shovel to fill the wheelbarrow. He is wearing a blue plaid shirt and yellow gloves. Just in front of them and in the center of the picture is a pile of dirt that the man on the left is digging into with the shovel. Behind the man on the left and to the far left of the picture is a stack of bricks and some wire. Just behind the pile of dirt is another stack of bricks and what looks like a wall is at the very back of the picture. I think both of these men are working on a big construction project because there are a lot of bricks there.

이 사진은 공사 현장에서 찍힌 것 같습니다. 가장 먼저 보이는 것은 그림 중앙에 있는 두 명의 공사장 인부들입니다. 그들은 노란색 안전모를 쓰고, 청바지를 입고 작업용 부츠를 신고 있습니다. 오른쪽 남성은 손수레의 손잡이를 잡고 있습니다. 그는 갈색 격자무늬 셔츠를 입고 갈색 벨트를 매고 있습니다. 왼쪽 남성은 손수레를 채우기 위해 삽을 사용하고 있는 것처럼 보입니다. 그는 파란색 격자무늬 셔츠를 입고 노란색 장갑을 착용하고 있습니다. 그들 바로 앞의 그림 중앙에는 왼쪽 남성이 삽으로 퍼 나르고 있는 흙더미가 있습니다. 왼쪽 남성 뒤 그림의 맨 왼쪽에는 벽돌 더미와 철사 뭉치가 있습니다. 흙더미 바로 뒤에는 또 다른 벽돌 더미가 있고, 그림 배경에는 벽처럼 보이는 것이 있습니다. 벽돌이 많은 것으로 미루어 보아 이 두 사람은 큰 규모의 공사 현장에서 작업을 하고 있는 것 같습니다.

|어 휘| **construction site** 공사 현장   **safety helmet** 안전모   **shovel** 삽
wheelbarrow 손수레   **pile of dirt** 흙더미   **stack** 쌓다, 더미   **hardhat** 안전모   **plaid** 격자무늬

Actual Test 02

Questions 4-6 Respond to Questions

Imagine that an American survey firm is conducting research in your country. You have agreed to participate in a telephone interview about repair work.

미국의 한 마케팅 회사가 당신의 나라에서 설문조사를 하고 있다고 가정해 보세요. 당신은 '수리 작업'에 관한 전화 인터뷰에 응하기로 동의했습니다.

Question 4
01-02-04

Q. When you have things break in your house, do you fix them on your own or call a repairman? 당신의 집에서 무엇인가 고장 났을 때, 당신은 스스로 그것을 수리합니까, 아니면 수리공을 부릅니까?

초·중급 Model Answer

A. When I have things break in my house, I usually call a repairman because it is more convenient and I don't waste my time trying to figure it out.

집에서 무엇인가 고장 났을 때, 저는 보통 수리공을 부릅니다. 왜냐하면 그렇게 하는 것이 더 편리하고, 고장 난 원인을 파악하거나 그것을 수리하기 위해서 시간을 낭비하지 않아도 되기 때문입니다.

고급 Model Answer

A. It depends on what breaks but as a general rule, I will look at it and try to fix it at first. If it is anything electronic then I automatically call a repairman. I am good with basic things but the more complicated something is the less I want to try.

어떤 물건이 고장 났는지에 따라 다르겠지만, 보통은 우선 처음에는 그 물건을 살펴보고 고쳐보려고 시도할 것입니다. 만약 전자제품이라면 저는 바로 수리공을 부릅니다. 간단한 것들은 고칠 수도 있겠지만, 복잡한 물건일수록 직접 고치는 것이 힘들게 마련입니다.

고득점 TIP | 실제 그렇지 않더라도, **말하기 쉬운 쪽으로 선택**해 순발력 있게 답변한다.

Question 5
01-02-05

Q. What was the last thing that had to be fixed in your house?

당신의 집에서 가장 최근에 고쳐야 했던 물건은 무엇이었습니까?

초·중급 Model Answer

A. My TV was broken last weekend and I called a repairman to fix it. The repairman came in and fixed it within about 30 minutes.

지난 주말에 제 TV가 고장 났고, 수리를 하기 위해 수리공을 불렀습니다. 수리공이 와서 30분도 채 안 되는 시간에 그것을 고쳐냈습니다.

고급 **Model Answer**

A. The last thing that had to be fixed was my washing machine. I tried to fix it for myself at first, but it was too complicated so I called a repairman in the end.

가장 최근에 고쳐야 했던 물건은 제 세탁기였습니다. 처음에는 제 스스로 고쳐보려고 노력했지만, 너무 복잡해서 결국에는 수리공을 불러야 했습니다.

|고득점|
T I P   **'가장 최근에 있었던 일'**에 대해 묻는 문제는 자주 출제된다. 실제로 언제였는지 기억을 떠올리려 하지 말고 **yesterday, last weekend** 등과 같은 쉬운 단어를 사용한다.

Question 6

🎧 01-02-06

Q. Why do you think some people do their own repair work as opposed to calling experts?

왜 어떤 이들은 전문가를 부르지 않고 직접 수리를 한다고 생각합니까?

초·중급 **Model Answer**

A. I think many people do their own repair work to save money. Usually the repair cost is very high if you have someone else to fix it. Two weeks ago my laptop computer was broken, so I called a repair shop and asked how much it would cost to fix. It was more than $50, which is too expensive. So I didn't call a repairman and tried to fix it for myself.

저는 많은 사람이 돈을 절약하기 위해 직접 수리를 한다고 생각합니다. 보통 누군가에게 수리를 맡길 경우, 수리비가 많이 듭니다. 2주일 전에 제 노트북 컴퓨터가 고장 나서 수리점에 전화해 수리 비용이 얼마나 들 것인지 물어보았습니다. 비용은 50달러가 넘었고, 너무 비쌌습니다. 그래서 저는 수리공을 부르지 않고 결국 직접 수리하려고 했습니다.

고급 **Model Answer**

A. In my opinion, some people like to be independent and feel a sense of power when they can solve their own problems. I think this is a good trait but like anything else it can be taken to an extreme. A person needs to know their limits and what they are capable of as well as what they enjoy. For me, dealing with technology is very frustrating and just creates stress so I usually call someone.

제 생각에는 어떤 사람은 자립심이 강하고, 그들의 문제들을 직접 해결하면서 무언가 힘이 있다는 느낌을 받는 것(성취감을 느끼는 것) 같습니다. 이것은 좋은 성향이라고 생각하지만, 다른 것과 마찬가지로 때로는 지나칠 수도 있습니다. 사람은 그들의 한계에 대해서 알아야 할 필요가 있고, 그들이 무엇을 즐길 수 있는가와 더불어 무엇을 할 수 있는지에 대해서도 알아야 합니다. 제 경우에는, 기술적인(기계와 관련된) 일을 하는 것이 너무 어렵고 스트레스를 받아서 보통 그럴 경우에 수리공을 부르곤 합니다.

|고득점|
T I P   두 가지 중 선택하는 선호 문제가 아니라, 한 가지 의견이나 현상에 대한 의견을 묻는 문제이다. **의견을 말하는 문제들의 경우 (Part 3, 5, 6) 아이디어가 잘 떠오르지 않으면 '돈, 시간, 사람'에 대해 생각해본다.**

|어 휘| **break** 고장 나다   **repairman** 수리공   **figure out** 알아내다   **as a general rule** 일반적으로   **electronic** 전자 장비와 관련된   **for oneself** 혼자 힘으로   **in the end** 결국   **as opposed to** ~와는 대조적으로   **trait** 특성   **extreme** 지나친   **be capable of** ~할 수 있다   **frustrate** 좌절감을 주다

Actual Test 02

Questions 7-9 Respond to Questions Using Information Provided

---

Storewide Veterans Day Sale

8 A.M.–8 P.M., November 11 ONLY

Department	Items	SALE
Home Furnishings	ALL TVs and freezers	30% off
Jewelry Counter	ALL watches and charm bracelets	25% off
Men's Shoe Department	ALL running shoes and hiking boots	30-40% off
Women's Shoe Department	ALL dress shoes	20% off

재향 군인의 날 기념 전 매장 할인행사

오전 8시~오후 8시, 11월 11일 단 하루!

매장	품목	할인율
홈 퍼니싱(실내 가구)	TV, 냉장고 전 품목	30%
귀금속	시계, 장식이 달린 팔찌류 전 품목	25%
남성화	운동화, 등산화 전 품목	30-40%
여성화	예복용 구두 전 품목	20%

Hello, this is Rick Jones. I'm calling to get more information about your Storewide Veterans Day Sale. Do you have time to answer some questions?

안녕하세요, 저는 Rick Jones입니다. '재향 군인의 날 기념 전 매장 할인행사'에 대해 추가로 궁금한 사항이 있어서 전화 드립니다. 답변해 주실 시간이 있으세요?

Question 7

 01-02-07

Q. What time will you open on Veterans Day for the sale? 재향 군인의 날에 할인행사는 몇 시부터인가요?

초·중급 Model Answer

A. On Veterans Day, we will be open from 8 A.M. to 8 P.M.

재향 군인의 날에, 저희는 오전 8시부터 오후 8시까지 문을 엽니다.

고급 Model Answer

A. We will open the Veterans Day Sale on November 11th only from 8 A.M. to 8 P.M.

저희는 재향 군인의 날 할인행사를 11월 11일 단 하루 오전 8시부터 오후 8시까지 진행합니다.

고득점 TIP 7번 문제는 6하원칙 질문이 자주 출제되는데, 그 중에서도 **표 윗부분의 행사 제목과 함께 나오는 일시, 장소와 관련된 질문**이 빈번히 출제된다.

Question 8

01-02-08

Q. So the discount on a new pair of running shoes is 25-30%, right?

그렇다면 신제품 운동화의 할인율이 25~30%가 맞나요?

초·중급 Model Answer

A. No actually. All running shoes and hiking boots will be 30-40% off.

아닙니다. 모든 운동화와 등산화의 할인율은 30~40% 입니다.

고급 Model Answer

A. Actually, we will save you even more! We will have a 30-40% discount on all running shoes and hiking boots.

실제로는 그 이상으로 할인해 드립니다! 저희는 모든 운동화와 등산화를 30~40% 할인된 가격에 제공합니다.

고득점 TIP 8번에 가장 많이 출제되는 유형인 **'잘못된 정보를 바탕으로 질문'**하는 경우이다. 우선 아니라는 답변을 한 후에, 실제 해당하는 정보에 대해 설명한다.

Actual Test 02

01-02-09

Q. Besides Men's shoes what else is on sale? 남성화 이외에 또 어떤 품목이 세일 중인가요?

초·중급 Model Answer

A. The Women's Shoe Department has 20% off on dress shoes. Additionally, Home Furnishings has 30% off on TVs and freezers and the Jewelry Counter has 25% off on watches and charm bracelets.

여성화 매장에서 예복용 구두를 20% 할인된 가격에 판매하고 있습니다. 또한, 실내 가구 매장에서 TV와 냉장고 제품들을 30% 할인가에 판매 중이며, 귀금속 매장에서는 시계와 장식이 달린 팔찌류 품목들을 25% 할인된 가격에 판매하고 있습니다.

고급 Model Answer

A. Besides Men's shoes, The Women's Shoe Department is offering 20% off on all dress shoes. Additionally, Home Furnishings will have 30% off on all TVs and freezers along with the Jewelry Counter which will have 25% off on all watches and charm bracelets.

남성화 이외에도 여성화 매장에서 모든 예복용 구두를 20% 할인된 가격에 판매하고 있습니다. 또한, 실내 가구 매장에서는 TV와 냉장고 전 제품들을 30% 할인가에 판매 중이며, 귀금속 매장에서는 시계와 장식이 달린 팔찌류 전 품목들을 25% 할인된 가격에 판매하고 있습니다.

고득점 TIP 9번 문제는 **열거하는 답변을 요구하는 문제**가 자주 출제된다. '첫째, 둘째' 혹은 '또한' 등과 같은 표현을 쓰면서 문장을 자연스럽게 연결시킨다.

|어 휘| **storewide** 점포 전체의, 전 매장의   **veteran** 재향 군인   **home furnishing** 실내 가구
charm bracelet 장식이 달린 팔찌   **additionally** 게다가

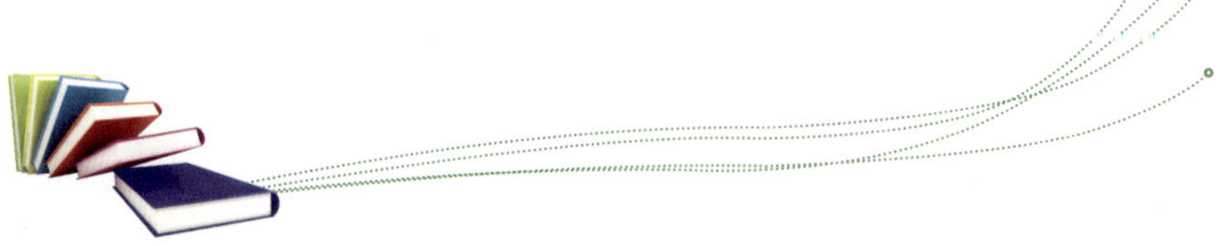

Question 10 Propose a solution

Hello, Phil this is Mr. Ryan from Jade's Jewelry. As you know, we have been one of your longest running tenants here in North Hills Mall and we haven't complained much. Well, now I am afraid I really must complain. The new tenant who moved in next to us just two months ago, Pete's Pets, has to do something about the smell! Look, I like pets and even have a dog myself, but the smell from the pet shop is distracting our customers. Please let me know what you are going to do about this. Again, this is Mr. Ryan from Jade's Jewelry.

안녕하세요, Phil 씨. 저는 Jade's 귀금속 매장의 Ryan입니다. 아시다시피, 저희는 이곳 North Hills Mall에서 가장 오래 머물고 있는 세입자 중 한 명이고, 그 동안 별다른 불만사항을 말씀 드린 적이 없습니다. 하지만 이번에는 무언가 짚고 넘어가야겠어요. 두 달 전에 저희 옆 매장으로 새로 이사온 세입자인 Pete's Pets 매장에서 지독한 냄새와 관련해 어떤 조치를 취해야 할 것 같아요! 저도 애완동물을 좋아하고 직접 개도 기르고 있지만, 이 애완동물 매장에서 나는 냄새 때문에 저희 고객들이 불편을 겪고 있습니다. 이 사태에 대해 어떠한 조치를 좀 취해주세요. 다시 한 번 말씀 드리면, 저는 Jade's 귀금속 매장의 Ryan입니다.

01-02-10

초 · 중급 Model Answer

Hello, Mr. Ryan. I am returning your call about your request. I got your message saying that you are suffering from the smell of the pet shop and you are asking me to deal with this issue. First of all, I apologize for the inconvenience. Besides you, some other tenants are complaining about this matter as well. So, why don't we all meet together and have a discussion about this issue. I will send out an email as to the exact time and ask the relevant tenants to meet in my office. I hope you can attend the meeting. Thank you for calling, if you have any questions please feel free to call me again.

안녕하세요, Ryan 씨. 요청하신 사안에 대해서 답변 드리고자 합니다. 애완동물 가게에서 나는 냄새 때문에 불편을 겪고 있고, 이 상황을 해결해달라고 제게 요청하셨죠. 무엇보다 불편을 드려서 죄송합니다. Ryan 씨 외에도 다른 세입자 몇 분께서도 같은 문제로 불평을 제기하셨습니다. 그래서 말인데, 저희 모두가 한 자리에 모여서 이 문제에 대해서 회의를 해보는 것이 좋을 것 같습니다. 관련이 있는 세입자들에게 정확한 모임시간을 공지하는 이메일을 보내서, 제 사무실에서 만나자고 요청을 하겠습니다. Ryan 씨께서도 참석해주셨으면 좋겠습니다. 연락 주셔서 감사합니다. 다른 궁금한 사항이 있으면 언제든 연락주십시오.

고급 Model Answer

Hello, Mr. Ryan. This is Phil from the management office. I'm returning your call about your situation. I got your message and understand that the smell from Pete's Pets is causing problems for you, especially for your customers. So you are asking me to deal with this matter. First of all, I apologize for the inconvenience. Let me go by and visit with Pete and see what we can do from there. Perhaps we could all sit down, talk about it and figure out an equitable solution. I promise I will keep you in the loop and get back to you as soon as I have more information to share. Thank you for calling and I hope to talk with you soon.

안녕하세요, Ryan 씨. 관리사무소의 Phil입니다. 요청하신 사안에 대해서 답변 드리고자 합니다. Pete's Pets 매장에서 나는 냄새 때문에 Ryan 씨께서, 특히 손님들께서 불편을 겪고 있다는 말씀을 들었습니다. 그래서 이 문제를 해결해달라고 제게 요청하셨죠. 무엇보다 불편을 드려서 죄송합니다. 제가 우선 Pete 씨의 매장에 찾아가서 해결방안을 강구해보도록 하겠습니다. 저희 모두가 함께 모여서 대화를 통해 서로가 납득할만한 해결책을 생각해낼 수도 있을 것 같습니다. Ryan 씨께 알려드릴 추가사항이 있으면 계속해서 말씀 드릴 것을 약속합니다. 연락주셔서 감사 드리고, 조만간 또 말씀 드리겠습니다.

|고득점|
|T I P| 상대방이 제기한 문제에 대해 **해결책을 함께 생각해보자**는 것도 자연스러운 방법이 될 수 있다. 이 문제의 경우, 전화를 건 상대방과 같은 처지에 있는 다른 세입자들도 있을 것이므로 다같이 모여 회의를 해보자는 해결책도 가능하다. 분량이 조금 부족할 경우, **공지 e-mail을 보내겠다**는 식의 e-mail 이야기를 하면 한 두 문장을 쉽게 덧붙일 수 있다.
(cf. e-mail로 이력서, 사진, 지도 혹은 특정 사안에 대한 상세정보를 보내라, 혹은 보내겠다)

|어 휘| **tenant** 세입자　　**distract** 신경 쓰이게 하다　　**suffer from** ~로 고통 받다
　　　　apologize 사과하다　　**inconvenience** 불편함　　**relevant** 관련 있는　　**figure out** 알아내다
　　　　equitable 공평한　　**keep someone in the loop** ~에게 계속해서 정보를 전달하다

Question 11 Express an Opinion

Do you think people are more focused on money today than they were in the past? Use specific reasons or examples to support your opinion.

요즘 사람들은 과거에 비해 돈에 더 연연한다고 생각합니까? 구체적인 근거나 예시를 들어 설명해보세요.

Question 11

01-02-11

초·중급 Model Answer

Yes, I agree that people are more focused on money today than they were in the past. There are several reasons to support my idea. First of all, the cost of living is constantly increasing these days. To be specific, the cost for food, housing and basic education is much higher than in the past. Second, in modern society, many people think money is the measure of success or happiness. For example, many jobseekers choose their jobs based only on the money. For these reasons, I go along with this opinion.

네, 저는 요즘 사람들이 과거에 비해 돈에 더 연연한다는 의견에 동의합니다. 제 의견을 뒷받침할 몇 가지 이유들이 있습니다. 무엇보다, 요즘에는 생활비가 지속적으로 상승하고 있습니다. 구체화하자면, 음식, 주거 그리고 기초적인 교육에 지출되는 비용이 과거에 비해 훨씬 많습니다. 두 번째로, 현대 사회에서는 많은 사람들이 돈이 성공과 행복의 척도라고 생각합니다. 예를 들어, 많은 구직자들이 오직 돈을 기준으로 그들의 직업을 선택합니다. 이러한 이유들 때문에 저는 이 의견에 동의합니다.

고급 Model Answer

Yes, I totally agree. Today people are much more concerned with money and the image of having money than they were in the past. This can be seen in several places. First, it is easy to see this happening with the cost of living that is constantly increasing. To be specific, the cost for food, housing and basic education is getting higher than in the past. Secondly, the materialism that we can see on TV and through the popular culture seems to be never ending. For example, many people think they can do anything with money and so they will do anything for money. Sometimes human rights are infringed on by this kind of attitude. For these reasons, I go along with this statement.

네, 저는 전적으로 동의합니다. 오늘날 사람들은 과거에 비해 돈과 돈을 소유하는 그 이미지에 대해서 훨씬 신경을 많이 씁니다. 이를 뒷받침하는 몇 가지 근거들이 있습니다. 첫째, 지속적으로 증가하고 있는 생활비 때문에 이러한 현상을 쉽게 볼 수 있습니다. 구체화하자면, 음식, 주거 그리고 기초적인 교육에 지출되는 비용이 과거에 비해 높아지고 있습니다. 둘째, TV와 대중문화에서 볼 수 있는 물질주의는 사라질 것 같지 않습니다. 예를 들어, 많은 사람이 돈으로 무엇이든 할 수 있고, 또 돈을 위해서는 무엇이든 할 것이라는 생각을 합니다. 가끔은 이러한 사람들의 마음가짐 때문에 인권이 침해 당하기도 합니다. 이러한 이유들 때문에 저는 이 의견에 동의합니다.

고득점 TIP '돈에 대한 생각'과 관련된 문제는 꾸준히 출제된다. 돈을 많이 받을 수 있지만 여가시간이 없는 직업을 고르겠는가, 혹은 인생에 있어 가장 중요한 것이 돈이라고 생각하는가 등. 돈에 대해 긍정적으로 답변할 경우, **요즘 사람들의 돈에 대한 인식**이나 **돈이 필요한 현실적인 이유들**을 들어 설명할 수 있다.

어휘 **cost of living** 생활비　**constantly** 지속적으로　**jobseeker** 구직자　**concern with** ～에 신경 쓰다　**materialism** 물질주의　**infringe** 침해하다

Actual Test 03

Questions 1-2 Read a Text Aloud

Question 1

01-03-01

BP is proud to **announce** / our **Absolutely** BP **Program results** ↗ / for this **year**. ↘ // **Our Community Relations Department** / has **distributed over 33 million dollars** ↗ / to **organizations** / **working** to preserve and **protect** / the oceans of the **world** / **through promotion**, ↗ / **education** ↗ / and **strategic** planning. ↘

저희 BP사는 올해 절대적 BP 프로그램의 결과를 발표하게 된 것을 자랑스럽게 생각합니다. 저희 지역사회 협력부에서는 홍보, 교육 그리고 전략적인 계획을 통해 전 세계의 바다를 보존하고 보호하기 위한 노력을 기울이는 단체들을 위해 3,300만 달러의 자금을 지원해왔습니다.

| 고득점 TIP | 기업의 **공지문**이다. **숫자는 강조**해서 읽고(**금액**, **날짜** 등 중요한 정보일 때), 특히 이 글처럼 **한 문장이 길게** 나오는 경우가 많으므로 **끊어 읽기**에 유의한다. (긴 주어, 전치사 앞, 열거하는 단어들 등) |

| 어휘 | **proud** 자랑스러운   **announce** 발표하다   **absolutely** 전적으로   **distribute** 나누어 주다
preserve 지키다   **strategic** 전략적인 |

Question 2

01-03-02

Here is **today's** / Inside the **Beltway Analysis**. ↘ // The **Republican Party** / wants to **get tough** / on **waste**, ↗ / **fraud** ↗ / and **abuse** / but are they tough enough / on their **own party members**? ↗ // This is the **precise** question / **now** being **raised** ↗ / by the **House Ethics Committee** / with regard to **Senator Bill Parbel**. ↘ // Until **further** notice, ↗ / **Senator Parbel** has been **suspended**. ↘ // **Stay tuned** / for **updates**.

오늘의 Inside the Beltway 분석입니다. 공화당은 국고낭비, 기만행위, 권력남용 등에 대해 강경하게 대처하겠다는 입장입니다만, 공화당원들에게도 충분히 강경한 잣대를 들이댈까요? 이 질문은 상원의원인 Bill Parbel과 관련해 현재 연방하원 윤리위원회에 의해 제기되고 있는 명확한 질문입니다. 추후 조치가 있을 때까지 Parbel 상원의원은 정직 조치를 받은 상황입니다. 새로운 소식들을 위해 채널 고정하세요.

| 고득점 TIP | **정계의 소식을 알리는 방송**이다. 내가 앵커가 되었다고 생각하고 느낌을 살려서 읽는다. 프로그램, 단체, 의원 이름과 같은 **고유명사는 천천히 강조**해서 읽고, **사람 이름**은 대부분 **첫 음절**에 **강세**를 준다. |

| 어휘 | **Inside the Beltway** 워싱턴 국회의사당을 중심으로 한 정세 권력들을 의미   **the Republican Party** 공화당
fraud 사기   **abuse** 남용   **precise** 정확한   **House Ethics Committee** 연방하원 윤리위원회
senator 상원의원   **further** 더 이상의   **be suspended** 정직되다   **stay tuned** 채널 고정하세요 |

 **Question 3** Describe a Picture

━ 도입　━ 중심　━ 주변　━ 마무리

|고득점|
|T I P|

사진에 등장한 4명의 **공통점**을 묘사한 후 **한 명씩 특징**을 잡아 이야기한다. 순서는 **앞에서 뒤쪽으로**, 혹은 **왼쪽에서 오른쪽으로** 선을 그리듯이 말한다. 노래를 부르거나 특히 **악기를 연주하는 사진**도 꾸준히 출제되고 있다.

Question 3

🎧 01-03-03

|초·중급 Model Answer|

This picture appears to be in a music room. The first thing I notice is four women playing musical instruments and singing. All of them are wearing white shirts. In the foreground, there is a young lady playing the piano and singing. On the right, a woman is playing something, listening to a headphone and singing. To her right, one girl is playing a guitar and another girl is playing a drum. These two ladies are smiling. In the background, I can see some bulletin boards with a lot of papers posted on them. This picture reminds me of my school days.

이 사진은 음악실에서 찍힌 것 같습니다. 가장 먼저 보이는 것은 악기를 연주하면서 노래를 부르고 있는 네 명의 여성들입니다. 모두 흰색 셔츠를 입고 있습니다. 사진 맨 앞쪽에는 피아노를 치면서 노래를 하고 있는 한 젊은 여성이 있습니다. 오른쪽에는 한 여성이 무언가를 연주하고 있고, 헤드폰을 끼고 있으며 노래를 부르고 있습니다. 그녀의 오른쪽에는 한 여성이 기타를 연주하고 있고, 또 다른 여성은 드럼을 연주하고 있습니다. 이 두 여성들은 미소를 짓고 있습니다. 배경에는 많은 종이가 붙어있는 게시판들을 볼 수 있습니다. 이 사진은 제 학창시절을 떠올리게 합니다.

|고급 Model Answer|

This picture appears to be in a music room at a school. The first thing I notice is four young ladies playing musical instruments and singing. They seem to be enjoying themselves and having a good time. All the ladies are wearing white shirts which look like school uniforms. In the foreground, I can see one young lady with red hair playing the piano and singing. To her left, I see another woman with long blond hair who is playing a drum and has a big smile. Next to her is another young lady who is playing an electric guitar. On the right, there is one last woman who is playing a maraca while listening to a headphone and singing. Behind the ladies are a couple of bulletin boards with various things posted on them.

이 사진은 학교 음악실에서 찍힌 것 같습니다. 가장 먼저 보이는 것은 악기를 연주하면서 노래를 부르고 있는 네 명의 여성들입니다. 그들은 즐거운 시간을 보내고 있는 것 같습니다. 모두 교복으로 보이는 흰색 셔츠를 입고 있습니다. 사진 맨 앞쪽에는 피아노를 치면서 노래를 하고 있는 붉은색 머리의 젊은 여성을 볼 수 있습니다. 그녀의 왼쪽에는 드럼을 치면서 활짝 웃고 있는 금발의 다른 여성이 보입니다. 이 여성의 옆에는 전자기타를 치고 있는 또 다른 젊은 여성이 있습니다. 오른쪽에는 나머지 한 여성이 헤드폰을 착용하고 노래를 부르면서 마라카스를 흔들고 있습니다. 이 여성들의 뒤에는 많은 게시물들이 붙어 있는 게시판이 몇 개 있습니다.

|어 휘| **music room** 음악실　**musical instrument** 악기　**bulletin board** 게시판　**school days** 학창시절
maraca 마라카스(쿠바 리듬 악기)　**a couple of** 두세 개　**various** 다양한

Actual Test 03

Questions 4-6 Respond to Questions

Imagine that an Australian marketing firm is conducting research in your country. You have agreed to participate in a telephone interview about being sick.

호주의 한 마케팅 회사가 당신의 나라에서 설문조사를 하고 있다고 가정해 보세요. 당신은 '아픈 것'에 관한 전화 인터뷰에 응하기로 동의했습니다.

Question 4
01-03-04

Q. How often do you see a doctor? 당신은 얼마나 자주 병원에 갑니까?

초·중급 Model Answer

A. I usually see a doctor once or twice a year. Last month, I caught a bad cold and I went to a hospital. 저는 보통 일 년에 한두 번씩 병원에 갑니다. 지난 달에 감기에 심하게 걸려서 병원에 간 적이 있습니다.

고급 Model Answer

A. I usually get a check-up once a year at least but in addition to that I usually see a doctor more than three times a year anytime I am sick. Most of the time I just see the doctor near my house.

저는 보통 적어도 일 년에 한번은 건강 진단을 받으며, 그 외에도 아플 때마다 일 년에 세 번 이상 병원에 갑니다. 대부분은 집 근처에 있는 병원들입니다.

고득점 TIP **How often~**은 4, 5번 문제에서 **가장 많이 등장**하는 육하원칙 문제이다. '한 달에 한 번, 일년에 한 번'처럼 **간단한 표현**을 익혀두고 활용한다. 실제 횟수가 몇 번인지는 전혀 중요하지 않다.

Question 5
01-03-05

Q. Do you use home remedies or prescription drugs when you are sick?

당신은 아플 때 민간요법을 활용합니까, 아니면 처방약을 씁니까?

초·중급 Model Answer

A. When I get sick I use prescription drugs. It works a lot quicker and easier. There is a doctor near my house and I get prescriptions from him.

저는 아플 때 처방약을 사용합니다. 사용하기가 쉽고 효과가 빠르기 때문입니다. 저는 집 근처에 있는 의사에게 처방전을 받습니다.

고급 Model Answer

A. While I try home remedies when I first get sick, I almost always have to get prescription drugs to fully get over the flu or a cold. Home remedies are only useful for me when I first start to get sick.

막 아프기 시작한 처음에는 민간요법을 시도하기도 하지만, 독감 등을 완전히 낫게 하기 위해서 저는 거의 항상 처방약을 사용합니다. 민간요법은 저에게 있어 아프기 시작한 처음에만 효력이 있습니다.

고득점 TIP 둘 중에 하나를 고르는 문제는, 평소 내가 하는 것이 아닐지라도 **말하기 쉬운 쪽으로 선택**한다.

Question 6

🔊 01-03-06

Q. What do you think is the worst thing about being sick?

아플 때 가장 안 좋은 점이 무엇이라고 생각합니까?

초·중급 Model Answer

A. The worst thing about being sick is that I feel annoyed. I don't feel like doing anything. I don't want to eat anything or meet anybody. Additionally, I don't like taking medicine. I don't have any energy and I feel sleepy after taking some medicine.

아플 때 가장 안 좋은 점은 짜증이 난다는 것입니다. 아플 때는 아무것도 하기 싫습니다. 아무것도 먹기 싫고 누구도 만나기 싫습니다. 게다가 저는 약을 복용하는 것을 좋아하지 않습니다. 약을 먹은 후에는 기운이 없고 졸음이 오기 때문입니다.

고급 Model Answer

A. I think the worst thing about being sick is the way it makes me feel. I don't like to cough or sneeze and I usually have body aches which annoy me. I even get angry with people around me without any specific reasons when I get sick. Additionally, when I get sick I usually fall behind at work. Then, I have to work overtime when I get back to catch up on my work.

아플 때 가장 안 좋은 점은 기분이 나빠진다는 것입니다. 저는 기침이나 재채기하는 것이 싫고, 보통 몸살이 날 경우가 많은데 그러면 정말 힘듭니다. 심지어 아플 때는 특별한 이유 없이 주위 사람들에게 화를 내기도 합니다. 또한 아플 때는 업무에 지장이 있게 마련입니다. 그러면 다시 업무에 복귀한 이후 뒤처진 일을 보충하기 위해 초과근무를 해야 합니다.

고득점 TIP 6번 문제는 몇 가지를 이야기해보라는 복수형 답변을 요구하는 경우를 제외하고, 근거나 이유를 한 개만 이야기해도 좋다. 그러므로 답변을 시작할 때 '안 좋은 점이 몇 가지 있다', '첫째는~, 둘째는~'처럼 이야기하지 말고, **우선 한 가지를 말하고 also, additionally 등의 표현을 하면서 자연스럽게 덧붙인다.**

|어 휘| **catch a cold** 감기 들다　**get a check-up** 건강검진을 받다　**at least** 적어도　**in addition to that** 그밖에
home remedy 민간요법　**prescription drug** 의사의 처방전이 필요한 약　**work** 효과가 있다
get over 극복하다　**flu** 독감　**annoy** 짜증나게 하다　**feel like ~ing** ~하고 싶다　**cough** 기침하다
sneeze 재채기하다　**ache** 아픔　**specific** 구체적인　**fall behind** ~에 뒤지다
work overtime 초과근무를 하다　**catch up on** ~을 만회하다

Questions 7-9 Respond to Questions Using Information Provided

Texas State Dog Show
Texas State Fairgrounds - Dallas Texas

Saturday December 3

9:00 A.M.	Opening Ceremony	Main Hall
10:30 A.M.	First Round Competition	San Antonio Hall
1:30 P.M.	Small Dogs Showing	Austin Hall
3:00 P.M.	Medium Dogs Showing	Houston Hall

Sunday December 4

10:00 A.M.	Second Round Competition	San Antonio Hall
11:00 A.M.	Large Dog Showing	Main Hall
1:30 P.M.	Finals for Best in Show	Main Hall
3:00 P.M.	Awards and Closing Ceremony	Main Hall

텍사스 주 애완견 대회
텍사스 주 축제 마당 – 텍사스, 댈러스

12월 3일 토요일

9:00 A.M.	개막식	대강당
10:30 A.M.	1차전 경기	샌 안토니오 홀
1:30 P.M.	소형 애완견 쇼	오스틴 홀
3:00 P.M.	중형 애완견 쇼	휴스턴 홀

12월 4일 일요일

10:00 A.M.	2차선 경기	샌 안토니오 홀
11:00 A.M.	대형 애완견 쇼	대강당
1:30 P.M.	최종 결승	대강당
3:00 P.M.	시상식 및 폐막식	대강당

Hello, this is Andy Meenk. I saw in the paper that there will be a dog show at the Texas State Fairgrounds. I am wondering if I could ask you a few questions.

안녕하세요, 저는 Andy Meenk입니다. 텍사스 주 축제 마당에서 애완견 대회가 개최된다는 기사를 읽었습니다. 혹시 몇 가지 질문을 해도 될지 궁금합니다.

Question 7

 01-03-07

Q. What time will day 2 get started? 둘째 날 행사는 몇 시에 시작됩니까?

초·중급 Model Answer

A. It will start on Sunday, December 4th at 10:00 A.M. in the San Antonio Hall.

행사는 12월 4일 일요일 오전 10시에 샌 안토니오 홀에서 시작합니다.

고급 Model Answer

A. The second day will start on Sunday, December 4th at 10:00 A.M. in the San Antonio Hall with the Second Round Competition.

둘째 날 행사는 12월 4일 일요일 오전 10시에 샌 안토니오 홀에서 열립니다. 첫 프로그램은 2차전 경기입니다.

고득점 TIP | **의문사 의문문**은 거의 매번 출제된다. 특히 7번 문제에 나오는 경우가 많으므로 어떤 의문사로 시작하는지 **첫 단어**를 주의 깊게 듣는다. 답변할 때는 **날짜 앞에 on, 시간 앞에 at(몇 시에)** 혹은 **from(몇 시부터)** 등 전치사 사용에 유의한다.

Question 8

01-03-08

Q. When is the best time to see the large dogs? 대형 애완견들을 보려면 언제가 가장 좋을까요?

초·중급 Model Answer

A. You can see the Large Dog Showing on the second day at 11 A.M. in the Main Hall.

대형 애완견 쇼는 둘째 날 오전 11시에 대강당에서 볼 수 있습니다.

고급 Model Answer

A. The best time to see just the large dogs would be at the Large Dog Showing. That will be at 11:00 A.M. on the second day December 4th in the Main Hall.

대형 애완견들을 볼 수 있는 가장 좋은 시간은 대형 애완견 쇼가 열리는 때일 것입니다. 그 쇼는 둘째 날인 12월 4일 오전 11시에 대강당에서 열릴 예정입니다.

고득점 TIP | Listening이 약하다고 너무 걱정하지 말 것. Part 4에서는 대부분의 문제가 전체 문장의 일부만 듣고도 답변할 수 있다. 이 문제의 경우 **When, large dogs**와 같은 **key words**만 듣고도 충분히 답변이 가능하다.

01-03-09

Q. What events are held in the Main Hall? 대강당에서는 어떤 행사들이 열리나요?

[초·중급 Model Answer]

A. On December 3rd, the Opening Ceremony will be held in the Main Hall. Additionally, on December 4th, there will be three events in the Main Hall. They are the Large Dog Showing, the Finals for Best in Show and the Awards & Closing Ceremony.

12월 3일에는 대강당에서 개막식이 열립니다. 또한 12월 4일에는 대강당에서 3종류의 행사가 열릴 예정입니다. 대형 애완견 쇼, 최종 결승, 그리고 시상식 및 폐막식입니다.

[고급 Model Answer]

A. On the first day, December 3rd, the Opening Ceremony will be held in the Main Hall at 9 A.M. Also, on the second day, December 4th, there are three exhibitions in the Main Hall. They are the Large Dog Showing at 11 A.M., the Finals for Best in Show at 1:30 P.M. and the Awards & Closing Ceremony at 3 P.M.

첫째 날인 12월 3일에는 대강당에서 개막식이 오전 9시에 열릴 예정입니다. 또한 둘째 날 12월 4일에는 대강당에서 3개의 행사가 있습니다. 대형 애완견 쇼는 오전 11시, 최종 결승은 오후 1시 30분, 그리고 시상식 및 폐막식은 오후 3시에 예정되어 있습니다.

| 고득점 TIP | 9번 문제는 **열거하는 내용**이 많으므로, 준비시간에 표를 보면서 **3번 이상 반복되는 정보**(특히 **사람 이름**이나 **장소**)들을 주의 깊게 보면서 그 단어를 듣고 바로 찾을 수 있도록 위치까지 파악해둔다.

| 어 휘 | **fairground** 박람회장　　**opening ceremony** 개막식　　**closing ceremony** 폐막식　　**wonder** 궁금하다
exhibition 전시회

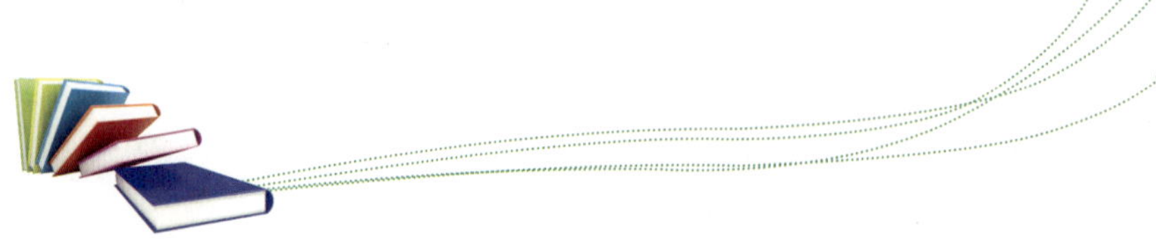

 **Question 10** Propose a solution

Hi, this is Hank from the warehouse and I am sorry to say we have a slight problem with the delivery to your store today. As you know, there were some bad storms overnight in the town right next to you. Well, I just got a call from our driver and according to him he can't get through due to the clean-up that is underway there. As a result, the order you have for the rugs will be late. I apologize for this again because I know your customers look forward to getting the rugs. I will keep you updated for sure, but please give me a call on this so we can coordinate our next move. My cell phone is 462-394-1867.

안녕하세요, 물류창고의 Hank입니다. 유감스럽게도 오늘 귀하 매장으로의 배달 건과 관련하여 작은 문제가 생겼습니다. 아시다시피 고객님 지역 바로 옆 도시에서 지난 밤에 심한 폭풍우가 있었습니다. 저희 운전사에게 방금 연락을 받았는데요, 그에 따르면 그 곳에서 진행 중인 청소 작업 때문에 현재 배송이 불가능하다고 합니다. 그래서 결국 주문하신 양탄자의 배송이 지연될 것 같습니다. 다시 한 번 죄송하다는 말씀을 드립니다. 왜냐하면 귀하의 고객들도 그 양탄자들을 계속해서 기다리고 있다는 것을 잘 알기 때문입니다. 물론 향후 상황에 대해 지속적으로 말씀을 드리겠지만, 추후 조치에 대한 의견을 나눌 수 있도록 연락 부탁 드립니다. 제 휴대폰 번호는 462-394-1867입니다.

Question 10

01-03-10

초·중급 Model Answer

Hello, Hank. I am returning your call about our delivery. I got your message saying that our shipment of rugs will be delayed because there were bad storms last night and you don't know how to deal with this situation. First of all, I am sorry to hear that and I don't think it's your fault. It can happen from time to time. Well, please let me know the estimated delivery time. I will ask the customers to understand this situation. Thank you for keeping in touch. Bye.

안녕하세요, Hank 씨. 배송과 관련해 답변 드리고자 합니다. 지난밤에 있었던 심한 폭풍우로 인하여 저희가 주문했던 양탄자의 배송이 늦어질 것이라고 말씀하셨죠. 그리고 이 상황을 어떻게 처리해야 될지 모르겠다고 하셨습니다. 우선은 일이 그렇게 되었다니 유감이고요, 저는 이 일이 Hank 씨의 잘못이 아니라고 생각합니다. 가끔 발생할 수도 있는 일이지요. 글쎄요, 그래도 대략적인 배송 시간은 알려주셨으면 합니다. 저도 고객들에게 연락을 취해서 이 상황에 대한 양해를 부탁 드리도록 하겠습니다. 계속해서 연락을 주신다니 감사 드립니다. 안녕히 계세요.

고급 Model Answer

Hello, Hank. This is Edward from the ABC rug store. I'm returning your call about the late delivery. I got your message and I understand that our shipment of rugs will be delayed due to the storms last night and you don't know how to deal with this situation. First of all, I am sorry to hear that and I assure you we know it's not your fault. Natural disasters are acts of God that no one can control. We understand and we will wait to hear from you for any updates. Just let us know the estimated delivery time. Then we will let our customers know the new delivery date and ask them to understand this situation. Also, we will make whatever adjustments we need to in order to accommodate the new delivery time. Thank you for keeping in touch. Bye.

안녕하세요, Hank 씨. ABC카펫의 Edward입니다. 배송지연과 관련해 답변 드리고자 합니다. 지난밤에 있었던 심한 폭풍우로 인하여 저희가 주문했던 양탄자의 배송이 늦어질 것이라고 말씀하셨죠. 그리고 이 상황을 어떻게 처리해야 될지 모르겠다고 하셨습니다. 무엇보다 그런 일이 있었다니 유감입니다. 그리고 이는 Hank 씨의 잘못이 아니라는 것을 말씀 드리고 싶네요. 천재지변은 불가항력적인 것이니까요. 충분히 이해하고, 이후 추가 사항들에 대한 업데이트를 부탁 드립니다. 우선 대략적인 배송 시간을 좀 알려주세요. 그러면 저희도 고객들에게 새로운 배송 날짜에 대해 공지하고, 현 상황에 대한 이해와 협조를 부탁 드려보겠습니다. 또한 새로운 배송 날짜에 맞추기 위해 저희 쪽에서 해야 할 일이 있으면 무슨 일이든지 협조하겠습니다. 계속해서 연락을 주신다니 감사합니다. 안녕히 계세요.

|고득점| **물품의 배송과 관련된 사안**도 꾸준하게 출제된다. (배송 지연, 배송 불가, 배송된 물건이 손상되거나 다른 물건이 오는 경우 등)
TIP 이 문제에서는 불가항력적인 이유 때문에 발생한 일이기 때문에, 상대방에게 특정 행동을 촉구하기 보다는 **대략적인 배송 날짜를 알려달라**고 하면서 **최종 고객에게 양해를 구하겠다**는 식으로 답변했다. 이처럼 **업무와 관련된 문제**의 경우 복잡한 솔루션을 꼭 내야겠다는 생각보다는 **상식적인 측면에서 접근**하면 된다.

|어 휘| **warehouse** 창고   **slight** 약간의   **delivery** 배송   **overnight** 밤사이에   **according to** ~에 의하면
due to ~때문에   **clean up** (~을) 치우다   **underway** 진행중인   **as a result** 결과적으로   **rug** 양탄자
apologize 사과하다   **look forward to** ~을 고대하다   **keep updated** 계속해서 소식을 알리다
coordinate 조정하다   **shipment** 수송   **deal with** 처리하다   **from time to time** 이따금
estimated 예상되는   **keep in touch** 계속해서 연락하다   **assure** 장담하다   **natural disaster** 자연재해
act of God 불가항력   **adjustment** 조정   **in order to** ~을 위하여   **accommodate** 수용하다

Question 11 Express an Opinion

What do you think of a competitive work environment as opposed to a cooperative work environment? Use specific reasons or examples to support your opinion.

경쟁적인 근무 환경과 그에 반대되는 협조적인 근무 환경에 대해 어떻게 생각하십니까? 당신의 주장을 뒷받침하기 위한 구체적인 근거나 예시를 제시해보세요.

초·중급 **Model Answer**

I think a competitive work environment is not as good as a cooperative work environment. There are several reasons to support my idea. First of all, people can't feel the sense of belonging in a competitive work environment. They don't think of others as teammates and they might leave that work place very easily just for money or better conditions. Second, it decreases work efficiency because it's difficult for employees to cooperate with each other. People don't share ideas with competitors or get feedback from them. That's why I don't think that the competitive work environment is useful at work.

저는 경쟁적인 근무 환경이 협조적인 근무 환경에 비해 좋지 않다고 생각합니다. 제 의견을 뒷받침할 몇 가지 이유들이 있습니다. 우선, 사람들은 경쟁적인 근무 환경에서 소속감을 느낄 수가 없습니다. 그들은 다른 이들을 팀 동료로 생각하지 않고, 단지 돈이나 다른 조건 때문에 해당 조직을 쉽게 떠날지도 모릅니다. 두 번째로, 직원들이 상호 협력하기 어렵기 때문에 작업의 효율성을 저하시킵니다. 사람들은 경쟁자들과 아이디어를 공유하거나 그들에게 피드백을 받지는 않을 것입니다. 이러한 이유들 때문에 저는 경쟁적인 근무 환경이 직장에서 바람직하다고 생각하지 않습니다.

고급 **Model Answer**

In my opinion, a competitive work environment is not as good as a cooperative work environment. There are a couple of reasons to support my idea. First, people can't feel the sense of belonging. They don't regard others as teammates and they will probably leave the organization the first time they are offered better conditions by another organization. There is a lack of connection between the employee and the corporation. In my case, I like to feel a sense of team work and effort toward common goals and that is definitely missing in this type of work environment. Second, it usually decreases work efficiency because people don't tend to share ideas or collaborate with anyone since they are competitors. Employees will always try to make others fail so they will look better and this creates a hostile work environment. These are the main reasons I don't feel like a competitive atmosphere is beneficial at work.

저는 경쟁적인 근무 환경이 협조적인 근무 환경에 비해 좋지 않다고 생각합니다. 제 의견을 뒷받침할 몇 가지 근거들이 있습니다. 우선, 사람들이 소속감을 느낄 수가 없습니다. 그들은 다른 이들을 팀원으로 여기지 않을 것이며, 다른 조직에서 더 나은 조건을 제시한다면 곧바로 기존에 몸담던 곳을 떠날지도 모릅니다. 직원과 회사 사이의 끈끈한 무언가가 결핍되어 있습니다. 제 경우에는, 소속감을 느끼며 공통된 목표를 향해 함께 노력하고 싶은데, 이러한 유형의 근무 환경에서는 물론 힘들 것입니다. 두 번째, 일반적으로 업무 효율성도 저하시킬 것입니다. 왜냐하면 사람들이 경쟁자들인 다른 이들과 아이디어를 공유하거나 협조하려 하지 않을 것이기 때문입니다. 직원들은 항상 다른 사람들이 실패하길 바라면서 그들을 밟고 올라가려 할 것이고 이런 상황들은 적대적인 근무 환경을 야기할 것입니다. 이러한 주된 이유들을 들어 저는 경쟁적인 근무 환경이 직장에서 유익하지 않다고 생각합니다.

고득점 TIP | 학생들이 이와 같은 **직장 생활과 관련한 문제**를 접하더라도 **상식적인 수준**에서 답하면 된다. 의견이 잘 생각나지 않는다면 '**돈**', '**시간**', '**사람**'을 떠올릴 것. 이 문제는 '협조적인 근무 환경에서 직원들이 서로 **소속감**을 갖고 **일의 효율성을 높일 수 있다**'는 식으로 필수 표현들을 사용해 어렵지 않게 답할 수 있다.

어휘 | **competitive** 경쟁적인　**work environment** 근무 환경　**as opposed to** ~와 대조적으로
cooperative 협조적인　**feel the sense of belonging** 소속감을 느끼다　**teammate** 팀 동료
work efficiency 작업 효율　**cooperate with** ~와 협력하다　**lack** 결핍　**common goal** 공통된 목표
definitely 분명히　**tend to** ~하는 경향이 있다　**collaborate with** ~와 공동으로 작업하다
competitor 경쟁자　**hostile** 적대적인　**atmosphere** 분위기　**beneficial** 유익한

 # *Actual Test* 04

Questions 1-2 Read a Text Aloud

Question 1

🎧 01-04-01

It's **time** / for the **Original Organic Chef's Buffet Sale**! ↘ // You will find a **smorgasbord** of **savings** ↗ / on all your **organic needs**. ↘ // Everything from **organic cocoa**, ↗ / **chocolate**, ↗ / **butter** ↗ / and **margarine** / are **all** / at **once a year reductions**. ↘ // Even our **storewide variety of tomatoes**, ↗ / **apples**, ↗ / **oranges** and **greens** / are at **drastic discounts**. ↘ // **Come by** / **today**! ↘

이제 Original Organic Chef's Buffet Sale 시간입니다! 다양한 유기농 음식들을 할인된 가격에 만날 수 있습니다. 유기농 코코아부터 초콜릿, 버터 그리고 마가린 등 수많은 제품들을 할인하는 1년에 단 한번 있는 기회입니다. 심지어 점포 전체에 걸쳐 다양한 토마토, 사과, 오렌지 그리고 녹색 야채들을 파격적인 가격에 세일 중입니다. 오늘 방문하세요!

고득점 TIP | 광고문답게 그 맛을 살려서 읽는다. 특히 **행사 이름, 광고 품목 등을 강조**한다. **품목을 나열할 경우 억양에 주의**하고, 특히 **variety of와 같은 빈출 표현**도 충분히 연습한다.

어휘 | **organic** 유기농의   **smorgasbord** 뷔페식 식사   **reduction** 할인   **storewide** 점포 전체의
variety of 다양한   **drastic** 과감한

Question 2

🎧 01-04-02

Welcome to **another edition** / of **Health Opportunity Now**! ↘ // **Today** ↗ / we have the **opportunity** to be **taught** / by **one** of the **leaders** in the field, ↗ / **Mr. Ben Penron**. ↘ // He will discuss / **how** to **make** our **diet** / **more precise** / for our **needs** ↗ / and **how to create nutritious recipes** ↗ / that will **facilitate** your **optimum balanced life**. ↘

Health Opportunity Now에 다시 오신 것을 환영합니다! 오늘은 분야의 리더 중 한 분인 Ben Penron 씨를 모시고 직접 배울 수 있는 기회를 갖게 되었습니다. 그는 우리에게 필요한 정확한 식단을 준비하는 방법과 당신이 최적의 균형 잡힌 삶을 영위할 수 있게 해주는 영양가 높은 조리법을 만드는 방법들에 대해서 논의할 것입니다.

고득점 TIP | 방송 프로그램이다. 내가 진행자라고 생각하고 그 **상황을 떠올리면서** 읽는다. **감탄문의 경우 마지막 부분을 강조**하긴 하지만 **억양은 내리면서 읽는다**. 사람을 소개하는 경우 **소개 받는 사람의 이름과 업적 등을 강조**한다.

어휘 | **edition** ~호, ~회(간행물, 방송물 등)   **diet** 식단, 식습관   **precise** 정확한   **nutritious** 영양가 높은
recipe 조리법   **facilitate** 가능하게 하다   **optimum** 최적의   **balanced** 균형 잡힌

Question 3 Describe a Picture

고득점 TIP 등장인물 3명의 **공통적인 모습을 먼저 묘사**하고, 그 후 각 인물의 주요 특징을 묘사한다. **인물 묘사를 다 끝낸 후 주변을 묘사**한다.

Question 3

01-04-03

초·중급 Model Answer

This picture appears to be in a yard. The first thing I notice is a family washing a dog. On the left, a woman is bending over and smiling. She is wearing a sleeveless shirt and blue jeans. Next to her, a child is holding a hose with her. On the right, a man is squatting down and washing the dog. In front of this family, there is a bull dog in a bucket. There is a lot of grass on the ground and in the background I can see a building. This picture reminds me of my childhood.

이 사진은 마당에서 찍힌 것 같습니다. 가장 먼저 보이는 것은 개를 목욕시키고 있는 한 가족입니다. 왼쪽에는 한 여성이 몸을 굽히고 웃고 있습니다. 그녀는 민소매 셔츠와 청바지를 입고 있습니다. 옆에는 한 아이가 그녀와 함께 호스를 들고 있습니다. 오른쪽에는 한 남자가 쪼그리고 앉아서 개를 씻기고 있습니다. 이 가족의 앞에는 불독 한 마리가 양동이 안에 있습니다. 바닥에는 잔디가 무성하며 배경에 한 건물이 보입니다. 이 사진은 저의 어린 시절을 떠올리게 합니다.

고급 Model Answer

This picture appears to be in a yard. The first thing that catches my eye is three people washing a dog. On the left is a lady who is dressed in a light blue tank top and blue jeans that she has rolled up to her knees. She is smiling and bending at the waist. In her right hand, she is helping an infant boy with a water hose. The little boy is wearing blue jean overalls and has light blond hair. On the right, there is a man smiling, squatting down and washing the dog. He is wearing an orange shirt and grey pants. Inside the bucket is a white and brown dog. It looks like a bulldog. In the background, I can see a building and there is a lot of grass on the ground. This picture reminds me of my childhood.

이 사진은 마당에서 찍힌 것 같습니다. 가장 먼저 보이는 것은 개를 목욕시키고 있는 세 사람입니다. 왼쪽에는 하늘색 민소매 셔츠와 무릎까지 접어 올린 청바지를 입고 있는 한 여성이 있습니다. 그녀는 웃으면서 허리를 구부리고 있습니다. 그녀는 오른손으로 한 아이가 호스로 물을 뿌릴 수 있도록 도와주고 있습니다. 그 어린 아이는 멜빵 청바지를 입고 있고, 머리는 밝은 금발입니다. 오른쪽에는 한 남자가 웃으면서 쪼그리고 앉아 개를 씻기고 있습니다. 그는 주황색 셔츠와 회색 바지를 입고 있습니다. 양동이 안에는 흰색과 갈색 털의 개가 있는데 불독인 것 같습니다. 배경에는 건물이 보이고 바닥에는 잔디가 무성합니다. 이 사진은 저의 어린 시절을 떠올리게 합니다.

|어 휘| **bend over** 몸을 굽히다   **sleeveless shirt** 민소매 셔츠   **squat** 쪼그리고 앉다   **bucket** 양동이
childhood 어린 시절   **roll up** 올리다   **bend at the waist** 허리를 구부리다   **infant** 유아
overalls 멜빵바지

Actual Test 04

Questions 4-6 Respond to Questions

> Imagine that a Canadian marketing firm is conducting research in your country. You have agreed to participate in a telephone interview about cultural events.
>
> 캐나다의 한 마케팅 회사가 당신의 나라에서 설문조사를 하고 있다고 가정해 보세요. 당신은 '문화행사'에 관한 전화 인터뷰에 응하기로 동의했습니다.

Question 4

 01-04-04

Q. How often do you go to a cultural event in your area?

당신은 당신이 살고 있는 지역에서 얼마나 자주 문화행사에 갑니까?

[초·중급 Model Answer]

A. I usually go to a cultural event once or twice a year. Last month, I went to the October Fest and enjoyed beer with my friends.

저는 보통 1년에 한두 번 문화행사에 갑니다. 지난 달에 October Fest에 가서 친구들과 함께 맥주를 즐겼습니다.

[고급 Model Answer]

A. I try to take in as many different events as I can. Usually about once a month in the warmer months but in the winter usually there isn't as much going on so I stay around the house.

저는 가능한 한 최대한 많은 문화행사에 참여하려고 합니다. 보통 따뜻한 계절에는 한 달에 한 번 정도, 하지만 겨울에는 대부분 행사가 많지 않아서 그냥 집에 있습니다.

[고득점 TIP] 육하원칙 문제 중 **How often~**이 가장 많이 출제된다. **실제 횟수를 생각하지 말고**, once a month, twice a year 등 **대답하기 쉬운 표현을 한다.**

Question 5

 01-04-05

Q. How do you find out about various events coming up?

당신은 다양한 문화행사에 대한 정보를 어떻게 얻습니까?

[초·중급 Model Answer]

A. I usually find out about various events on the Internet. My favorite website is www.eventsforyou.com.

저는 주로 다양한 문화행사에 대한 정보를 인터넷을 통해 얻습니다. 제가 가장 좋아하는 웹사이트는 www.eventsforyou.com입니다.

[고급 Model Answer]

A. I subscribe to several email notification services that keep me updated. Additionally, I have some good friends with similar taste as mine and we talk about upcoming events.

저는 새로운 정보를 계속해서 얻을 수 있는 이메일 알림 서비스들을 몇 개 이용하고 있습니다. 또한 저와 비슷한 취향을 가진 좋은 친구들이 몇 명 있는데 우리는 앞으로 있을 행사들에 대해 대화를 하곤 합니다.

Question 6

01-04-06

Q. What was the last special event you went to? Please describe what it was like.

가장 최근에 참여했던 특별한 행사는 무엇이었고, 어떠했는지 설명해주세요.

초·중급 Model Answer

A. Last month, I went to the October Fest event. It's a German traditional event. I enjoyed various kinds of beer with foreign friends. Also, I watched some cultural shows and danced with a bunch of people on a stage. It was such a great time and I want to invite my friends next time.

지난달에 저는 October Fest에 다녀왔습니다. 그것은 독일의 전통문화행사입니다. 저는 외국인 친구들과 다양한 종류의 맥주를 즐겼습니다. 또한, 문화 공연들을 관람했고, 무대 위에서 많은 사람들과 춤을 추기도 했습니다. 정말 흥겨운 시간이었고, 다음 번에는 친구들을 초대하고 싶습니다.

고급 Model Answer

A. The last event I went to was the St. Patrick's Day celebration that was put on by the Irish Society of Korea. It was a great day of music and dancing in an outdoor stage area near downtown Seoul. I took my girlfriend, several other friends and we grabbed some food on the way. It was kind of like a picnic but it had all this amazing Irish music and lots of foreigners were there. We all had a great time.

제가 가장 최근에 다녀온 문화행사는 한국에 있는 아일랜드 단체 사람들이 주도한 St. Patrick's Day(성 패트릭의 날) 축하 행사였습니다. 서울 시내 근처의 야외 무대에서 음악과 춤을 즐길 수 있었던 멋진 날이었습니다. 저는 제 여자친구와 다른 친구들 몇 명을 데려갔고, 도중에 음식을 사먹기도 했습니다. 마치 소풍 같은 느낌이었지만, 놀라운 아일랜드 음악과 수많은 외국인들과 함께할 수 있었습니다. 우리 모두 정말 좋은 시간을 보냈습니다.

| 어휘 | **cultural event** 문화행사　　**October Fest** 옥토버페스트(독일 뮌헨지역에서 유래한 맥주 축제)
take in (쇼 등을) 보러 가다　　**stay around the house** 집에 머무르다
subscribe to (인터넷 서비스 등) 가입하다　　**notification** 알림, 통지
keep updated 소식을 계속해서 알려주다　　**taste** 취향　　**a bunch of** 다수의
St. Patrick's Day 성 패트릭의 날(아일랜드에 처음 그리스도교를 전파한 인물인 성 패트릭을 기념하는 축제)
Irish 아일랜드의 (사람들)

 **Questions 7-9** Respond to Questions Using Information Provided

Lou Phillips School of Film Acting
Classes Offered Fall Term

Day	Time	Class	Instructor
Mondays	5-7 P.M.	Intro to Film Acting	Tom Meeks
Tuesdays	6-9 P.M.	Intermediate Film Acting I	Rick Bell
Tuesdays	9-10 P.M.	Intermediate Film Acting II	Rick Bell
Thursdays	6-10 P.M.	Advanced Film Acting I	Lou Phillips
Fridays	6-10 P.M.	Advanced Film Acting II	Lou Phillips

* Class tuition is $300 for two hour classes, $400 for three hour classes and $500 for four hour classes.

Lou Phillips 영화 연기 학원
가을 학기 개설 수업

요일	시간	수업	강사
월요일	오후 5~7시	영화 연기 개론	Tom Meeks
화요일	오후 6~9시	영화 연기 중급 I	Rick Bell
화요일	오후 9~10시	영화 연기 중급 II	Rick Bell
목요일	오후 6~10시	영화 연기 고급 I	Lou Phillips
금요일	오후 6~10시	영화 연기 고급 II	Lou Phillips

* 수업료는 2시간 수업은 300달러, 3시간 수업은 400달러, 그리고 4시간 수업은 500달러입니다.

Hello, this is Kate Harder. I would like to get some information about your classes. Is this a good time?

안녕하세요, 저는 Kate Harder입니다. 수업들에 관해 문의하고 싶은 게 있는데요, 시간 괜찮으신지요?

Question 7

01-04-07

Q. What days of the week do you offer classes? 무슨 요일에 수업이 있나요?

[초·중급 Model Answer]

A. We offer classes on Monday, Tuesday, Thursday and Friday. There are no classes on Wednesday.

저희는 월요일, 화요일, 목요일 그리고 금요일에 수업을 합니다. 수요일에는 수업이 없습니다.

[고급 Model Answer]

A. We offer classes on Monday, Tuesday, Thursday and Friday. Classes, times and instructors vary but all the classes are in the evening.

저희는 월요일, 화요일, 목요일 그리고 금요일에 수업을 합니다. 수업 내용, 시간 그리고 강사는 다르지만 모든 수업은 저녁에 있습니다.

[고득점 TIP] 의문사로 시작하는 의문문이다. **What days of the week~?**라고 질문했으므로 **요일 관련 정보**를 언급한다.

Question 8

01-04-08

Q. What day is your beginner class? 초급 수업은 무슨 요일에 하나요?

[초·중급 Model Answer]

A. We offer the 'Intro to Film Acting' class on Monday from 5 to 7 P.M. for beginners.

초급자들을 위한 '영화 연기 개론' 수업은 월요일 오후 5시부터 7시까지입니다.

[고급 Model Answer]

A. Our 'Intro to Film Acting' class which is for beginners is held on Monday from 5 to 7 P.M. and it's taught by Tom Meeks.

초급자들을 위한 '영화 연기 개론' 수업은 월요일 오후 5시부터 7시까지이며 강사는 Tom Meeks 입니다.

[고득점 TIP] 표를 분석하는 준비시간에 미리 문제를 예측해야 한다. **class**의 등급(난이도)이 나누어져 제시되는 경우(초/중/고급) 거의 대부분 그 중 한 등급에 대한 질문이 출제된다.

Question 9

01-04-09

Q. What classes are taught by Lou Phillips? Lou Phillips 씨가 가르치시는 수업은 무엇이 있나요?

초·중급 **Model Answer**

A. Lou teaches two classes. The first one is 'Advanced Film Acting I' on Thursday, from 6 to 10 P.M. The other class is 'Advanced Film Acting II' on Friday from 6 to 10 P.M. as well.

Lou 강사님께서는 두 가지 수업을 맡으셨습니다. 첫 번째는 '영화 연기 고급 I' 수업으로 목요일 오후 6시부터 10시까지입니다. 나머지 하나는 '영화 연기 고급 II' 수업이며 금요일에 역시 오후 6시부터 10시까지 진행됩니다.

고급 **Model Answer**

A. Lou Phillips offers two classes. He has the 'Advanced Film Acting I' class on Thursday from 6 to 10 P.M. He also teaches 'Advanced Film Acting II' on Friday from 6 to 10 P.M. Please remember that the class tuition is $500 for all our four hour classes.

Lou 강사님께서는 두 가지 수업을 맡으셨습니다. 그는 목요일 오후 6시부터 10시까지 '영화 연기 고급 I' 수업을 합니다. 또한 금요일 오후 6시부터 10시까지 '영화 연기 고급 II' 수업을 진행합니다. 모든 4시간 수업의 수업료는 500 달러임을 기억하세요.

고득점 TIP 사람 이름을 언급하는 질문은 가장 많이 나오는 유형 중 하나이다. 준비시간에 미리 표에 있는 고유명사(이름, 지명 등)를 소리 내 읽어봄으로써, 질문이 나왔을 때 빨리 찾을 수 있도록 한다.

|어 휘| **term** 학기   **intro** 도입부   **intermediate** 중급 수준의   **advanced** 고급 수준의   **instructor** 강사
tuition 수업료   **vary** 서로 다르다   **beginner** 초보자

 **Question 10** Propose a solution

Hello, this is Thomas Jenkins from the Marketing department up on the third floor. Next week all of the public transportation workers are supposed to go on strike in the city. I would like to suggest as a result that we put out some sort of car-pool list. Since your department, the Communications department handles all in-house communications I thought perhaps I should check with you and collaborate with you to make the car-pool list. Please let me know what you think of the idea and if I could help in any way. Again this is Thomas Jenkins and my extension is 729.

안녕하세요, 저는 3층 마케팅 부서의 Thomas Jenkins입니다. 다음 주에 모든 대중교통 운전기사들이 도시 내에서 파업을 할 예정이라고 하네요. 그래서 말인데요, 카풀 목록을 작성해 보는 것이 어떨까 합니다. 커뮤니케이션 부서에서 모든 회사 내부의 커뮤니케이션을 담당하시잖아요. 그래서 카풀 목록을 만들기 위해서는 아마도 당신과 상의하고 협조를 구해야 할 것이라고 생각했습니다. 제 의견에 대해서 어떻게 생각하시는지, 그리고 제가 도울 일이 있는지 연락 부탁 드립니다. 다시 말씀 드리면, 저는 Thomas Jenkins이고 제 내선 번호는 729입니다.

 01-04-10

초·중급 Model Answer

Hello, Mr. Jenkins. This is Joshua. I am returning your call about your request. I got your message saying that there will be a strike by the public transportation workers, so you are asking me to collaborate with you on car-pool list. First of all, thank you for calling us. We have the basic information for the entire staff to include: department, name, phone number and address. I think it's better to make the car-pool list together based on employees' addresses. Let's have a meeting and work on this. Please let me know when you are available.

안녕하세요, Jenkins 씨. 저는 Joshua입니다. 요청하신 사안에 대해서 답변 드리고자 합니다. 대중교통 운전기사들이 파업을 할 예정이고, 그래서 카풀 목록과 관련해 협조를 구하신다는 메시지를 잘 들었습니다. 우선 전화 주셔서 감사합니다. 저희는 전 직원들의 부서, 성명, 전화번호 그리고 주소와 같은 기본적인 신상정보를 보유하고 있습니다. 제 생각에는 직원들의 주소지를 바탕으로 카풀 목록을 함께 작성하는 것이 좋을 것 같습니다. 우선 만나서 작업을 시작해 봅시다. 가능하신 시간을 알려주시기 바랍니다.

고급 Model Answer

Hello, Mr. Jenkins. This is Ralph Kearney from the Communications department. I'm returning your call about the car-pool list. I got your message and understand that the public transportation workers are supposed to go on strike next week, so you are asking me to collaborate with you to make the car-pool list. First of all, thank you for calling us. Fortunately, we have the basic information for the entire staff which includes department, name, phone number and address. I think it's possible to make the car-pool list based on employees' addresses. We would love to send out a ride share or car-pool list to everyone but right now we are working several large projects that we have to complete. If you could develop some sort of list through a word based document we would be more than happy to send it out and give you the credit for it. Please let me know if this would be possible. Thank you.

안녕하세요, Jenkins 씨. 저는 커뮤니케이션 부서의 Ralph Kearney입니다. 말씀하셨던 카풀 목록에 대해서 답변 드리고자 합니다. 대중 교통 운전기사들이 다음 주에 파업을 할 예정이고, 그래서 카풀 목록 작성과 관련해 협조를 구하신다는 메시지를 잘 들었습니다. 우선 전화 주셔서 감사합니다. 다행히도 저희는 전 직원들의 부서, 성명, 전화번호 그리고 주소와 같은 기본적인 신상정보를 보유하고 있습니다. 직원들의 주소지를 근거로 카풀 목록을 만드는 것이 가능할 것 같습니다. 저희도 물론 카풀 목록을 모든 직원들에게 송부하고 싶지만, 지금 당장은 완수해야 할 몇 가지 큰 프로젝트들 때문에 정신이 없습니다. 만약 Jenkins 씨께서 워드 파일로 목록을 만들어 주신다면 저희가 직원들에게 기꺼이 송부토록 하고, 이 모든 공로를 Jenkins 씨께 돌릴 것입니다. 제가 말씀 드린 이 제안이 혹시 가능할지 여부에 대해 답변 부탁 드립니다. 감사합니다.

고득점 TIP   **Part 5 답변**은 '**요약+해결책**'이다. **요약** 부분에서는 2~3줄로 간단히 사건의 발단이나 전화를 건 이유를 언급한다. **해결책**은 이렇게 특정 사안에 대해 **요청을 하는 문제일 때는 상대가 요청하는 내용을 들어준다**고 하고 **부연 설명**을 덧붙이는 것이 가장 쉬운 답변 방법이다.

|어 휘| **public transportation** 대중교통   **be supposed to** ~하기로 되어 있다   **go on strike** 파업하다
as a result 결과적으로   **some sort of** 일종의   **car pool** 승용차 함께 타기   **handle** 다루다
in-house 회사 내부의   **collaborate on A with B** A에 대해 B와 협력하다   **extension** 내선 번호
entire staff 전 사원   **based on** ~에 근거하여   **work on** 착수하다   **available** 시간 여유가 있는
fortunately 다행스럽게도   **complete** 완료하다   **send out** 발송하다   **give credit for** 공로를 인정하다

 **Question 11** Express an Opinion

In your opinion which of the following do you think has the biggest impact on modern society:

a) Smart Phones
b) Social Networking sites
c) Instant Messaging

Give specific reasons or examples to support your opinion.

다음 중 현대 사회에 가장 큰 영향을 준 것이 무엇이라고 생각하나요?

a) 스마트폰
b) 소셜 네트워킹 사이트(SNS)
c) 인스턴트 메시징
당신의 주장을 뒷받침하기 위한 구체적인 근거나 예시를 제시해보세요.

초·중급 **Model Answer**

In my opinion, smart phones have the biggest impact on modern society among these three. There are some reasons to support my opinion. First of all, it has changed how people work. People can easily check and send e-mails at home or wherever they may be even after work. It increases work efficiency but some people feel stressed to work like this. Second, smart phones created a new industry. To be specific, many IT guys are trying to make applications such as games, messaging devices, maps and so on. For these reasons, I would choose the smart phone.

저는 세 가지 항목들 중에서 스마트폰이 현대 사회에 가장 큰 영향을 끼쳤다고 생각합니다. 제 의견을 뒷받침할 몇 가지 근거들이 있습니다. 무엇보다, 스마트폰은 사람들이 일하는 방식을 변화시키고 있습니다. 사람들은 심지어 퇴근 후에도 집에서 혹은 장소에 관계없이 손쉽게 이메일을 확인하고 보낼 수 있습니다. 이러한 변화는 업무 효율성을 증가시키지만 어떤 이들은 이와 같은 업무 방식 때문에 스트레스를 받기도 합니다. 둘째, 스마트폰은 새로운 산업을 탄생시켰습니다. 구체적으로 말하자면, 정보기술 분야에서 일하는 많은 이들이 게임, 메신저, 지도 등과 같은 어플리케이션들을 제작하기 위해 노력하고 있습니다. 이러한 이유들 때문에 저는 (현대 사회에 가장 큰 영향을 미친 품목으로 보기 중에서) 스마트폰을 고르고 싶습니다.

고급 **Model Answer**

In my opinion, Smart Phones have had the biggest impact on modern society. This can be seen in several places. First of all, people can easily upload anything they see on the Internet with smart phones. To be specific, if something is happening in another part of the world someone can film it and post it on the Internet and suddenly everyone in the world can see it as well. This has changed countries from dictatorships to democracies. Second, smart phones have changed how people work. These days, many people carry their phones everywhere and send e-mails or even participate in meetings using them. Obviously it can increase the work efficiency but people might get more stressed because they can never really leave work. That's why I would choose smart phones as having the biggest impact on modern society.

저는 스마트폰이 현대 사회에 가장 큰 영향을 끼쳤다고 생각합니다. 몇 가지 측면에서 그 이유들을 살펴볼 수 있습니다. 무엇보다, 사람들은 그들이 본 것들을 스마트폰을 사용해 인터넷에 쉽게 업로드할 수 있습니다. 구체화하자면, 만약 지구 반대편에서 무슨 일이 발생할 경우 누군가 그것을 촬영해 인터넷에 올리면 곧 세상 사람들도 그 장면을 볼 수 있을 것입니다. 이러한 현상은 독재 국가들을 민주주의 국가로 변화시키는 데에도 영향을 미쳤습니다. 둘째, 스마트폰은 사람들이 일하는 방식을 변화시켰습니다. 요즘에는, 많은 사람이 스마트폰을 항상 소지하면서 이메일을 보내거나 심지어 전화기를 이용해 미팅에 참여하기도 합니다. 스마트폰이 일의 효율성을 증가시킨 것은 분명해 보이지만, 사람들은 잠시라도 일과 떨어져 있을 수 없기 때문에 더 많은 스트레스를 받을지도 모릅니다. 이러한 이유들 때문에 저는 현대 사회에 가장 큰 영향을 준 것이 스마트폰이라고 생각합니다.

| 고득점 TIP | 2개가 아닌 3개 중 1개를 고르는 문제이다. 혹시 3개 중에 모르는 어휘가 나와도 당황하지 말고, 나머지 2개 중에서 고르면 된다. **가장 범위가 큰 개념이거나 평소 본인과 친숙한 소재**를 선택하면 그만큼 할 말이 더 많아진다. |

|어 휘| **modern society** 현대 사회　**instant** 즉각적인　**after work** 퇴근 후에　**work efficiency** 업무 효율
feel/get stressed 스트레스를 받다　**application** 응용프로그램　**device** 장치, 기구
and so on 기타 등등　**film** 촬영하다　**post** 게시하다　**dictatorship** 독재 국가　**democracy** 민주 국가
carry 휴대하다　**participate in** ~에 참가하다　**obviously** 분명히

Actual Test 05

Questions 1-2 Read a Text Aloud

Question 1

01-05-01

Hello ↗ / and **thank you** / for **coming** to the **product launch** ↗ / for <u>this</u> **amazing** new **phone**. ↘ // **Motorphona** Corp. is **proud** / to **launch** this **precise**, ↗ / **well-organized** ↗ / and **versatile line** of **phones** ↗ / <u>called the</u> **Tiger Line**. ↘ // <u>As you</u> can **see**, / this **sleek**, ↗ / **stylish** ↗ / and **sexy phone** / **looks great**, ↗ / but <u>wait</u> till you **see** / <u>what it</u> **can do**! ↘ // For **individual** **product demonstrations** ↗ / **see** our **Associates** / **up** front **now**. ↘

안녕하세요? 이 놀라운 새 전화기의 신제품 출시 행사에 와주셔서 감사합니다. 저희 Motorphona사는 이 정밀하면서도 잘 조직화되어 있으며 다양한 용도로 사용될 수 있는 전화기 제품 라인인 Tiger Line을 출시하게 된 것에 대해 자부심을 느끼고 있습니다. 보시다시피 이 매끄럽고, 스타일리시하며, 섹시하기까지 한 전화기는 보기에도 훌륭하지만 그 기능을 보기 전까지는 기다려주시기 바랍니다! 개별 제품 시연을 위해 이제 앞에 있는 저희 직원들을 봐주십시오.

| 고득점 TIP | **광고글**이므로 **광고의 느낌**을 살려서 읽고 **기업명, 제품의 이름** 및 **기능** 등을 강조한다. **열거하는 부분**의 **억양**에 주의한다. 준비 시간에 이러한 부분에 주의하면서 몇 번씩 반복해 연습해둔다. |

| 어휘 | **launch** 출시하다   **amazing** 놀라운   **precise** 정밀한   **versatile** 다용도의   **sleek** 매끄러운   **individual** 각각의   **demonstration** 시범, 설명   **associate** (직장) 동료 |

Question 2

01-05-02

KHOO FM100 / is **your station** / for the **latest** news, ↗ / **sports**, ↗ / **weather** ↗ / and **hits** from the **70s**, ↗ / **80s** ↗ / and **90s**. ↘ // <u>In addition</u>, ↗ / **don't forget** <u>about our</u> **variety of talk shows** ↗ / **available** on **Sunday** ↗ / **including** our **recently** added **Dr. Tom's wisdom** / on **what to eliminate** from **your life** ↗ / for the **health** <u>of</u> It. ↘ // **All this** / and **so much more** ↗ / **only here** at **KHOO**. ↘

KHOO FM100은 최신 뉴스, 스포츠, 날씨와 70, 80, 90년대의 히트곡들을 만날 수 있는 당신의 쉼터입니다. 또한 최근에 추가된, 건강을 위해 당신의 삶에서 제거해야 할 것들을 소개해주는 Dr. Tom의 조언들을 비롯해, 일요일에 다양한 토크쇼가 마련되어 있다는 것을 잊지 마세요. 이 모든 것들과 그 이상의 것들은 오직 여기 KHOO에서만 만나보실 수 있습니다.

| 고득점 TIP | 라디오 방송 프로그램을 광고하는 내용이다. 본인이 진행자가 되었다는 기분으로 그 느낌을 살려 읽는다. variety of, available, recently와 같이 자주 등장하는 어휘의 **연음** 및 **강세**에 주의한다. |

| 어휘 | **latest** 최신의   **variety of** 다양한   **available** 이용할 수 있는   **eliminate** 제거하다 |

Question 3 Describe a Picture

고득점 TIP **공항 검색대**의 광경이다. **맨 앞 오른쪽 두 명**에 대해 **먼저** 말하고, 그 후에 왼쪽에 줄을 서 있는 사람들을 간단하게 묘사한다. **'마주보다, 팔을 올리다, 팔짱을 끼다, 주머니에 손을 넣고 있다'** 등 자주 출제되는 동작 표현에 유의한다.

Question 3   🎧 01-05-03

초·중급 Model Answer

This picture appears to be at an airport. The first thing I notice is two men facing each other. On the right, a man is searching another man. It seems that he is a security officer. In front of him, a man with short hair is holding out his arms. On the left, a woman is frowning at him with her arms folded. She is wearing an orange short sleeved shirt. Behind her, a man has his hands in his pockets. Behind him, there are two other women. In the background, I can see some windows.

이 사진은 공항에서 찍힌 것 같습니다. 가장 먼저 보이는 것은 마주보고 있는 두 남자입니다. 오른쪽에는 한 남자가 다른 남자를 수색하고 있습니다. 그는 보안요원으로 보입니다. 그의 앞에는 짧은 머리의 한 남성이 양 팔을 들고 있습니다. 왼쪽에 한 여성이 팔짱을 낀 채 그를 보며 찡그리고 있습니다. 그녀는 주황색 반팔 셔츠를 입고 있습니다. 그 여자 뒤에 한 남성은 주머니에 손을 넣고 있습니다. 그 남자 뒤에는 두 명의 다른 여자들이 있습니다. 배경에는 창문들이 보입니다.

고급 Model Answer

This picture appears to be at an airport. The first thing I notice is two men facing each other. On the right, a man is searching another man. It seems that he is a security officer. He is standing with his back toward us. Right in front of him, a man with short hair is holding out his arms. He looks nervous. On the left, some people are standing in a line and waiting to go through the screening. A woman is standing at the head of the line. She is frowning at the two guys on the right, she has her arms folded and she is wearing an orange short sleeved shirt. Behind her, a man has his hands in his pockets. Behind him, there are two other women with blonde hair. In the background, I can see some windows.

이 사진은 공항에서 찍힌 것 같습니다. 가장 먼저 보이는 것은 마주보고 있는 두 남자입니다. 오른쪽에는 한 남자가 다른 남자를 수색하고 있습니다. 그는 보안 요원으로 보입니다. 그는 등을 우리 쪽으로 한 채 서 있습니다. 그의 바로 앞에는 짧은 머리의 한 남성이 팔을 들어올리고 있습니다. 그는 긴장한 것처럼 보입니다. 왼쪽에는 몇몇 사람들이 줄을 서서 검색대를 통과하길 기다리고 있습니다. 한 여성이 줄 맨 앞에 서 있습니다. 그녀는 오른쪽의 두 남자들을 보고 찡그리고 있습니다. 그 여성은 팔짱을 끼고 있으며 오렌지색 반팔 셔츠를 입고 있습니다. 그녀 뒤에 한 남성은 주머니에 손을 넣고 있습니다. 그 뒤에는 금발의 다른 두 여자가 있습니다. 배경에는 창문들이 보입니다.

| 어 휘 | **face** 향하다 **search** 수색하다 **hold out** ~을 내밀다 **frown** 찡그리다 |

Actual Test 05

Questions 4-6 Respond to Questions

Imagine that a Canadian marketing firm is conducting research in your country. You have agreed to participate in a telephone interview about sunglasses.

캐나다의 한 마케팅 회사가 당신의 나라에서 설문조사를 하고 있다고 가정해 보세요. 당신은 '선글라스'에 관한 전화 인터뷰에 응하기로 동의했습니다.

Question 4

01-05-04

Q. When was the last time you bought sunglasses and where did you go to shop for them?

마지막으로 언제 선글라스를 샀으며, 어디서 샀습니까?

[초·중급 Model Answer]

A. Last month, I bought sunglasses at a department store. They were on sale so I could buy them at a reasonable price.

저는 지난달 백화점에서 선글라스를 샀습니다. 세일 중이어서 합리적인 가격에 구입할 수 있었습니다.

[고급 Model Answer]

A. The last time I bought sunglasses was last summer. I usually go through one pair at least every summer because I break or lose them frequently. I generally buy a pair on the street.

마지막으로 선글라스를 구입했던 것은 작년 여름이었습니다. 저는 선글라스를 자주 부러뜨리거나 잃어버리기 때문에 매 여름마다 적어도 한 개는 삽니다. 주로 길거리에서 구입합니다.

[고득점 TIP] **When was the last time~** 으로 시작하는 문제는 when과 관련된 문제 중 가장 많이 출제되었다. **과거형**으로 대답하고, **바로 답부터** 말하는 것이 쉽다.

Question 5

01-05-05

Q. How long did it take to choose the sunglasses that you bought?

구매하신 그 선글라스를 고르는 데 얼마나 시간이 걸렸습니까?

[초·중급 Model Answer]

A. It took about 20 minutes to choose the sunglasses. At first I couldn't find what I wanted, so I went around several different shops.

그 선글라스를 고르는 데 20분 정도 걸렸습니다. 처음에 원하는 것을 찾지 못해서 여러 곳의 다른 매장들을 돌아다녔습니다.

[고급 Model Answer]

A. It took me about 30 minutes to pick out the exact pair I wanted. I kept going back and forth to a couple of different street vendors so I could get the best price by negotiating with them.

제가 정확히 원하는 것을 고르기 위해 30분 정도 걸렸습니다. 길거리의 두 세 군데 노점상을 계속 왔다 갔다 하며 상인들과 흥정한 결과 최고의 가격에 구입할 수 있었습니다.

Question 6

🎧 01-05-06

Q. Can you describe your decision making process when you buy sunglasses?

선글라스를 구매할 때 당신의 구매 결정 과정에 대해서 설명해줄 수 있습니까?

초·중급 Model Answer

A. Let me tell you about my decision making process. First, I think of some brands and designs that I like. Then, if a shop has some sunglasses like the ones I am thinking of, I try them on to see how they look. If I like them, I ask how much they are. If the prices are not reasonable enough, I start to negotiate with shopkeepers or visit another shop.

제 구매 결정 과정에 대해서 말해보겠습니다. 우선, 저는 제가 좋아하는 몇 개의 브랜드와 디자인에 대해 생각해봅니다. 그런 다음, 매장에 제가 생각하는 것과 같은 선글라스들이 있으면 제게 어울리는지를 보기 위해서 그것들을 써봅니다. 만약 그 선글라스가 마음에 들면 가격이 얼마인지 물어봅니다. 가격이 만약 적당하지 않을 경우에는, 매장 직원과 흥정을 시작하거나 다른 매장으로 갑니다.

고급 Model Answer

A. Well, at first I have an idea of the style that I am looking for and I check to see if the street vendor has it. Next, I try on a couple of that style to see how they look and feel. Then, I ask how much and usually walk away even if I like them a lot just to see if they will bargain. After that, I look for the same ones at another vendor to see if I can make a better deal. Finally, I take the lowest priced pair.

우선 제가 찾는 스타일에 대한 생각을 해보고, 길거리 노점에 그것들이 있는지 확인해봅니다. 그 다음, 원하던 스타일의 선글라스들을 몇 개 써 보고 괜찮은지 봅니다. 그 후에 얼마인지 물어보고, 선글라스가 아주 마음에 들더라도 다른 곳에서 더 싸게 파는지 보기 위해 가게에서 나옵니다. 그런 다음에 다른 노점에서 내가 더 좋은 가격에 살 수 있는지 알아보기 위해 같은 것들이 있는지 살펴봅니다. 마침내 저는 가장 싼 가격의 선글라스를 삽니다.

|어 휘| **shop** 쇼핑하다　**be on sale** 할인 판매 중인　**at a reasonable price** 적당한 가격으로
go through 살펴보다　**at least** 적어도　**frequently** 자주　**go around** 돌아다니다
pick out (신중하게) 고르다　**back and forth** 왔다 갔다　**a couple of** 두세 가지 정도
street vendor 거리의 노점상　**negotiate** 협상하다　**try on** ~을 해보다　**shopkeeper** 상점 주인
walk away 떠나버리다　**bargain** 흥정하다　**make a deal (with)** ~와 거래하다

 **Questions 7-9** Respond to Questions Using Information Provided

Smokey Mountain Resort and Conference Center
Restaurant Availability

New Year's Weekend Dec.31-Jan.2

Date	Restaurant	Seating availability - Total/Available
December 31	Mountain View	250 / 9
	Creek Café	175 / 22
	Boulder Bistro	150 / 15
January 1	Mountain View	250 / 12
	Creek Café	175 / 8
	Boulder Bistro	150 / 10
January 2	Mountain View	250 / 55
	Creek Café	175 / 80
	Boulder Bistro	150 / 50

* All restaurants will close by 9 P.M. on December 31st to prepare for the New Year's Eve party.

Smokey Mountain 리조트 및 회의장 레스토랑 예약

연말 마지막 주말 12월 31일~1월 2일

날짜	레스토랑	좌석 수 - 전체/가능 좌석
12월 31일	Mountain View	250 / 9
	Creek Café	175 / 22
	Boulder Bistro	150 / 15
1월 1일	Mountain View	250 / 12
	Creek Café	175 / 8
	Boulder Bistro	150 / 10
1월 2일	Mountain View	250 / 55
	Creek Café	175 / 80
	Boulder Bistro	150 / 50

* 모든 레스토랑은 신년 전야제 파티를 준비하기 위해 12월 31일 오후 9시에 문을 닫습니다.

Hi, this is Tricia Adams. We come to your New Year's Eve party every year. This year we have a total of 10 people with us and I have a few questions.

안녕하세요, 저는 Tricia Adams입니다. 우리는 해마다 당신들의 신년 전야제 파티에 참석하고 있습니다. 이번엔 총 10명의 사람들이 함께 가려고 하는데요, 몇 가지 질문이 있습니다.

Question 7
01-05-07

Q. What are our choices for New Year's Eve dinner?

새해 전날 저녁식사를 위해서 어떤 레스토랑들을 이용할 수 있습니까?

초·중급 Model Answer

A. On December 31, we have two restaurants available, Creek Cafe and Boulder Bistro.

12월 31일에 두 개의 레스토랑을 이용하실 수 있습니다. Creek Cafe와 Boulder Bistro 입니다.

고급 Model Answer

A. On New Year's Eve, the only two restaurants still available are the Creek Cafe and the Boulder Bistro.

새해 전날에 유일하게 이용 가능한 두 개의 레스토랑은 Creek Cafe와 Boulder Bistro입니다.

고득점 TIP 이처럼 **레스토랑**이나 **호텔**에서 **이용 가능한 좌석(객실) 수**를 묻는 문제도 꾸준히 출제되는 편이다. 우선 **intro 부분**에 나오는 **의뢰인을 포함한 인원**이 몇 명인지 잘 기억한 후, **해당 날짜**에 그 **인원과 같거나 더 많은 좌석**이 남아 있는 레스토랑을 언급한다.

Question 8
01-05-08

Q. What time will the restaurants close on New Year's Eve for the party?

파티를 위해 새해 전날 레스토랑들은 몇 시에 문을 닫습니까?

초·중급 Model Answer

A. All restaurants will close by 9 P.M. on December 31st to prepare for the New Year's Eve party.

신년 전야제 파티를 준비하기 위해 모든 레스토랑은 12월 31일 오후 9시에 문을 닫을 것입니다.

고급 Model Answer

A. On December 31st, all the restaurants will close early, at 9 P.M. in order to prepare for the New Year's Eve party.

12월 31일에 모든 레스토랑은 신년 전야제 파티를 준비하기 위해 오후 9시에 일찍 문을 닫을 것입니다.

Question 9

01-05-09

Q. What are our dining options for January 1st and 2nd?

1월 1일과 2일에는 어떤 레스토랑을 선택할 수 있나요?

초·중급 Model Answer

A. On January 1st, you could dine at Mountain View restaurant or Boulder Bistro, but on January 2nd, you could enjoy any of our restaurants; Mountain View, Creek Cafe or Boulder Bistro.

1월 1일에는 Mountain View 혹은 Boulder Bistro 레스토랑에서 식사를 하실 수 있습니다. 그러나 1월 2일에는 Mountain View, Creek Cafe 또는 Boulder Bistro 모두 이용하실 수 있습니다.

고급 Model Answer

A. On January 1st, you have two choices. Both Mountain View restaurant and Boulder Bistro are available. January 2nd, you have an additional choice and that one is Creek Cafe which is also open.

1월 1일에는 두 가지 중에서 선택하실 수 있습니다. Mountain View와 Boulder Bistro 레스토랑 두 곳을 이용하실 수 있습니다. 1월 2일에는 그 외에도 Creek Cafe도 문을 엽니다.

고득점
TIP
9번 문제는 답변 시간이 넉넉하므로 **dining options, January 1st, 2nd**와 같은 **핵심 단어**를 잘 듣고 침착하게 하나씩 답한다. 똑같은 말을 반복하는 것보다 **you could dine at, ~be available** 등 **다양한 표현**을 사용하는 것이 좋다.

어휘 **availability** 이용, 예약   **creek** 개울, 시내   **boulder** 바위   **bistro** 작은 식당   **prepare for** ~를 준비하다
in order to ~하기 위해   **dining** 식사   **dine** 식사하다   **additional** 추가의

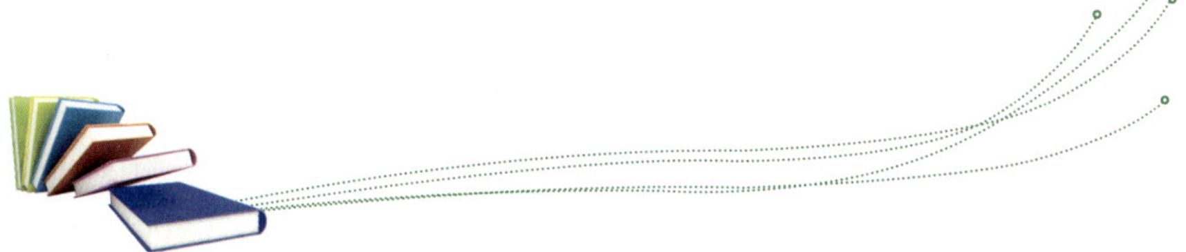

Actual Test 05

Question 10 Propose a solution

Hello, this is Andy Falcon from The Learning Tree on the 3rd floor. I am trying to get in touch with someone from the maintenance department for our building at 601 Main Street, Suite 305. Apparently something is wrong with our heating unit. I don't know about the rest of the building but the 3rd floor is freezing cold. In addition, the water in the restroom wasn't running when I was in there a moment ago. I have some important customers coming in today at 1:30 P.M. and I was hoping something could be done to fix the situation with this heating and water system before that time. Please call me on my mobile as I will be in and out of the office until they get here due to the cold. My number is 598-298-6173. Thank you very much.

안녕하세요? 3층 Learning Tree의 Andy Falcon입니다. 저는 601 Main Street Suite 305에 있는 우리 건물의 관리부서 직원과 통화를 하고 싶습니다. 우리 난방시스템에 분명히 문제가 있는 것 같습니다. 나머지 층은 모르겠지만 3층은 너무 춥습니다. 뿐만 아니라, 좀 전에 화장실에 갔을 때 물이 나오지 않았습니다. 중요한 고객들이 오늘 오후 1시 반에 오기로 되어 있기 때문에, 그전에 난방과 수도를 수리해주시길 부탁 드립니다. 그들이 이 곳에 도착할 때까지 추위로 인한 문제 때문에 제가 사무실을 들락거릴 것 같으니 제 휴대폰으로 연락 주시기 바랍니다. 제 번호는 598-298-6173 입니다. 감사합니다.

Question 10 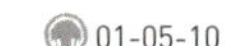 01-05-10

초·중급 Model Answer

Hello, Mr. Falcon. This is Terry from the maintenance department. I'm returning your call about your request. I got your message saying that something is wrong with the heating unit on the 3rd floor and the water in the restroom so you are asking us to deal with this situation. First of all, we apologize for this inconvenience. I will send one of the best technicians to your office to check it out and fix the whole system. He will be there in about an hour before your customers come. If you have any questions please call me anytime. Thank you.

안녕하세요? Falcon 씨. 관리부서의 Terry입니다. 요청하신 사안에 대해서 답변 드리고자 합니다. 3층 난방 시스템과 화장실 수도에 문제가 있으니 해결해 달라는 메시지를 들었습니다. 먼저, 불편을 드려 죄송합니다. 저희 최고의 수리공 중 한 명을 당신의 사무실로 보내서 문제를 점검하고, 전체 시스템을 고치도록 하겠습니다. 그 수리공은 당신의 고객들이 오기 1시간 전에 도착할 것입니다. 질문이 더 있으시면 언제든 연락주십시오. 감사합니다.

고급 Model Answer

Hello, Mr. Falcon. This is Terry from the maintenance department. I'm returning your call regarding your request. I got your message and understand that the heater in the building or at least on your floor isn't working. It sounds like the water in the restroom has some malfunction as well. First of all, we apologize for this inconvenience. All of this could have been caused by the freeze last night but I would like to check out the whole system. I am on my way and it shouldn't take too long as I am right here at 603 Main Street, so I think I can check the system out before your customers show up to your place this afternoon. It would be best if I could get into your office to ensure that the problem is resolved. Just in case we miss each other, my direct mobile is 598-374-2761.

안녕하세요? Falcon 씨. 관리부서의 Terry입니다. 요청하신 사안에 대해서 답변 드리고자 합니다. 건물의 난방기가, 혹은 적어도 당신의 층에서 난방기가 작동하지 않는다는 메시지를 들었습니다. 또한, 화장실의 수도도 제 기능을 하지 못한다고 들었습니다. 우선은, 불편을 끼쳐 드려 죄송합니다. 이 모든 문제는 지난 밤 한파 때문인 것으로 보이지만 제가 전체 시스템을 점검해보도록 하겠습니다. 저는 지금 그 곳으로 가는 길이며, 이미 603 Main Street에 와 있기 때문에 그리 오래 걸리지 않을 것입니다. 제 생각에 오늘 오후에 당신의 고객들이 그곳으로 오시기 전에 시스템 점검을 마칠 수 있을 것 같습니다. 문제가 해결되었는지 확실하게 하기 위해 제가 당신의 사무실로 가는 것이 최선일 것 같습니다. 혹시 길이 엇갈릴 수도 있으니 제 개인번호를 알려드리겠습니다. 598-374-2761입니다.

|고득점|　**건물 관리**와 관련한 **고객 불만** 유형이다. 건물의 **관리 부서**나 **경비실**에 불만을 제기하는 문제도 자주 출제된다. **사과의 표현을**
| T I P |　먼저 한 후에, **다른 직원**을 보내거나 아니면 **직접** 가서 해결하겠다는 식으로 답변할 수 있다.

|어　휘|　**get in touch with** ~와 연락하다　　**maintenance** (건물, 기계 등) 유지, 관리　　**apparently** 분명히
　　　　　freezing (얼음이 얼 정도로) 추운　　**in addition** 게다가　　**a moment ago** 방금　　**due to** ~때문에
　　　　　apologize 사과하다　　**inconvenience** 불편　　**malfunction** 고장　　**on one's way** 도중에
　　　　　ensure 보장하다　　**resolve** 해결하다　　**just in case** 만약을 위해서

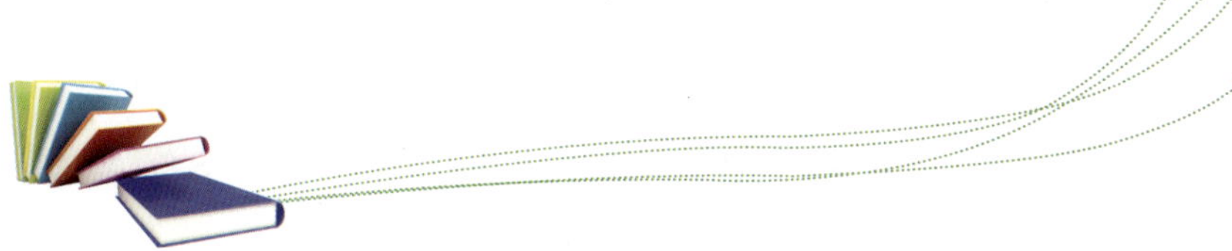

Actual Test 05

Question 11 Express an Opinion

> Some people think that it is better to stay in the same workplace while other people prefer to work at various workplaces. What are your thoughts and why? Use specific reasons or examples to support your opinion.
>
> 어떤 사람들은 한 직장에 머무는 것이 낫다고 생각하는 반면, 다른 이들은 다양한 직장에서 일하는 것을 선호합니다. 당신 생각은 어떠하며, 그 이유는 무엇입니까? 당신의 의견을 뒷받침할 구체적인 근거나 예시를 사용하세요.

Question 11

01-05-11

초·중급 Model Answer

I prefer to work at various workplaces for the following reasons. First, people can experience and learn many things from trial and error. To be specific, as they get used to new workplaces they can become generalists. It helps them get promoted faster in some companies. Second, employees can get along with many kinds of people and develop interpersonal skills. In my case, I have worked at various workplaces so I can network with many people and we can help each other. For these reasons, I think working at various workplaces is better.

저는 다음과 같은 이유로 다양한 직장에서 일하는 것이 좋다고 생각합니다. 첫째, 사람들은 시행착오로부터 많은 것을 경험하고 배울 수 있습니다. 구체적으로, 그들이 새로운 직장에 익숙해져 감에 따라 그들은 제너럴리스트(다방면에 걸쳐 많이 아는 사람)가 될 수 있습니다. 이는 그들이 어떤 회사에서는 더 빨리 승진할 수 있도록 도와주는 요인이 됩니다. 둘째, 직원들은 다양한 종류의 사람들과 어울릴 수 있으며 대인관계 기술을 익힐 수 있습니다. 제 경우에, 저는 다양한 일터에서 일해왔기 때문에 많은 사람들과 네트워크를 쌓을 수 있고 서로 도울 수도 있습니다. 이런 이유들 때문에, 저는 다양한 직장에서 일하는 것이 더 좋다고 생각합니다.

고급 Model Answer

My thought is that it's usually better to get experience at various workplaces. The primary reason for this is that it makes a person more marketable to a company since they come to a company with innovative ideas. Employees working at just one place can be short-sighted. Secondly, it helps people become generalists. In some companies, the generalist can get promoted more easily than others. In the case of my boss, he has worked at various departments and became an executive director faster than any other. Finally, I believe multiple workplaces are better for a person as it builds their group of friends and colleagues for possible positions later. Networking with various people is very important at work. That's why I think a person should usually have multiple workplaces.

저는 보통 다양한 직장에서 경험을 얻는 것이 더 좋다고 생각합니다. 이에 대한 주된 이유로, 이러한 직원들은 혁신적인 아이디어들을 회사에 제시하기 때문에, 다양한 경험을 하는 것은 회사에게 있어 직원을 더 경쟁력이 있도록 만들어 줄 수 있습니다. 한 장소에서만 근무하는 직원들은 근시안적이 될 수 있습니다. 둘째로, 이는 사람들이 제너럴리스트가 되도록 도움을 줍니다. 어떤 회사에서는 제너럴리스트들이 다른 이들보다 더 쉽게 승진할 수 있습니다. 제 상사의 경우에, 그는 다양한 부서에서 일을 해왔고 다른 누구보다도 빠르게 전무로 승진했습니다. 마지막으로, 다양한 직장 근무 경험은 향후 가능성이 있는 일자리를 위한 친구나 동료를 얻을 수 있게 해주므로 더 낫다고 생각합니다. 다양한 사람들과의 네트워크는 직장에서 매우 중요합니다. 저는 이러한 이유들 때문에 다양한 직장에서 근무해야 한다고 생각합니다.

Actual Test 06

Questions 1-2 Read a Text Aloud

Question 1

🎧 01-06-01

Good Morning / and **welcome** to the **New York Public Library**. ↘ // **Please** listen to **this message** ↗ / **before** proceeding. ↘ // **You** are **currently** / in **front** of the **Sawyer Lion sculpture**. ↘ // Your **options** are **fiction**, ↗ / **non-fiction**, ↗ / **periodicals** ↗ / and **information-tion desk**. ↘ // For **fiction** and **nonfiction**, ↗ / **proceed** to the **3rd** floor. ↘ // For **periodicals**, ↗ / **proceed** to the **second** floor ↗ / and for **all other information** ↗ / please see the **information desk** / **behind** this **sculpture**. ↘ // Thank you ↗ / and we **hope** you **enjoy your visit**. ↘

안녕하세요, 뉴욕 공공 도서관에 오신 것을 환영합니다. 이동하시기 전에 잠시 드릴 말씀이 있습니다. 현재 여러분은 Sawyer Lion 조각상 앞에 계십니다. 소설, 논픽션, 정기간행물 섹션이나 안내데스크 쪽으로 가실 수 있습니다. 소설과 논픽션 섹션은 3층으로 가시면 됩니다. 정기간행물 섹션은 2층에 있으며, 다른 모든 필요한 사항이 있으시면 이 조각상 뒤에 있는 안내데스크로 가셔서 문의해 주시길 바랍니다. 다시 한 번 감사의 말씀을 드리며 즐거운 시간 되시길 바랍니다.

| 고득점 TIP | 도서관 이용객들을 위한 **공지글**이다. **섹션**이나 **층수, 이동 방향** 등 **주요 정보**를 강조해서 읽는다. **열거하는 부분**에서 **억양**에 주의하고, **currently**와 같이 **~ly로 끝나는 부사**들은(ex. recently, approximately 등) 자주 등장하므로 발음이나 **강세**에 특히 주의한다. |

| 어휘 | **proceed** 나아가다   **currently** 현재   **sculpture** 조각품   **fiction** 소설   **non-fiction** 실화
periodical 정기간행물 |

Question 2

🎧 01-06-02

Good evening. ↘ // On this **edition** of **Teacher's Tip's**, ↗ / we will **hear** the **latest** / from **Tom Rippen**. ↘ // **Tom** is the **man** ↗ / who is getting **students excited** / about **math analysis functions**. ↘ // **Today** / he is going to **share** with **us** / his **precise methodology** ↗ / on **how** to **help students** / **analyze**, ↗ / **calculate**, ↗ / **draw a graph** ↗ / and **keep smiling** / through it **all**. ↘

안녕하세요. 이번 Teacher's Tip 시간에는 Tom Rippen 씨로부터 최근 이야기를 들어보도록 하겠습니다. Tom은 수학 분석 함수로 학생들에게 큰 호응을 얻고 있습니다. 오늘 그는 학생들이 손쉽고 즐겁게 분석 및 계산을 하고 그래프를 그릴 수 있도록 도움을 줄 수 있는 그의 정밀한 방법론에 대해 저희와 공유해 주실 것입니다.

| 고득점 TIP | **방송**에서 강사를 **소개**하는 내용이다. 소개받는 사람의 **이름, 업적** 및 **방송 내용**을 강조한다. 단어를 **열거하는 부분의 억양** 및 analysis, precise, analyze 등 자주 나오는 어휘들의 **발음**이나 **강세**에 주의하며 연습해본다. |

| 어휘 | **edition** (방송) ~회   **latest** 가장 최근의   **analysis** 분석   **function** 함수, 기능   **precise** 정밀한
methodology 방법론   **analyze** 분석하다   **calculate** 계산하다 |

 **Question 3** Describe a Picture

━ 도입 ━ 중심 ━ 주변 ━ 마무리

고득점 TIP 사람들 몇 명이 **테이블 주위에 앉아 있는 구도**는 **도서관, 회의실, 레스토랑** 등에서 자주 등장한다. 우선 **앞의 세 사람**을 중심으로 **공통점**을 이야기하고 **각각의 특징**을 언급한 후, 그 앞의 **테이블**과 뒤쪽의 **배경**을 묘사한다.

🎧 01-06-03

초·중급 Model Answer

This picture appears to be in a library. The first thing I notice is three people sitting at a table. They are holding pens and looking at a book on the table. It seems that they are studying the same book. The man in the middle is smiling and pointing at something in the book. On the left, there is a woman with blonde hair and on the right I can see an elderly man wearing a blue long sleeved shirt. In front of them, some books are stacked up on the table. In the background, I can see other people sitting around a table and many books on a bookshelf.

이 사진은 도서관에서 찍힌 것 같습니다. 가장 먼저 보이는 것은 테이블에 앉아있는 세 사람입니다. 그들은 펜을 들고 책상에 있는 책을 보고 있습니다. 그들은 같은 책으로 공부하는 중인 것 같습니다. 가운데 남자는 미소를 지으며 책에 있는 무언가를 가리키고 있습니다. 왼쪽에는 금발의 여자가 있고, 오른쪽에는 푸른색 긴 팔 셔츠를 입고 있는 나이가 지긋한 한 남자를 볼 수 있습니다. 그들의 앞에는 책 몇 권이 테이블에 쌓여져 있습니다. 배경에는 테이블 주위에 앉아 있는 다른 사람들과, 책장에 있는 많은 책들이 보입니다.

고급 Model Answer

This picture appears to be in a library. The first thing I notice is three people sitting at a table with several books stacked up on it. They are holding pens and looking at a book that the middle guy is pointing at. It seems that they are studying the same book. The man in the middle is smiling and wearing a green long sleeved shirt. On his right, there is a woman with blonde hair and on his left I can see an elderly man wearing a blue long sleeved shirt and pants. Behind them, I can also see a bookshelf full of books and another table with three people.

이 사진은 도서관에서 찍힌 것 같습니다. 가장 먼저 보이는 것은 몇 권의 책들이 쌓인 테이블에 앉아 있는 세 사람입니다. 그들은 펜을 들고 있고 가운데 남자가 가리키고 있는 책을 바라보고 있습니다. 그들은 같은 책으로 공부하고 있는 것 같습니다. 가운데 남자는 미소를 짓고 있으며 녹색 긴 팔 셔츠를 입고 있습니다. 그의 오른쪽에는 금발의 여자가 있고, 그의 왼쪽에는 푸른색 긴 팔 셔츠와 바지를 입고 있는 나이가 지긋한 남자가 있습니다. 그들의 뒤에는 책들로 가득 찬 책장과 세 사람들이 있는 또 다른 테이블이 보입니다.

어휘 **point at** ~을 가리키다　**elderly** 나이가 지긋한　**long sleeved shirt** 긴 소매 셔츠　**stack up** 쌓이다
bookshelf 책장

Actual Test 06

Questions 4-6 Respond to Questions

Imagine that a British marketing firm is conducting research in your country. You have agreed to participate in a telephone interview about sports.

영국의 한 마케팅 회사가 당신의 나라에서 설문조사를 하고 있다고 가정해 보세요. 당신은 '스포츠'에 관한 전화 인터뷰에 응하기로 동의했습니다.

Question 4　　01-06-04

Q. What sport was the most popular in your high school?

당신의 고등학교에서 가장 인기 있었던 운동은 무엇이었습니까?

초·중급 Model Answer

A. It was soccer. In my case, I used to eat lunch very quickly so I could play soccer with my classmates during the lunch time.

가장 인기 있었던 운동은 축구였습니다. 저는 반 친구들과 점심시간에 축구를 하기 위해서 점심을 아주 빨리 먹었습니다.

고급 Model Answer

A. In my high school, the most popular sport by far was soccer. If a guy played soccer well in my school he was considered a "women magnet." All the guys wanted to be like him and all the girls wanted to date him.

고등학교 때 가장 인기 있었던 운동은 단연 축구였습니다. 만약 학교에서 남학생이 축구를 잘하면 그는 인기가 많을 것으로 간주되곤 했습니다. 모든 남학생들은 그와 같이 되기를 바랬고 모든 여학생들은 그와 데이트하길 원했습니다.

고득점 TIP 최상급 질문이므로 **한 가지만 이야기**하고 **부연 설명**을 간단히 덧붙인다. 설령 실제와 다르더라도 축구나 농구처럼 **이야기하기 쉬운 주제**를 택하는 것도 좋은 방법이다.

Question 5　　01-06-05

Q. Did you play sports? Which ones? What positions?

당신은 운동을 했었습니까? 어떤 종목이었나요? 어떤 포지션이었죠?

초·중급 Model Answer

A. I played baseball in high school. I was a good pitcher who was able to throw fastballs and curve balls. Baseball is still my favorite sport.

저는 고등학교 때 야구를 했습니다 저는 강속구와 커브를 던질 수 있는 좋은 투수였습니다. 야구는 여전히 제가 가장 좋아하는 운동입니다.

고급 Model Answer

A. I played a couple of sports when I was in high school. I played basketball and baseball. In basketball I was a forward and on the baseball team I was a catcher.

고등학생일 때 저는 두 가지 정도의 운동을 즐겼습니다. 저는 농구와 야구를 했습니다. 농구를 할 때는 포워드였고 야구팀에서는 포수였습니다.

Question 6

🎧 01-06-06

Q. If you had to describe the perfect coach what would they be like?

만약 훌륭한 코치에 대해서 묘사한다면, 그들은 어떠해야 합니까?

초·중급 Model Answer

A. I think the perfect coach should listen to players carefully. If they communicate with each other well, they can perform better. Additionally, the coach should put the right man in the right place. For example, my basketball coach was almost perfect. He knew every player's potential exactly and helped them to develop their skills for the game.

저는 훌륭한 코치는 선수들의 말에 귀 기울일 줄 알아야 한다고 생각합니다. 만일 그들이 의사소통을 원활하게 한다면 그들은 더 잘 해낼 수 있습니다. 또한, 코치는 필요한 선수를 적재적소에 투입할 수 있어야 합니다. 예를 들어, 저희 농구팀 코치는 거의 완벽한 분이셨습니다. 그는 모든 선수들의 잠재력을 정확히 알고 있었고, 경기를 위해 그들이 능력을 개발할 수 있도록 도와주셨습니다.

고급 Model Answer

A. In my opinion, the perfect coach should keep motivating players. My basketball coach was almost perfect. He was kind and understanding but he wouldn't let you slack off or get lazy. He really helped young people to focus on and think about what they were doing right then and there. Additionally, the perfect coach should be open-minded. We all knew we could talk with the coach about anything and he would take time to listen to and give us his advice.

제 생각에 훌륭한 코치는 선수들에게 꾸준히 동기를 부여할 수 있어야 합니다. 저희 농구팀 코치는 거의 완벽한 분이셨습니다. 그는 친절하고 이해심이 많은 분이었지만 게으름을 부리거나 나태해지는 것을 용납하지 않았습니다. 그는 젊은이들이 집중하고 그들의 현 위치에서 무엇을 하고 있는지에 대해 생각할 수 있도록 도움을 주었습니다. 또한, 훌륭한 코치는 포용력이 있어야 합니다. 우리 모두는 무엇이든 코치님과 상의할 수 있다는 것을 알고 있었고, 그는 우리의 말을 듣고 조언을 해줄 시간을 가지려 했습니다.

|어 휘| **used to** ~하곤 했다　　**classmate** 반 친구　　**by far** 단연코　　**magnet** 자석, 매력적인 사람
pitcher 투수　　**catcher** 포수　　**potential** 잠재력　　**motivate** 동기를 부여하다　　**understanding** 이해심이 있는
slack off 게으름을 부리다　　**get lazy** 게을러지다　　**then and there** 그때 그곳에서
open-minded 마음이 열린

Museum of Natural History
National Teachers Appreciation Day

Date: May 8
Admission: Free to all teachers and their families
Location: Central Park West at 79th Street, New York, NY, 10024-5192

09:00 - 10:30	Real Science - Larry Gould (CBS "Science Guy")
10:30 - 12:00	Film - Mysteries of the Deep
12:00 - 13:00	Free Lunch sponsored by NYC Teachers Credit Union
13:00 - 15:30	Browse the museum at your leisure
15:30 - 16:30	Teacher Appreciation Awards - Mayor of NYC

* All scheduled events will happen in the Main Auditorium

자연사 박물관
스승의 날 행사

날짜: 5월 8일
입장: 모든 선생님들과 그 가족들은 무료 입장
위치: 뉴욕, 센트럴 파크 서부 79번가, 10024-5192

09:00~10:30	진짜 과학 - Larry Gould (CBS 방송 "Science Guy" 프로그램)
10:30~12:00	영화 상영 – 바다의 신비
12:00~13:00	무료 점심 – 뉴욕시 교원공제회 후원
13:00~15:30	여유롭게 박물관 둘러보기
15:30~16:30	스승의 날 시상 – 뉴욕 시장

* 예정된 모든 행사는 대강당에서 열립니다.

Hello, this is Sam Brady. I teach in the Bronx. I am considering coming to the Teacher's Day Appreciation Event. Could I get some more information from you?

안녕하세요, 저는 Sam Brady 입니다. 저는 Bronx에서 학생들을 가르치는 일을 하고 있습니다. 스승의 날 행사에 참석하려고 생각 중인데요. 몇 가지 정보를 더 얻을 수 있을까요?

Question 7

Q. What is the cost for my family of four? 저희 가족은 4명인데요, 비용이 얼마나 될까요?

 **초·중급 Model Answer**

A. The National Teachers Appreciation event is free to all teachers and their families.

스승의 날 행사는 모든 교사들과 그들의 가족들은 무료로 참여하실 수 있습니다.

고급 Model Answer

A. This event is free to all teachers and their families. Additionally, there is a free lunch for them sponsored by NYC Teachers Credit Union.

이 행사는 모든 교사들과 그들의 가족들은 무료로 참여하실 수 있습니다. 또한 뉴욕시 교원공제회 후원으로 점심 식사가 무료로 제공됩니다.

고득점 TIP 표 윗부분에 나오는 정보는 출제될 확률이 크므로, 표를 분석하는 준비시간에 미리 대비한다. 해당 내용을 바탕으로 문장을 완벽하게 만들어 답한다.

Question 8

Q. Will we have time to just look around the museum? 저희가 박물관을 돌아볼 시간이 있을까요?

 **초·중급 Model Answer**

A. Yes, there is time to browse the museum at your leisure from 1 to 3:30 P.M.

네, 1시부터 3시 30분 사이에 편안하게 박물관을 관람하는 시간이 있습니다.

고급 Model Answer

A. Yes, after lunch, there are two and a half hours, from 1 to 3:30 P.M for you and your family to browse at your leisure.

네, 점심 식사 후 가족들과 함께 1시부터 3시 30분까지 2시간 30분 동안 여유롭게 관람하실 수 있습니다.

고득점 TIP 조동사(Will, Can)나 Be동사(Am, Are, Is)로 질문할 경우, 대답은 Yes/No로 시작한다. 표에 있는 browse란 단어를 look around로 변형해 질문했다. 이렇게 특히 8번에서는 비슷한 뜻의 단어나 상위 단어를 사용해 질문하는 경우가 많다.

Q. What events are in the morning and where will they be held?

오전에는 어떠한 행사들이 어디에서 열리나요?

초·중급 Model Answer

A. There are two programs in the morning. The first one is 'Real Science' by Larry Gould from "Science Guy" on CBS. Then you can watch a film called "Mysteries of the Deep". All scheduled events will happen in the Main Auditorium.

오전에는 두 개의 프로그램이 있습니다. 첫 번째는 CBS 'Science Guy' 프로그램의 Larry Gould 가 진행하는 'Real Science(진짜 과학)'입니다. 그 다음엔 'Mysteries of the Deep(바다의 신비)'라는 영화를 관람하실 수 있습니다. 예정되어 있는 모든 행사는 대강당에서 진행됩니다.

고급 Model Answer

A. There are two programs scheduled for the morning. The first program will be 'Real Science' by Larry Gould from "Science Guy" on CBS that will go from 9 to 10:30 A.M. The second program, a film called "Mysteries of the Deep" is from 10:30 A.M. to noon. Both programs will be held in the Main Auditorium.

두 개의 프로그램이 오전에 예정되어 있습니다. 첫 번째 프로그램은 CBS 'Science Guy' 프로그램의 Larry Gould가 오전 9시부터 10시 반까지 진행하는 'Real Science(진짜 과학)'입니다. 두 번째 프로그램으로 'Mysteries of the Deep(바다의 신비)'라는 영화를 오전 10시 반부터 오후 12시까지 상영합니다. 두 프로그램 모두 대강당에서 진행됩니다.

고득점 TIP 의문사와 in the morning 같은 key word를 잘 듣고 답한다. **열거하는 답변**이므로 **몇 개의 프로그램이 있는지를 먼저** 말하고, **각각의 내용**에 대해 차근차근 언급한다. **전치사**나 **동사의 수 일치**와 같은 세부 사항에 유의한다.

어휘 **appreciation** 감사   **admission** 입장   **deep** 바다   **sponsor** 후원하다   **credit union** 신용조합   **browse** 둘러보다   **at leisure** 한가하게   **main auditorium** 대강당   **look around** 둘러보다

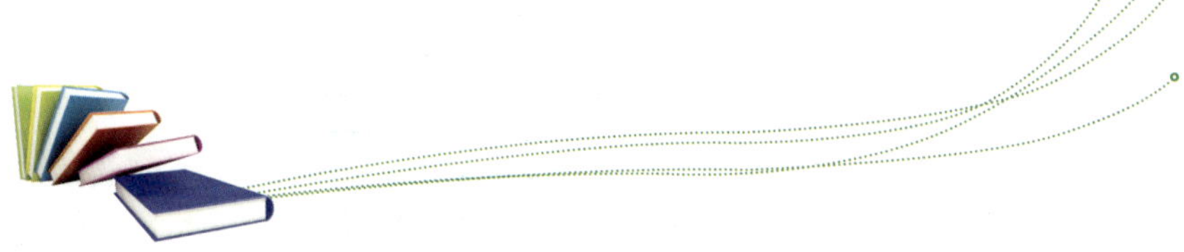

Question 10 Propose a solution

Hello, this is Tom Paxton. I went to the Jazz concert in the Chicago stadium yesterday. When I arrived I gave my coat to one of your staff and I saw him hang it on the clothes rack before the concert started. After the concert, which was terrific by the way, your staff gave me what I thought was my coat and I came home. The next morning, to my surprise, I found out that the coat wasn't mine. It's the same brand, color and size but there was a wallet and an ID with this coat and they are not mine. Perhaps there was some confusion by your staff. I work downtown and I am keeping the coat with me but I can't afford the time to go back to the stadium and try to exchange this coat for mine. Would it be possible for you to help me out? If at all possible I would like to get my coat back for an important meeting this evening. My number is (555)246-5987. Thank you.

안녕하세요, 저는 Tom Paxton 이라고 합니다. 어제 시카고 경기장에서 있었던 재즈 콘서트에 갔습니다. 그 곳에 도착해서 저는 직원 중에 한 분에게 제 코트를 맡겼고, 콘서트가 시작되기 전에 그 직원이 제 코트를 옷걸이에 거는 것을 보았습니다. 콘서트가 끝난 후에, 아 그런데 그 콘서트는 정말 멋졌어요, 한 직원이 제가 생각할 때 제 코트였던 것을 주셨고, 전 집에 왔습니다. 다음 날 아침에 너무 놀랍게도, 저는 그 코트가 제 것이 아니라는 것을 알게 되었습니다. 브랜드, 색상, 사이즈도 같았지만, 코트 안에는 제 것이 아닌 지갑과 신분증이 있었어요. 아마 직원께서 혼동했던 것 같습니다. 저는 시내에서 일하고 있고 지금 그 코트를 가지고 있지만, 시간이 없어서 제 코트와 바꾸기 위해 다시 경기장에 가는 것은 힘들 것 같습니다. 좀 도와주시겠어요? 가능하다면 오늘 저녁에 있는 중요한 미팅 전에 그 코트를 받고 싶습니다. 제 번호는 (555)246-5987 입니다. 감사합니다.

01-06-10

초·중급 Model Answer

Hello, Sir. This is Jack Dill from the customer service department of Chicago stadium. I'm returning your call about your request. I got your message saying that you got the wrong coat after the concert so you are asking us to help you exchange the coat. First of all, we apologize for this inconvenience. It seems that one of our staff members made a mistake. However, please don't worry about it. We are keeping your coat and I can bring it to you today because I'm supposed to go downtown for a meeting this afternoon. Please let me know your office address. If you have any questions you can reach my cell phone at 010-7942-9413. We apologize for our mistake again and thank you for coming to our concert.

안녕하세요, 저는 시카고 경기장 고객 지원 부서의 Jack Dill입니다. 말씀하신 사항에 대해서 답신 전화 드립니다. 콘서트 후에 다른 사람의 코트를 가져가셨고 그래서 저희에게 원래 본인의 코트를 되돌려 받을 수 있도록 도움을 요청하셨죠. 우선 불편을 끼쳐드려 죄송합니다. 저희 직원 중 한 명이 실수를 한 것 같습니다. 하지만 걱정하지 마세요, 저희가 코트를 잘 보관하고 있고, 마침 제가 오늘 오후에 미팅 건으로 시내에 갈 일이 있어서 코트를 가져다 드릴 수 있을 것 같습니다. 사무실 주소를 좀 알려주세요. 궁금하신 사항이 있으시면 제 휴대폰 010-7942-9413 으로 연락 주시길 바랍니다. 저희의 실수에 대해서 다시 한 번 사죄 드리며, 저희 콘서트에 와주셔서 감사 드립니다.

[고급 Model Answer]

Hello, Mr. Paxton. This is Jack Dill from customer service department of the Chicago stadium. I'm returning your call about the coat. I got your message and understand that the coat you got after the concert is not yours. You figured that out from finding a wallet and an ID of another person and you want to get your coat back but can't afford the time to come all the way back to the stadium. First of all, we sincerely apologize for this inconvenience. One of our staff members might have made this mistake because the concert was so crowded. However, you don't have to worry about it. We are keeping your coat with us and there is no problem for me to exchange the coats because I have a staff meeting at our company headquarters downtown this afternoon. Please leave the address of your office. If you have any questions you can reach me at 010-7942-9413. We apologize for our mistake again and thank you for coming to the event yesterday.

안녕하세요, Paxton 씨. 저는 시카고 경기장 고객 지원 부서의 Jack Dill입니다. 코트와 관련해서 답신 전화 드립니다. 콘서트 후에 가져가신 코트가 본인의 것이 아니라는 메시지를 들었습니다. 다른 사람의 지갑과 신분증을 보고 그 사실을 알게 되셨고, 코트를 되돌려 받고 싶지만 다시 이 곳 경기장으로 오실 시간적인 여유가 없다고 말씀하셨죠. 무엇보다 불편을 끼쳐드려 죄송합니다. 아마도 콘서트장이 너무 혼잡했기 때문에 저희 직원이 실수를 했던 것 같습니다. 하지만, 걱정 안 하셔도 될 것 같습니다. 저희가 코트를 잘 보관하고 있고, 제가 코트를 가져가서 현재 가지고 계신 것과 교환해 드릴 수 있습니다. 왜냐하면 오늘 오후에 시내 본사에서 직원 미팅이 있기 때문입니다. 사무실 주소를 좀 남겨주세요. 궁금하신 사항이 있으시면 010-7942-9413으로 연락 주시길 바랍니다. 저희의 실수에 대해서 다시 한 번 사죄 드리며 어제 저희 공연에 와주셔서 감사 드립니다.

[고득점 TIP] 불만이나 요청에 해당하는 문제 유형이다. 우리의 잘못을 인정했다면 '**직원의 실수**'와 같은 **잘못의 원인**을 간단하게 언급한다. 상대방이 현재 위치를 알려주었고 우리 쪽으로 올 수가 없다고 했으므로, 내가 직접 그쪽으로 가겠다는 식으로 답했다. 이와 같이, '**내가 직접 하겠다**'라는 대답도 많은 문제에 적용시킬 수 있다.

[어휘] **clothes rack** 옷걸이　**terrific** 훌륭한　**by the way** 그런데　**on one's surprise** 놀랍게도
ID 신분증(identification)　**confusion** 혼동　**downtown** 시내에서　**afford** 여유가 되다
be supposed to ～하기로 되어있다　**figure out** 알아내다　**sincerely** 진심으로　**headquarters** 본부

Question 11 Express an Opinion

Do you agree or disagree that new employees should have to work a certain period before being considered for a promotion? Give specific reasons or examples to support your opinion.

신입사원들은 승진 기회를 갖기 위해서 일정한 기간 동안 근무해야 한다는 의견에 동의하십니까 반대하십니까? 당신의 의견을 뒷받침할 구체적인 근거나 예시를 제시하세요.

초·중급 Model Answer

I disagree that new employees should have to work a certain time before being considered for a promotion. First, I think everyone is different and some people want to work harder than others. Those employees should be rewarded. Second, I think if a person thinks they have to wait to get promoted they might lose the desire to work hard at first when they have the most energy. In the case of my coworker, Mr. Kim, after he found that he should wait to get promoted to the next level, he started to focus more on his leisure activities, not on work. For these reasons, I'm against this statement.

저는 신입사원들이 승진 기회를 갖기 위해서 일정한 기간 동안 근무해야 한다는 의견에 동의하지 않습니다. 우선 개개인은 다 다를 수 밖에 없고 어떤 이들은 다른 사람들보다 더 열심히 일하고 싶어합니다. 이러한 직원들은 그에 상응하는 보상을 받아야 합니다. 두 번째로 제 생각에는 만약에 사람들이 승진하기 위해서 반드시 기다려야 한다면, 특히 입사 초기에 열정이 충만할 때 열심히 일해야겠다는 의욕을 상실할지도 모릅니다. 제 직장 동료인 Mr. Kim의 경우 진급을 하기 위해 기다려야만 한다는 사실을 알게 된 이후, 일이 아닌 여가 활동에 더 관심을 갖기 시작했습니다. 이러한 이유들 때문에 저는 이 의견에 동의하지 않습니다.

고급 Model Answer

I disagree with this opinion. First of all, I think each individual should be evaluated on their merits or lack of them. To be specific, no two people are alike and just like we shouldn't hold back someone with drive and ambition. I wouldn't want to see someone with no desire to grow be put in charge of the company just because of a certain period of time. Secondly, I think it takes away the initial desire to work hard when someone first starts at a company. If the person thinks they can impress someone and move ahead it might create strong motivation at work. For these reasons, I'm against the idea of having to have a mandatory time without any possibility of promotion.

저는 이 의견에 동의하지 않습니다. 무엇보다, 저는 직원들이 각자의 가치나 장점 유무에 따라서 평가 받아야 한다고 생각합니다. 구체화하자면, 두 명의 사람도 서로 같을 수 없고, 그렇기 때문에 추진력이나 야망을 가진 사람을 저지해서는 안될 것입니다. 성장하려는 의욕도 없는 사람이 일정 기간이 지났다고 해서 회사의 중책을 맡게 되는 것을 보고 싶지는 않습니다. 둘째로, 그렇게 하는 것은 처음 입사했을 때 열심히 일하려고 하는 그 첫 마음가짐을 무색하게 만들 수 있습니다. 만약 한 직원이 누군가에게 좋은 인상을 남길 수 있고 앞으로 전진할 수 있다고 생각한다면, 이러한 점은 그 직원에게 일터에서의 강한 동기부여가 될 수 있을 것입니다. 이러한 이유들 때문에 저는 승진에 대한 아무 가능성도 없이 일정 기간을 의무적으로 보내야 한다는 생각에 동의할 수 없습니다.

고득점 TIP 학생들의 경우 이와 같이 **직장에서 일어나는 사안들**에 대해 그 동안 생각해본 적이 없겠지만, **할 말이 더 많은 쪽**으로 의견을 정해서 쉽게 이야기하려고 노력한다. 이 문제의 경우에는 반대하는 쪽이 더 말하기 쉽다. 사람은 모두 다르기 때문에 그 **능력과 기여도에 따른 보상**이 이루어져야 한다는 것, 그리고 **상대편 의견을 비판**하면서 꼭 일정 기간 동안 근무해야 승진이 가능한 제도 하에서는 직원들의 의욕이 꺾일 수 있고 **동기부여**가 힘들다는 점 등을 근거로 들 수 있다.

어휘 **certain** 특정한 **consider** 고려하다 **promotion** 승진 **reward** 보상하다 **desire** 욕구
coworker 직장동료 **individual** 개인 **evaluate** 평가하다 **merit** 장점 **lack** 결핍 **alike** 아주 비슷한
hold back 저지하다 **drive** 추진력 **ambition** 야망 **in charge of** ~을 담당해서 **take away** 제거하다
initial 처음의 **impress** 인상을 주다 **motivation** 동기부여 **mandatory** 의무적인

Actual Test 07

Questions 1-2 Read a Text Aloud

Question 1
01-07-01

Attention Edwin Mart shoppers. ↘ // We <u>have a</u> **red light sale** / going on **right now** ↗ / in the **sporting goods department**. ↘ // <u>Get an</u> **automatic 25% off** of **bats**, ↗ / **balls** ↗ / and **bases** / **as long as** the **red light** is **flashing**. ↘ // **Additionally,** ↗ / **don't forget** our **Daily Hot Item** / in our <u>Bed and</u> **Bath department**. ↘ // **See** any <u>**Sales Associate**</u> <u>around you</u> ↗ / for **more information**. ↘

Edwin Mart 고객 여러분께 알려드립니다. 스포츠용품점에서 지금 빨간 불 세일을 진행하고 있습니다. 빨간 불이 깜빡이는 동안 야구방망이, 야구공 및 Base(루) 품목에 대해 자동적으로 25% 할인을 받으실 수 있습니다. 추가로, 침대 및 욕조 코너에 있는 오늘의 핫 아이템을 잊지 마세요. 추가 정보는 주위에 있는 영업사원에게 문의해주시기 바랍니다.

고득점 TIP 매장에서 **세일을 알리는 공지글**이다. **세일 품목, 할인폭** 등의 주요 정보를 강조해서 읽고, **열거하는 표현의 억양**에 주의한다. r, l 발음이 들어간 **red, light**와 같이 자주 등장하는 어휘들은 **준비 시간에 몇 번씩 연습**해본다.

어휘 **attention** 주목(하세요)   **as long as** ~하는 동안은   **flash** 번쩍이다   **additionally** 추가로   **associate** 직원

Question 2
01-07-02

Attention passengers, ↗ / <u>this is</u> your **Captain** speaking / **one more** time. ↘ // I <u>wanted to</u> <u>update</u> you / on some **gates** for **transfers**. ↘ // The **flights** <u>that I</u> have / are for **Vicksburg**, ↗ / **Pittsburg** ↗ / and **Baltimore**. ↘ // **Flight 101** for **Vicksburg** / will be <u>**out of**</u> gate 7, ↗ / **Pittsburgh flight 345** / will **leave** from **gate 9** ↗ / <u>and the</u> **Baltimore flight 478** / will be <u>**out of**</u> gate 3. ↘ // We will be **arriving at gate 1**, ↗ / and <u>if you</u> **need further information,** ↗ / a **screen** for **departing flights** / <u>is on</u> your **right** / <u>as you</u> **exit** the **gate**. ↘

승객 여러분, 주목해주시기 바랍니다. 다시 한번 기장이 승객 여러분께 알려드립니다. 환승 게이트에 대해 알려드리고자 합니다. 빅스버그, 피츠버그 및 볼티모어 행에 대한 비행편들에 대해 알려드립니다. 빅스버그행 101 항공편은 게이트 7에서 출발하고, 피츠버그행 345편은 게이트 9에서 출발하며 볼티모어행 478편은 게이트 3에서 출발합니다. 저희는 게이트 1에 도착할 예정입니다. 추가정보가 필요하신 경우 게이트를 나가시면서 우측에 있는 출발 항공편 스크린을 참고하시기 바랍니다.

고득점 TIP 비행기 안에서 **기장이 승객들에게 환승 게이트**에 대해 **공지**하는 글이다. **행선지와 게이트 번호** 등 핵심 정보를 강조해서 읽는다. 특히 f, v, p, b 발음이 자주 나오는데, 이렇게 **반복되는 발음이나 어휘**는 **중요한 채점 요소**이므로 준비시간에 반복해서 연습해보고 답변 시간에 좀 더 주의해서 읽는다.

어휘 **passenger** 승객   **captain** 기장   **transfer** 환승   **further** 추가의   **depart** 출발하다   **exit** 나가다

Question 3 Describe a Picture

|고득점|
|T I P|

두 명이 마주하고 있는 구도의 사진도 자주 출제된다. (상점, 사무실, 공원 등) **두 명의 공통점을 먼저 언급**한다. '**쪼그리고 앉다, 몸을 구부리다, 손을 담그다**' 등의 표현에 유의하고, **사람 묘사를 먼저 한 후에 주위에 있는 사물 및 배경을 묘사**한다.

🎧 01-07-03

[초·중급 Model Answer]

This picture appears to be at the water's edge. The first thing I notice is two people looking into the water. On the right, a man is sitting with his body crouched over and he is dipping his hand in the water. He is wearing khaki clothes. On the left, a boy with blonde hair is bending over the man. He is holding a stick with a net pocket at the end. There are some rocks around them. This picture reminds me of my father.

이 그림은 물가에서 찍힌 것으로 보입니다. 처음 보이는 것은 물속을 바라보고 있는 두 사람입니다. 우측에는 한 남자가 쪼그리고 앉아서 손을 물속에 넣고 있습니다. 그는 카키색 옷을 입고 있습니다. 쇠측에는 금발머리의 신녀이 남자 쪽으로 허리를 구부리고 있습니다. 그는 끝에 그물 주머니가 달려있는 막대기를 들고 있습니다. 그들 주변에 몇 개의 돌이 있습니다. 이 사진은 제 아버지가 생각나게 합니다.

[고급 Model Answer]

This picture appears to be at a beach or someplace right at the water's edge. The first thing I notice is two people looking into the water. One is a young boy and the other is a middle aged man, possibly his father. The man on the right is crouching over and pointing into the water. The boy on the left has blonde hair, and he is bending at the waist while looking intently at where his father is pointing. The boy is holding what appears to be a bamboo pole with a green net on one end. There are several rocks around them and a red bucket behind the boy. It seems like a very fun and peaceful father-son outing.

이 사진은 해변 혹은 물가에서 찍힌 것으로 보입니다. 처음 보이는 것은 물속을 바라보고 있는 두 사람입니다. 한 명은 남자아이, 다른 사람은 중년 남자인데 그의 아버지인 것 같습니다. 우측에 있는 남자는 쪼그리고 물 속을 가리키고 있습니다. 왼쪽의 소년은 금발이며, 몸을 구부린 채 그의 아버지처럼 보이는 사람이 가리키는 곳을 열심히 바라보고 있습니다. 이 소년은 한쪽 끝에 녹색 그물이 달린 대나무 장대처럼 생긴 것을 들고 있습니다. 이들 주변에는 여러 개의 돌이 있고 소년의 뒤에 빨간 양동이가 있습니다. 아버지와 아들의 즐겁고 평화로운 나들이인 것 같습니다.

|어 휘| **edge** 가장자리   **look into** ~속을 들여다보다   **crouch** 쪼그리다   **dip** 살짝 담그다   **bend** 굽히다
　　　 middle aged 중년의   **intently** 골똘하게   **bamboo** 대나무   **pole** 장대   **bucket** 양동이   **outing** 나들이

Actual Test 07

Questions 4-6 Respond to Questions

Imagine that an Australian marketing firm is conducting research in your country. You have agreed to participate in a telephone interview about visiting museums.

호주의 한 마케팅 회사가 당신의 나라에서 설문 조사를 하고 있다고 가정해 보세요. 당신은 '박물관 방문'에 관한 전화 인터뷰에 응하기로 동의했습니다.

Question 4
01-07-04

Q. How often do you visit a museum? 얼마나 자주 박물관에 갑니까?

[초·중급 Model Answer]

A. I visit a museum two or three times a year. There is the National Museum near my school and sometimes I visit it with friends.

1년에 두세 번 박물관에 갑니다. 학교 근처에 국립박물관이 있고 가끔씩 친구들과 함께 갑니다.

[고급 Model Answer]

A. I typically go to a museum two or three times a year. There are several good museums in my city that regularly change exhibits.

1년에 보통 두세 번 박물관에 갑니다. 제가 사는 도시에는 주기적으로 전시물을 교체하는 좋은 박물관이 몇 군데 있습니다.

[고득점 TIP] **How often~** 질문은 육하원칙 질문 중 **가장 자주** 출제된다. **첫 문장에 직접적인 대답**을 하고, **두 번째 문장**은 **예**를 들거나 **where, when** 등 **다른 육하원칙 질문에 대한 답**을 만들어 간단하게 답한다.

Question 5
01-07-05

Q. When was the last time you visited a museum, and what did you see there?

마지막으로 박물관에 간 적이 언제였고, 거기서 무엇을 봤습니까?

[초·중급 Model Answer]

A. Last month, I visited the National Museum and saw many items there. I saw a lot of famous paintings and sculptures.

지난 달에 국립박물관에 가서 많은 작품들을 봤습니다. 유명한 그림들과 조각품들을 많이 볼 수 있었습니다.

[고급 Model Answer]

A. The last time I visited a museum was last month. My friend and I went to the National Museum and saw many artifacts that were very old. It was such a great experience.

마지막으로 박물관에 간 것은 지난달입니다. 제 친구와 저는 국립박물관에 갔었고 아주 오래된 유물을 많이 봤습니다. 정말 좋은 경험이었습니다.

[고득점 TIP] **When was the last time~**도 빈출 문제 유형으로 **과거시제로 답변**한다. **의문사 질문이 두 개**이므로 각각에 대해 한 문장씩만 답변해도 분량은 충분하다.

01-07-06

Q. Are you more likely to tour a museum by yourself or with a tour group? Why?

당신은 혼자 박물관에 가는 것을 좋아합니까, 혹은 그룹 단위로 가는 것을 좋아합니까? 그 이유는 무엇입니까?

초·중급 Model Answer

A. I prefer to tour a museum with a tour group. I can share information with other people and they can take pictures of me. I don't like to go somewhere or have a meal by myself. It's so lonely. When I visited a museum with a tour group last year, I could make some friends, and we still go to museums together these days.

저는 단체로 박물관에 가는 것을 선호합니다. 다른 사람들과 정보를 나눌 수 있고 그들이 제 사진을 찍어줄 수도 있습니다. 저는 혼자서 어떤 곳에 가거나 밥을 먹는 것을 싫어합니다. 그건 너무 외롭습니다. 작년에 단체와 함께 박물관을 갔을 때, 친구들을 몇 명 사귈 수 있었고, 요즘에도 여전히 우리는 함께 박물관에 갑니다.

고급 Model Answer

A. I would probably go tour a museum by myself. The main reason I like going solo or with just a friend or two is that I like to check things out that interest me. If I am with a tour group or even just a large group that has to meet a certain schedule then I have to go along with the rest of the group. In addition to that I might not be able to really check out the piece of art or the exhibit because other people would be in the way. For me a museum is not just something to go through but it's a place to look, think and wonder about the things there. Because of that I like to go through the museum by myself.

저는 아마 혼자서 박물관에 갈 것 같습니다. 제가 혼자서 가거나, 단지 한 두 명의 친구들과 함께 가는 것을 좋아하는 주된 이유는, 제 관심을 끄는 것들을 보고 싶기 때문입니다. 투어 그룹이나 정해진 일정을 따라야 하는 큰 단체와 함께 있으면 그 그룹의 다른 사람들과 함께 이동해야 합니다. 게다가 다른 사람들이 시야를 가려서 예술 작품이나 전시물을 제대로 볼 수 없을지도 모릅니다. 제게 박물관은 그냥 지나가는 곳이 아니라 거기에 있는 작품들을 보고, 생각하고 경탄하는 곳입니다. 그렇기 때문에 저는 박물관에 혼자 가는 것을 좋아합니다.

고득점 TIP 특정 장소나 여행을 갈 때 혼자 가는 것을 좋아하는지, 단체로 혹은 가이드와 함께 가는 것을 좋아하는지에 대한 질문으로, 이러한 유형도 자주 출제된다. **함께 간다**고 답하고 **정보 공유, 사진 찍기 등 함께 있을 때의 장점**을 말하는 것이 쉽다. **혼자 가는 것**이 좋다고 답할 경우는 **결정을 내가 원하는 대로** 할 수 있다거나 **단체로 움직일 때의 단점**을 지적한다.

|어 휘| **the National Museum** 국립박물관　**typically** 일반적으로　**regularly** 정기적으로　**exhibit** 전시품　**sculpture** 조각품　**artifact** 유물　**wonder** 궁금해하다

 **Questions 7-9** Respond to Questions Using Information Provided

Sarah Jameson

sjisawinner@hatmail.com
382 Main Apt. A Idyllwild CA. 68945
Phone: 294-398-4718

Desired Position: Intern or entry level position, Marketing Department for YG

Experience: (2007-2010) Marketing and Campus Sales Rep. for Zale's Jewelry on

University of Texas Campus

Education: BBA (University of Texas 2008), MBA (UT 2010)

Certifications: Social Media Management Certification-2009, Microsoft Suite Certification-

2010

Sarah Jameson

sjisawinner@hatmail.com
382 Main Apt. A Idyllwild CA. 68945
전화번호: 294-398-4718

희망 직책: 인턴 또는 신입사원, **YG** 마케팅 부서

경력: (2007-2010) **Zale's Jewelry** 텍사스대학교점 마케팅 및 캠퍼스 영업사원

학력: 경영학 학사(텍사스대학교 **2008**), 경영학 석사 (텍사스대학교 **2010**)

자격증: 소셜미디어 관리 자격증 – **2009**, MS Suite 자격증 – **2010**

Question 7

 01-07-07

Q. What kind of job is she looking for? 그녀는 어떤 직책을 찾고 있나요?

초·중급 Model Answer

A. She is looking for the intern or entry level position in the Marketing Department.

그녀는 마케팅 부서에 인턴 또는 신입사원 자리를 찾고 있습니다.

고급 Model Answer

A. She is seeking an intern or entry level position in our Marketing Department.

그녀는 저희 마케팅 부서에 인턴 또는 신입사원 자리를 찾고 있습니다.

 이력서에 있는 **Desired Position** '희망 직책'을 **look for** '찾다'라는 다른 표현을 사용해 물어보고 있다. 주어와 동사를 사용해 **완벽한 문장**으로 답한다.

Question 8

 01-07-08

Q. Does she have much experience? 그녀는 경력이 많은가요?

초·중급 Model Answer

A. Yes. She was the marketing and campus sales representative for Zale's Jewelry on University of Texas Campus.

예, 그녀는 Zale's Jewelry 텍사스대학교점에서 마케팅 및 캠퍼스 영업사원이었습니다.

고급 Model Answer

A. Yes. She worked as a marketing and campus sales representative for Zale's Jewelry. According to her resume she did that from 2007 to 2010 at The University of Texas.

예, 그녀는 Zale's Jewelry에서 마케팅 및 캠퍼스 영업사원으로 일했습니다. 이력서에 따르면 텍사스대학교에서 2007년부터 2010년까지 그 일을 했습니다.

 **조동사**로 질문했으므로 **대답은 Yes/No로 시작**한다. 핵심 어휘인 **experience**에 해당하는 정보를 언급한다.

Question 9

01-07-09

Q. Does she have any other qualifications? 그녀에게 기타 (참고해야 할) 자격(증)이 있나요?

초·중급 Model Answer

A. Yes, she got a BBA and MBA. Also, she has a social media management certification and Microsoft suite certification.

예, 그녀는 경영학 학사와 경영학 석사 학위를 받았습니다. 또한 그녀는 소셜미디어 관리 자격증과 MS Suite 자격증을 갖고 있습니다.

고급 Model Answer

A. Yes, she got her BBA at the University of Texas in 2008 and MBA at UT in 2010. Additionally, she got certifications in Social Media Management and Microsoft Suite in 2009 and 2010 respectively.

예, 그녀는 2008년에 텍사스대학교에서 경영학 학사 학위를 받았고, 2010년 텍사스대학교에서 경영학 석사 학위를 취득했습니다. 또한 2009년에 소셜미디어 관리 자격증을, 2010년에 Microsoft Suite 자격증을 각각 취득했습니다.

고득점 TIP 이력서의 **Education, Certifications**를 qualification '자격, 자격증'이란 다른 표현을 사용해서 질문하고 있다. 이렇게 Part 4에서는 **비슷한 의미의 다른 표현으로 물어보는 경우**(paraphrasing)가 많다. **연도 앞에는 전치사 in, 학교 이름 앞에는 전치사 at**을 사용하며, **추가 내용**을 말할 때는 also, additionally 등으로 시작한다.

어휘 **desire** 바라다 **entry** 입장, 참가 **Rep.(representative)** 대표
BBA(Bachelor of Business Administration) 경영학 학사
MBA(Master of Business Administration) 경영학 석사 **certification** 자격증 **favor** 부탁
candidate 지원자 **fill in** 정보를 주다 **look for** ~을 찾다 **seek** 구하다 **according to** ~에 따르면
qualification 자격(증) **respectively** 각각

 **Question 10** Propose a solution

Hello this is Tom Larson, the vice president. I have recently been made aware of the fact that our raw material cost will be sharply increased next quarter by 8% and I am a little concerned about our bottom line. What I am most concerned about is how this will affect our product on the shelf and our profit margin. Since you are the head of accounting, please analyze this for me and let me know what you find out about the final price. As you know, we have a new product line coming out this spring. I'm worried that even some of our loyal customers would turn away from our products. I want to hear any ideas from the accounting department if any adjustments are needed in order to keep our profits up. Again, this is Tom Larson. Thank you.

안녕하세요, 저는 Tom Larson 부사장입니다. 저희 원재료 가격이 다음 분기에 8%나 급증한다는 소식을 최근에 들었고, 그래서 우리 제품의 최종 가격에 대해 조금 염려가 됩니다. 가장 걱정되는 부분은 이러한 점이 시장에서의 우리 제품과 이윤 폭에 어떠한 영향을 미칠 것인가 입니다. 회계 부서의 책임자로서 본 상황을 분석하고 최종 가격에 대해 파악되는 사항이 있으면 알려주기 바랍니다. 아시다시피 이번 봄에 신제품이 출시될 것입니다. 심지어 우리 단골고객들 중 일부가 우리 제품을 외면하지는 않을까 걱정됩니다. 수익을 올리기 위해 필요한 조정 사항이 있는지에 대해 회계 부서에서 의견이 있다면 말씀해주시기 바랍니다. 다시 말씀드리면, 저는 Tom Larson입니다. 감사합니다.

01-07-10

초 · 중급 Model Answer

Hello, Mr. Larson. This is George from the accounting department. I'm returning your call about your request. I got your message saying that you are worried about the final price and our profit about the new product. So, you are asking us to give you some ideas about them. Well, you don't have to worry about it, sir, because the final price of our new product will not increase. These days more and more people recognize our company and products, so we can save the marketing expenses. I will send you the estimated final price and other related information by e-mail by 5 P.M. If you have any questions, please call me anytime. Thank you.

Larson 씨, 안녕하십니까. 회계부서의 George입니다. 부사장님의 요청에 대해 답변을 드립니다. 신제품의 최종 가격과 수익에 대해 염려된다고 하셨고, 그것에 대한 아이디어를 내보라고 말씀하셨습니다. 글쎄요, 너무 걱정 안 하셔도 될 것 같습니다. 왜냐하면 저희 신제품의 최종 가격이 상승하지 않을 것이기 때문입니다. 요즘 들어 더 많은 사람이 저희 기업과 제품을 알아보기 때문에 마케팅 비용을 절약할 수 있습니다. 오후 5시까지 이메일로 예상 최종 가격 및 기타 관련 정보를 보내 드리겠습니다. 추가 문의 사항이 있으시면 언제든 전화주십시오. 감사합니다.

[고급 **Model Answer**]

Hello, Mr. Larson. This is George in accounting. I'm returning your call regarding our new product. I got your message and understand that our raw material cost will be increased by 8% so you are concerned what this will mean to our bottom line and profit margin. Well, Sir, I think you don't have to worry about it too much because the final price of our new product will not increase. I contacted the marketing department and found out that we can cut down the marketing expenses thanks to the steady increase of our brands' awareness among customers. I will give you some rough estimates later today with other related information by e-mail. If you have any questions please call me anytime. Thank you.

Larson 씨 안녕하십니까. 회계 부서의 George입니다. 신제품과 관련해서 답신 전화를 드립니다. 저희 원자재 비용이 8% 상승할 것이고, 그래서 저희 제품의 최종 가격과 이윤 폭에 어떤 영향을 미칠지 염려된다고 하셨습니다. 신제품의 최종 가격이 상승하지 않을 것이기 때문에 너무 많은 걱정을 하지 않으셔도 될 것 같습니다. 마케팅 부서에 알아보니 고객들 사이에서 저희 브랜드 인지도가 점증하고 있기 때문에 마케팅 비용을 줄일 수 있다고 합니다. 금일 내에 이메일을 통해 대략적인 견적가 및 기타 관련 정보를 보내 드리겠습니다. 추가 문의 사항이 있으시면 언제든지 전화주십시오. 감사합니다.

[고득점 **TIP**] 최종 제품 가격의 상승을 우려해 **예상 가격과 대응책에 대한** 조언을 구하는 문제이다. 이렇게 어떠한 특정 상황에 대한 **조언을 구하는 문제** 역시 자주 출제된다. 원자재 가격이 상승했다고 했으므로, **다른 가격 요소를 언급하면서 답변**한다. 접근하기 쉬운 마케팅 비용에 대해 말하면서 최종 가격에는 큰 변화가 없을 것이라고 답했다. 듣기를 할 때는 **What I am most concerned about is~**와 같이 **바로 그 다음에 중요한 내용이 나오는 표현들**에 더 집중하고, 내 **직책**에 대한 표현(**Since you are the head of accounting**)도 잘 기억해서 답변에 활용한다.

|어 휘| **vice president** 부사장　**be aware of** ~을 알고 있다　**raw material** 원료　**sharply** 급격히
quarter 분기　**be concerned about** ~을 걱정하다　**bottom line** 최종 가격　**affect** 영향을 미치다
profit margin 이윤 폭　**accounting** 회계(부)　**analyze** 분석하다　**royal** 충성스러운　**turn away** 외면하다
adjustment 조정　**recognize** 알아보다　**cut down** 삭감하다　**steady** 꾸준한　**awareness** 인지도
rough 대략적인

 **Question 11** Express an Opinion

What do you think is the most important thing for parents to educate their children about? Choose one of the options provided below and give some specific reasons or examples to support your idea.

- how to achieve goals
- how to learn from mistakes
- how to socialize with others

부모가 아이들에게 교육해야 하는 것들 중 가장 중요한 것이 무엇이라고 생각합니까? 아래 제시된 항목 중 한 가지를 선택하고 당신의 의견을 뒷받침할 구체적인 근거나 사례를 제시하세요.

· 목표를 달성하는 방법
· 실수로부터 배우는 방법
· 타인과 잘 어울리는 방법

초·중급 Model Answer

In my opinion, the most important thing for parents to educate their children about is how to socialize with others. There are some reasons to support my idea. First of all, social skills are very important in any organization. Their children should cooperate with other students in school or coworkers at work. In my case, I learned interpersonal skills from my parents and they are very helpful when I am working with other teammates now. Second, the real friends can help someone to achieve goals and also give them good advice on their mistakes. As the saying goes, 'A life without a friend is a life without a sun.' For these reasons, I think how to socialize with others is most important.

제 생각에는, 부모가 아이들에게 교육해야 하는 것들 중 가장 중요한 것은 사람들과 교제하는 방법에 대한 것입니다. 제 생각을 뒷받침할 만한 몇 가지 이유가 있습니다. 첫째, 어떤 조직에서든 사교성은 매우 중요합니다. 자녀들은 학교에서는 다른 학생들과, 또 직장에서는 동료들과 협력해야 합니다. 제 경우에는, 부모님으로부터 대인관계 기술을 배웠고 현재 팀원들과 함께 일할 때 많은 도움이 됩니다. 둘째, 진정한 친구들은 목표를 달성하는데 도움을 줄 수 있고 실수에 대해서 조언을 해줄 수 있습니다. 속담에 이르길, "친구 없는 삶은 태양이 없는 삶과 같다."라고 했습니다. 이러한 이유로, 저는 다른 사람들과 교제하는 방법이 가장 중요하다고 생각합니다.

고급 Model Answer

In my opinion, the most important lesson that a child can take from home is how to learn from their mistakes. The main reason is that life is full of ups and downs and mistakes are made each and every day. We have to learn from them and move on. If a person is unable to do this, as a general rule their life will be a constant cycle of making the same mistake again and again. Another reason is that this one is relatively easier than the others for parents to teach their children. Setting a goal and trying to achieve it using all possible means is not a simple process. Getting socialized with other different people is also difficult to teach at home. However, learning from mistakes can be taught at home because children make mistakes every single day, and there is something to learn from every mistake. For these reasons, I think learning from mistakes is most important.

제 생각에는 아이가 가정에서 배울 수 있는 것 중에 가장 중요한 교훈은 실수로부터 배우는 방법입니다. 주된 이유는, 인생에는 우여곡절이 많고 우리는 매일 실수를 하기 때문입니다. 우리는 실수로부터 교훈을 얻고 앞으로 나아가야 합니다. 이렇게 하지 못한다면 일반적으로 그 사람의 삶은 같은 실수의 끊임없는 반복이 될 것입니다. 또 다른 이유는, 부모들이 아이들에게 가르치기에 다른 항목보다 이 항목이 상대적으로 수월합니다. 목표를 세우고 가능한 수단들을 사용해 그 목표를 달성하기 위해 노력하는 것은 단순한 과정이 아닙니다. 다양한 사람들과 교제하는 방법 또한 가정에서 가르치기 힘듭니다. 하지만, 실수를 통해 배우는 것은 가정에서 배울 수 있습니다. 왜냐하면 아이들은 매일 실수를 하고 모든 실수에서는 배울 점이 있기 때문입니다. 이러한 이유로, 저는 실수로부터 배우는 것이 가장 중요하다고 생각합니다.

고득점 TIP | 세 가지 중 선택해야 하는 문제는, 항목 중에서 가장 포괄적인 개념이 무엇인지부터 생각해본다. 예컨대 타인과 잘 어울려 진정한 내 사람들이 생긴다면 그들이 목표를 달성하는 방법과 실수로부터 배우는 방법과 관련해서도 도움을 줄 수 있다. 또한 많은 문제에서 '사람', 즉 '사람들 사이에서의 관계'에 관한 아이디어를 선택하면 cooperate with, work with, interpersonal skill 등과 같은 표현들을 사용해 쉽게 답할 수 있다.

어 휘 | **achieve** 달성하다 **socialize** 어울리다 **coworker** 직장동료 **interpersonal skill** 대인 관계 기술 **teammate** 팀 동료 **constant** 끊임없는 **relatively** 비교적 **means** 수단

Actual Test 08

Questions 1-2 Read a Text Aloud

Question 1

🎧 01-08-01

The **Sports Academy** is **happy** / to **announce** the **Grand Opening** ↗ / of **another** store in **Seattle**. ↘ // This means **huge savings** / on **all** men's, ↗ / **women's** ↗ / and **children's sporting apparel**. ↘ // **Everything** / from our **famous retro jerseys** / to our **Bell's basketball** and **baseball equipment** / has been **drastically reduced** ↗ / and is **marked down** even **further** / this **weekend only**. ↘ // **Come** to the **Sports Academy** today! ↘

Sports Academy는 시애틀에 또 하나의 매장을 개점하게 된 것을 알려 드리게 되어 기쁘게 생각합니다. 남성, 여성, 그리고 아동용 스포츠 의류에 많은 돈을 절약하실 수 있습니다. 저희의 유명한 복고풍 저지에서부터 Bell's 농구 및 야구 장비까지 가격을 대폭 낮췄고 이번 주말에 한해 더욱 낮췄습니다. 오늘 Sports Academy로 오시기 바랍니다!

| 고득점 TIP | 광고문이다. **광고 대상, 형용사, 부사, 명령문** 등을 강조해서 **광고의 느낌**을 살린다. **열거하는 내용들의 억양**이나 **긴 문장의 끊어 읽기** 등 Part 1 에서 강조되는 **포인트**들을 상기하면서 읽는다. |

| 어휘 | **announce** 알리다   **apparel** 의복   **retro** 복고풍   **jersey** (운동복 같은) 셔츠   **equipment** 장비   **drastically** 과감하게   **mark down** 가격을 인하하다 |

Question 2

🎧 01-08-02

Hello, Mr. **Jackson**. ↘ // This is **Belinda Packard** ↗ / from **Tim's Terrific Temps**. ↘ // I am **calling** to let **you** know / that based on your **resume** and **experience** ↗ / we might have a **long term temp position** for **you**. ↘ // It's for a **company** / that is **solid**, ↗ / with a **relaxed work environment** ↗ / and seems to be **growing**. ↘ // Please **call** me / at **898-3425** ↗ / if this is **something** / you might be **interested** in. ↘

Jackson 씨 안녕하세요. Tim's Terrific Temps 사의 Belinda Packard입니다. 귀하의 이력서와 경력을 고려해 보았을 때, 귀하를 위한 장기 임시직 자리가 있을 것 같아서 전화 드렸습니다. (재정적으로) 탄탄하고, 편안한 근무환경을 가졌으며 성장하고 있는 기업입니다. 관심이 있으시면, 898-3425로 연락바랍니다.

| 고득점 TIP | **자동응답기**의 녹음 메시지이다. 항상 **글의 종류와 대략적인 내용**을 준비 시간에 미리 파악하고 그 느낌을 살리도록 노력한다. 주요 내용인 **사람 이름**을 강조해서 읽고, **전화번호**는 **한 자리씩 끊어서 읽는다**. 이 지문에서는 **t가 들어가는 어휘**가 많이 나왔는데, 이렇게 **반복되는 발음**은 **채점 포인트**이므로 더욱 신경 써서 읽도록 한다. |

| 어휘 | **based on** ~에 기초한   **resume** 이력서   **long term** 장기간의   **temp** 임시 직원 |

Question 3 Describe a Picture

고득점 TIP 주방 사진도 꾸준히 출제되고 있다. '**요리 도구** 및 **재료, 선반, 앞치마**' 등의 관련 어휘를 기억한다. **3명의 공통점을 먼저 묘사**하고, 그 후에 앞의 **2명의 공통점을 따로 묘사**한다.

01-08-03

초·중급 Model Answer

This picture appears to be in a restaurant kitchen. The first thing I notice is three people wearing white uniforms. It seems that they are cooks and very busy preparing food. On the left a man with glasses is holding a pan and another cooking tool. Behind him, an African-American woman with a pony tail is holding some ingredients. These two people are wearing black aprons and standing back to back. Behind them, there is another man looking at the woman on the right. In the background, I can see many cooking utensils placed on the shelves.

이 사진은 식당 주방에서 찍힌 사진처럼 보입니다. 처음 눈에 들어오는 것은 흰색 유니폼을 입은 세 사람입니다. 그들은 요리사로 보이며 음식을 준비하느라 매우 바빠 보입니다. 왼쪽에는 안경을 낀 남자가 팬과 또 하나의 조리 도구를 들고 있습니다. 그 남자 뒤에는 말총머리를 한 흑인 여성이 요리 재료를 들고 있습니다. 이 두 사람은 검은 앞치마를 두르고 있고 등을 맞대고 서있습니다. 그들 뒤쪽에는 우측 여성을 바라보고 있는 또 다른 남자가 있습니다. 배경에는 선반에 많은 조리 기구가 놓여 있습니다.

고급 Model Answer

This picture appears to be in a restaurant kitchen. The first thing I notice is three people wearing white smocks or uniform tops and two of them in the foreground are also wearing blue aprons with white stripes on in front of their pants. They appear to all be cooks. One man on the left is wearing glasses and working with a small pan on a stove. Behind him, facing the other direction is a woman holding some freshly chopped ingredients. Behind them, there is another man facing the stove but looking back to see what the woman is doing. It seems like he might be teaching them or supervising them as they work preparing the food.

이 사진은 식당 주방에서 찍힌 사진처럼 보입니다. 처음 눈에 들어오는 것은 흰색 스목(기다란 셔츠) 또는 유니폼 상의를 입은 세 사람이고, 그들 중에 앞쪽에 있는 두 사람은 바지 위에 흰 줄무늬가 있는 파란색 앞치마를 두르고 있습니다. 그들 모두 요리사로 보입니다. 왼쪽에 있는 한 남자는 안경을 쓰고 있고 레인지 위에서 작은 팬으로 일을 하고 있습니다. 그의 뒤에는, 반대 방향을 향해 있는 한 여성이 신선하게 잘라 놓은 음식 재료를 들고 있습니다. 그들 뒤에는, 몸은 레인지를 향해 있지만 여성이 무엇을 하고 있는지 확인하기 위해 뒤를 돌아보고 있는 또 다른 남자가 있습니다. 이 남자는 그들을 가르치고 있거나 음식 준비를 감독하고 있는 것처럼 보입니다.

|어 휘| **cook** 요리사   **pony tail** 포니테일(뒤에서 묶어 늘어뜨린 머리모양)   **ingredient** 재료   **apron** 앞치마
utensil 도구   **shelf** 선반   **smock** 기다란 셔츠   **chopped** 잘게 썬   **supervise** 감독하다

Actual Test 08

Questions 4-6 Respond to Questions

Imagine that a British marketing firm is conducting research in your country. You have agreed to participate in a telephone interview about drinking beverages.

영국의 한 마케팅 회사가 당신의 나라에서 설문 조사를 하고 있다고 가정해 보세요. 당신은 '음료를 마시는 것'에 관한 전화 인터뷰에 응하기로 동의했습니다.

Question 4
01-08-04

Q. What kind of beverages do you like to drink the most often and when do you usually drink them? 어떤 음료를 가장 자주 마시고 주로 언제 마십니까?

초·중급 **Model Answer**

A. I like to drink coffee most often and I usually drink coffee every day after meals.

저는 커피를 가장 자주 마시고 주로 매일 식사 후에 커피를 마십니다.

고급 **Model Answer**

A. I usually drink 3 or 4 cups of coffee throughout the day. My first cup is as soon as I wake up and then when I feel my energy is getting low at work I grab another cup.

저는 하루에 주로 커피를 3잔에서 4잔 마십니다. 첫 잔은 일어나자 마자 마시고 직장에서 힘이 없다고 느껴지면 한 잔 더 마십니다.

고득점 TIP │ **두 개의 의문사**가 나올 경우 빠짐없이 꼼꼼하게 답변한다. **most** 등의 **최상급** 표현이 나오면 **한 가지**만 말해도 되고, **when do you usually**와 같이 **습관적인 사항**에 관해서 질문할 경우 **현재형**으로 답변한다.

Question 5
01-08-05

Q. Where do you usually buy the beverages that you like? 당신이 좋아하는 음료를 주로 어디서 구매합니까?

초·중급 **Model Answer**

A. I usually buy coffee at a coffee shop. It is located near my office. They have very good coffee.

저는 주로 커피숍에서 커피를 삽니다. 사무실 근처에 위치해 있습니다. 그곳 커피가 정말 맛있습니다.

고급 **Model Answer**

A. I usually buy a cup of coffee on the way to my office at a Starbucks that is close. I like the taste of the coffee and the shop is very convenient.

저는 주로 사무실에 출근하는 길에 근처에 있는 스타벅스에서 커피를 삽니다. 커피 맛이 좋고 매장이 매우 편리합니다.

고득점 TIP │ **일반적인 성향**을 물어보는 질문이므로 **현재형**으로 답한다. **실제 사실과 달라도** 괜찮으니 순발력 있게 대답하고, **실존하는 브랜드 이름**을 거론해도 상관 없다.

Q. What is the most important thing to consider when you drink beverages?

음료를 마실 때 가장 중요하게 고려하는 것이 무엇입니까?

초·중급 Model Answer

A. I think the most important thing is taste. Although the price is reasonable, if it doesn't taste good then I don't want to buy it again. There is a coffee shop near my office and I can get very delicious coffee there. They sell coffee at high prices but there are always many customers because of the good taste.

가장 중요한 것은 맛이라고 생각합니다. 가격이 합당해도 맛이 없다면 저는 다시 구매하고 싶지 않습니다. 사무실 근처에 커피숍이 있고 정말 맛있는 커피를 살 수 있습니다. 커피 가격이 비싸지만 맛이 좋아서 항상 손님이 많습니다.

고급 Model Answer

A. The taste of anything I drink or eat is the factor that I consider above anything else. If I enjoy what I am drinking then everything else like price or the shape of bottle take a back seat. The reason I will come back to get a second cup of anything is that it has a wonderful taste. There is a coffee shop near my office which offers thoroughly delicious coffee and I drop by there every single day.

제가 무엇인가를 마시거나 먹을 때 무엇보디 가장 우선적으로 고려하는 요소는 바로 '맛'입니다. 제가 마시고 있는 것을 즐긴다면, 가격이나 용기의 모양 등 기타 모든 것들은 우선순위에서 밀립니다. 어떤 음료든 두 번째 다시 사러 오는 이유는 훌륭한 맛 때문입니다. 사무실 근처에 아주 맛있는 커피를 파는 커피숍이 있는데 저는 그곳에 매일 갑니다.

고득점 TIP **최상급** 질문이므로 **한 가지**를 우선 대답한다. 어렵게 생각하지 말고 '**맛, 가격**' 등으로 쉽게 접근할 수 있다. 덜 고려하는 다른 사항들(브랜드, 용기 모양 등)에 대해 말할 수도 있고, 사무실 근처에 훌륭한 맛의 커피를 판매하는 매장이 있다는 식으로 **예를 들면서** 쉽게 **부연 설명**을 할 수 있다.

어휘 **beverage** 음료　**throughout** ~에 걸쳐서　**as soon as** ~하자 마자　**be located** 위치해 있다
　　　factor 요소　**take a back seat** 부차적인 것이 되다　**thoroughly** 완전히　**drop by** 잠깐 들르다

 **Questions 7-9** Respond to Questions Using Information Provided

---

Hero Fitness Center

289 Main Street
Sacramento, California
207-1764
Hours: Monday to Saturday 6 A.M. – 11 P.M.

★ **June Specials:**
New members – first month free
3 classes of Aerobic & Jazz dance free (Group Exercise)

★ **July Specials:**
Early class free (6 A.M. – 8 A.M.)
All beverages and snacks at The Health Bar 10% off

★ **August Specials:**
Club dance 5% off
Personal training 10% off

* "Club Dance" is our unique class of high intensity, fast paced club music that makes a great workout and a lot of fun with other group members!

Start Being a Hero Today!!

Hero 피트니스센터

289 Main Street

캘리포니아 주 새크라멘토

207-1764

시간: 월요일부터 토요일까지 오전 6시~오후 11시

★ **6월 특별 행사:**

신규 멤버 – 첫 달 무료

에어로빅 및 재즈댄스 강좌 3회 무료 (단체 운동)

★ **7월 특별 행사:**

아침 수업 무료 (오전 6시~8시)

The Health Bar의 모든 음료 및 간식 10% 할인

★ **8월 특별 행사:**

클럽 댄스 5% 할인

개인 훈련(PT) 10% 할인

* "클럽 댄스"는 강도가 높고 빠른 클럽 음악의 특별한 강좌이며 운동이 많이 되고 다른 그룹 멤버들과 함께
  즐길 수 있습니다!

Here(영웅)가 되는 것, 바로 오늘 시작하세요!

Hello. This is Bob. I had a sales flyer of your fitness center. I put it somewhere but I don't know where it is now. I am wondering if I could ask you a few questions.

안녕하세요. Bob이라고 합니다. 그곳 피트니스센터의 전단지를 갖고 있었습니다. 어디엔가 두었는데 지금 어디에 있는지 모르겠네요. 몇 가지 문의해도 되는지 궁금합니다.

Question 7
🎧 01-08-07

Q. Could you tell me where your fitness center is located and what time I can use it?

피트니스센터의 위치와 사용할 수 있는 시간이 어떻게 되는지 알려주시겠어요?

초·중급 Model Answer

A. Hero Fitness Center is at 289 Main Street in Sacramento California. We are open from 6 A.M. to 11 P.M.

Hero 피트니스센터는 캘리포니아 주 새크라멘토 시 289 Main Street에 있습니다. 오전 6시부터 오후 11시까지 운영합니다.

고급 Model Answer

A. Sure, no problem. We are located in Sacramento California at 289 Main Street. Our hours of operation are from Monday to Saturday from 6 A.M. to 11 P.M.

물론입니다. 전혀 문제가 되지 않습니다. 저희 위치는 캘리포니아 주 새크라멘토 시 289 Main Street입니다. 저희 운영 시간은 월요일에서 토요일, 오전 6시부터 오후 11시까지 입니다.

고득점 TIP | **where, what time** 등의 **의문사**를 잘 듣고 답한다. **위치**와 **요일**, **시간**을 묘사할 때 **전치사** 표현에 특히 주의한다.

Question 8
🎧 01-08-08

Q. I heard something about free classes in July as part of your July specials. Is this right?

제가 듣기로는 7월에 특별 행사의 일환으로 피트니스센터를 무료로 사용할 수 있다는데, 맞습니까?

초·중급 Model Answer

A. No, that is not correct. New members can join in June for free. In July, our early classes are free.

아닙니다. 그렇지 않습니다. 신규 멤버는 6월에 무료로 가입할 수 있습니다. 7월에는 아침 강좌가 무료입니다.

고급 Model Answer

A. No, I am sorry but that is incorrect. Our June specials have one month free membership to all new members. In July however, our early classes are free

아닙니다. 죄송하지만 정확하지 않습니다. 저희 6월 특별 행사의 일환으로 모든 신규 멤버에게 1개월간 무료 멤버십을 제공합니다. 그러나 7월에는 아침 강좌가 무료입니다.

고득점 TIP | 이처럼 **잘못된 정보**에 대해 질문하는 경우에는 우선 **'아니다'라는 답변**을 하고, 다음 문장에서 **상대에게 필요한 정보**를 정확하게 언급한다. 표에 있는 내용들을 조합해 문장을 만들 때는 수 일치, 전치사 등에 특히 유의한다.

Q. A friend of mine swears by group exercise. Could you tell me what kind of group exercises you offer?

제 친구 중에 한 명이 단체 운동이 참 좋다고 하던데요. 어떠한 종류의 단체 운동을 제공하는지 알려줄 수 있나요?

초·중급 Model Answer

A. There are two group exercises. First, in June, you can take 3 classes of Aerobic and Jazz dance for free. Second, we offer Club Dance. In August, you can get a 5% discount for it. Club Dance is our unique class of high intensity, fast paced club music that makes a great workout and a lot of fun with other group members.

두 가지 단체 운동이 있습니다. 첫째, 6월에 에어로빅 및 재즈댄스 강좌 3회를 무료로 수강할 수 있습니다. 둘째, 클럽댄스 강좌가 있습니다. 8월에는 5% 할인을 받을 수 있습니다. 클럽 댄스는 강도가 높고 빠른 클럽 음악의 특별한 강좌이며 운동이 많이 되고 다른 회원들과 함께해서 매우 재미있습니다.

고급 Model Answer

A. Sure, we offer two kinds of group exercises. The first one is Aerobic & Jazz dance. You can take 3 classes of Aerobic and Jazz dance for free in June. The other one is Club dance. Our August Specials offer a 5% discount for it. Club Dance is our unique class of high intensity, fast paced club music that makes a great workout and a lot of fun with other group members.

물론입니다. 저희는 두 종류의 단체 운동을 제공합니다. 첫 번째는 에어로빅 및 재즈댄스입니다. 6월에 에어로빅 및 재즈댄스 강좌에 무료로 3회 참가할 수 있습니다. 다른 것은 클럽 댄스입니다. 8월 특별 행사로 5%를 할인해드립니다. 클럽 댄스는 강도가 높고 빠른 클럽 음악의 특별한 강좌이며 운동이 많이 되고 다른 회원들과 함께해서 매우 재미있습니다.

고득점 TIP 문제에서 제시된 **group exercise**라는 **key word**를 듣고 **Aerobic & Jazz dance**는 쉽게 찾을 수 있다. 하지만 그 외에 표의 하단에 있는 **with other group members**라는 표현도 **group exercise**와 관련이 있기 때문에 **club dance** 또한 함께 언급해야 한다. 이처럼 **표에 있는 내용을 표현만 다르게 해서 문제에 제시하는 경우**가 많으니 주의하자.

| 어 휘 | **fitness** 건강　　**beverage** 음료　　**intensity** 강렬함　　**workout** 운동　　**flyer** 전단
swear by ～의 효능을 확신하다

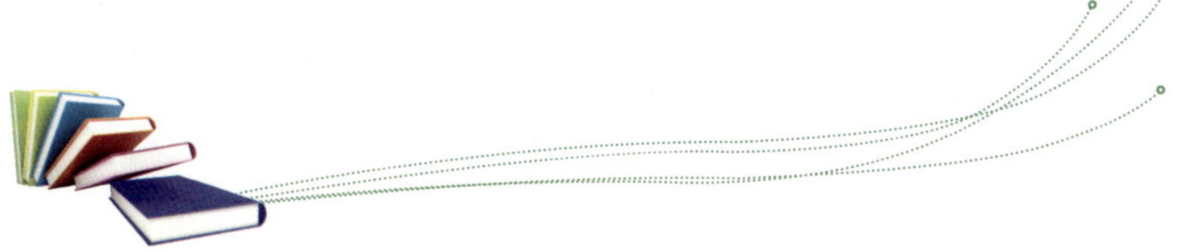

Actual Test 08

Question 10 Propose a solution

Hello, this is Jake from the city parks office. Do you remember the fire that occurred a few months ago in one of our parks? According to the investigation, it was started from a cigarette. Thanks to the fire a new policy has come out that prohibits smoking in any city park and from next month it will be rigorously enforced. Personally, I think this is a great idea as smokers leave a mess in our parks and I think the smoking disturbs the children who are playing there so I am sure that this is a change for the better. All our staff already know about this upcoming change but my concern is that most people who use our parks do not. I really don't want to have a lot of angry people when we start enforcing this new code so I need your advice. Do you have any ideas how we could notify the general public, and let them know? Please give me a call; you can reach me at 765-8901. Thank you very much.

안녕하세요, 시립 공원 사무실의 Jake라고 합니다. 저희 공원 중 한 곳에서 몇 개월 전에 발생한 화재 사건 기억하시나요? 조사에 의하면 담배로 시작되었다고 합니다. 그 화재 사건 덕분에 모든 시립 공원에 흡연을 금지하는 새 정책이 나왔고 다음 달부터 엄격하게 실시될 것입니다. 개인적으로는 좋은 아이디어라고 생각합니다. 왜냐하면 흡연자들이 저희 공원을 더럽히고 공원에서 노는 아이들을 방해하기 때문에 좋은 변화라고 확신합니다. 저희 모든 직원은 앞으로 있을 이 변경 사항에 대해 이미 알고 있지만, 공원을 이용하는 대부분의 사람들은 모르고 있어서 염려됩니다. 새로운 방침을 새롭게 시행함에 있어 화를 내는 사람들이 많이 없었으면 해서 당신의 조언을 구하고자 합니다. 일반 대중들에게 공지해서 이 사실을 알리기 위한 아이디어가 있나요? 전화 부탁드립니다. 765-8901로 연락 주시면 됩니다. 감사합니다.

Question 10　　　　　　　　　　　　　　　　　　　　　　　　01-08-10

초·중급 **Model Answer**

Hello, this is Jason. I am returning your call about your request. I got your message saying that a new policy which prohibits smoking in the city park came out and you think this is great so you are asking me how to let people know about this policy. We usually suggest putting up some signs about any policy or code change. Additionally, you could get some announcement on the city radio station perhaps. I think I could help you with these options but maybe it would be best to meet and discuss this first. Could you call me on my mobile phone and we could set up a time and place. Please call me at 010-765-3890. Thank you.

안녕하세요, Jason입니다. 당신의 요청에 대해 답신을 드립니다. 시립 공원에서 흡연을 금지하는 새 정책이 나왔다는 메시지를 받았고, 당신은 잘된 일이라고 생각하며 사람들에게 본 정책에 대해 어떻게 알려야 하는지 저에게 문의하셨습니다. 저희는 어떠한 정책 또는 방침 변경에 대해 보통 표지판을 세울 것을 제안합니다. 추가적으로, 아마 도시 라디오 방송을 통해 공지를 할 수 있을 것입니다. 제가 이러한 방안들을 통해 도움을 드릴 수 있을 것으로 생각되지만, 그래도 먼저 만나서 논의를 해보는 것이 가장 좋을 것 같습니다. 제 휴대 전화로 연락주실 수 있을까요? 그럼 (미팅에 관한) 시간과 장소를 정할 수 있을 것 같습니다. 010-765-3890으로 전화 부탁드립니다. 감사합니다.

Hello Jake, this is Jason from the code enforcement department. Sorry I was out when you called. Yes, I do remember that fire and it was a tragedy. As far as your question goes, let me say that I can understand why you would want to let the general public know about this before the enforcement begins. I would start by placing signs at the entrance and exit of every city park. Additionally, I would make a public service announcement through radio, TV and newspapers. Perhaps if we sat down and discussed this together that would help come up with some more ideas. Could you call me on my cell phone at 010-765-3890? Let's try to find a time that we can sit down and discuss this.

Jake 씨 안녕하세요. 규정 집행부서의 Jason이라고 합니다. 전화하셨을 때 부재중이었네요. 예, 그 화재 사건에 대해 물론 기억하고 있습니다. 정말 비극이었습니다. 당신의 질문에 대해서, 규정이 시행되기 전에 왜 일반 대중에게 알리고 싶어 하시는지 충분히 이해가 갑니다. 저는 우선 모든 시립 공원의 입구 및 출구에 표지판을 설치하는 것으로 시작할 것입니다. 추가적으로 라디오, 텔레비전 그리고 신문을 통해 공익 광고를 낼 것입니다. 아마도 함께 앉아서 논의해보면 더 많은 아이디어를 생각해내는 데 도움이 될 것입니다. 제 휴대 전화번호 010-765-3890으로 전화주실 수 있나요? 앉아서 논의할 수 있는 시간을 정해봅시다.

|고득점 TIP| 이처럼 '새로운 정책이나 제품 가격 할인, 매장 위치 등에 대해 **어떻게 하면 대중에게 홍보를 잘할 수 있을까**'에 대한 문제도 자주 출제된다. '**대중 매체를 통한 광고**'도 쉽게 접근할 수 있는 방법이고, 이 문제에서는 '**공원 입구에 표지판을 설치**'하는 것도 현실적인 방안이 될 수 있다.

|어 휘| **occur** 발생하다　**investigation** 조사　**cigarette** 담배　**policy** 정책　**prohibit** 금지하다
rigorously 엄격하게　**enforce** 집행하다　**mess** 지저분하고 엉망인 상태　**disturb** 방해하다
upcoming 다가오는　**code** 법규　**additionally** 추가적으로　**announcement** 공지
tragedy 비극　**come up with** 생각해 내다

Actual Test 08

Question 11 Express an Opinion

Do you agree or disagree with the following statement?
'Young people today are more interested in helping others than they have been in the past.'
Use specific reasons or examples to support your opinion.

다음 문장에 동의하십니까 아니면 반대하십니까?
'요즘 젊은이들은 남을 돕는 것에 과거보다 더 많은 관심을 갖는다.'
당신의 의견을 뒷받침할 구체적인 근거나 사례를 제시하세요.

Question 11

01-08-11

초·중급 Model Answer

I disagree that young people today are more interested in helping others than they have been in the past. There are several reasons to support my idea. First, young people these days are more selfish than before. For example, most of them are indifferent to problems in their own neighborhood. Second, although a lot of college students are participating in volunteer activities and helping poor people, many of them are doing it because they are forced to do it. To be specific, many companies require social service experience when they hire employees, so many applicants pretend to help other people just because they have to do it. For these reasons, I'm against this opinion.

저는 요즘 청년들이 남을 돕는 것에 과거보다 더 많은 관심을 갖는다는 말에 동의하지 않습니다. 제 생각을 뒷받침할 만한 이유가 몇 가지 있습니다. 첫째, 요즘 젊은이들은 예전보다 더 이기적입니다. 예를 들면, 그들 대부분은 이웃들의 문제들에 대해 무관심합니다. 둘째, 많은 대학생들이 봉사 활동에 참여하고 가난한 사람들을 돕고 있지만, 대부분은 그렇게 하도록 강요당해서 하는 것입니다. 정확히 말하자면, 많은 기업들이 직원 채용 시 봉사 활동 경험을 요구하기 때문에 많은 지원자들은 할 수 없이 남을 돕는 척하는 것입니다. 이러한 이유로 저는 이 의견에 반대합니다.

고급 Model Answer

I agree with this opinion. There are a couple of reasons why I agree with this. First is the number of young people and in particular college students that are going places every time they get vacation. They aren't going places just to sit on a beach. More and more they seem to be going places to help others. Secondly, because of so much information online, I think more young people than ever before are seeing needs and finding ways to help out. In the case of my sister, after she saw the lives of refugees in Africa online, she joined an international relief organization. For these reasons, I would absolutely agree with this statement.

저는 이 의견에 동의합니다. 동의하는 이유가 몇 가지 있습니다. 첫째는 방학 때마다 어딘가로 떠나는 많은 청년들 특히 대학생들의 수입니다. 그들은 해변에 앉아있기 위해 떠나지는 않습니다. 점점 더 많은 청년들이 남을 돕기 위한 장소로 가는 것 같습니다. 둘째, 온라인 상에 정말 많은 정보가 있기 때문에 그 어느 때보다 많은 청년들이 도움이 필요한 상황을 확인하고 도움을 줄 수 있는 방법을 찾고 있습니다. 제 여동생의 경우에는 온라인상에서 아프리카 난민들의 삶을 본 후, 국제 구호단체에 가입했습니다. 이러한 이유로, 저는 이 문장에 전적으로 동의합니다.

|고득점|
TIP **요즘 대학생들의 다양한 봉사활동**을 언급하면서 주어진 의견에 동의할 수 있다. 만약 반대한다면, 그러한 봉사활동의 대부분이 '**취업을 위해 어쩔 수 없이 이루어지는 것**이다'라는 의견도 설득력이 있다. **본인이나 주변 지인들의 예**를 들면서 부연설명을 한다.

|어 휘| **selfish** 이기적인　　**indifferent** 무관심한　　**neighborhood** 이웃　　**volunteer** 자원 봉사자　　**force** 강요하다
applicant 지원자　　**pretend to** ～인 체하다　　**against** ～에 반대하여　　**in particular** 특히　　**refugee** 난민
relief organization 구호단체　　**absolutely** 전적으로

 **Questions 1-2** Read a Text Aloud

Question 1

01-09-01

Are **you up** <u>for a</u> **challenge**? ꜛ // Do you **crave** <u>a</u> **new adventure**? ꜛ // <u>**Check out**</u> / **Beach Boys Power Scuba**! ꜜ // We have **professional instructors** / who can <u>take **anyone**</u> / <u>from an</u> **absolute amateur** ꜛ / to the **seasoned vet** / and get **them** to the **next level**. ꜜ // Our **well organized staff** ꜛ / and **immaculate facilities** / will **give you** the **opportunity** ꜛ / to **experience** <u>an</u> **amazing world**. ꜜ // **Call now** / at **982-8364**! ꜜ

도전을 해보시겠습니까? 새로운 모험을 갈망하십니까? Beach Boys Power Scuba를 경험해 보세요! 저희에겐 완전 초보를 숙달된 베테랑으로 만들어 주고 다음 단계로 승격시켜 줄 수 있는 전문 강사들이 있습니다. 저희의 잘 조직화된 직원들과 깔끔한 시설은 당신으로 하여금 놀라운 세계를 경험할 수 있는 기회를 제공해 줄 것입니다. 지금 982-8364로 전화하세요!

| 고득점 TIP | 전형적인 **광고문이다. 의문문의 억양**에 주의하고, **명령문 동사** 및 **광고 대상**, 그리고 **수식하는 표현들**을 강조한다. amateur, facilities, opportunity와 같은 빈출 단어의 발음 및 강세에 주의한다. |

| 어휘 | **crave** 열망하다   **instructor** 강사   **absolute** 절대적인   **seasoned** 노련한   **vet(veteran)** 전문가   **immaculate** 결점이 없는 |

Question 2

01-09-02

Hello, ꜛ / Mr. **Prichard**. ꜜ // <u>This is</u> **Bob Sheffield** / with **Exhibition Auto parts**. ꜜ // I **recently** <u>**met you**</u> / at the <u>**Dallas Auto**</u> **Exhibit**. ꜜ // We manufacture **quality antennas**, ꜛ / **batteries**, ꜛ / **horns** / and **rear-view mirrors** ꜛ / for <u>**all**</u> sorts of **vehicles**. ꜜ // We **talked** <u>for a while</u> / <u>about</u> <u>your</u> **diesel truck repair shops** ꜛ / <u>and if</u> possible ꜛ / I <u>would like</u> to **get back** / <u>in</u> **touch** <u>with</u> <u>**you**</u>. ꜜ // Please feel free to <u>**contact me**</u> ꜛ / at **975-2310**. ꜜ

Prichard 씨, 안녕하세요. Exhibition Auto parts(엑시비션 자동차 부품 사)의 Bob Sheffield입니다. 최근 Dallas 주 자동차 전시회에서 귀하를 만났습니다. 저희는 다양한 종류의 자동차를 위한 고품질의 안테나, 배터리, 경적 및 백미러를 제조합니다. 귀하의 트럭 정비소에 대해 잠시 얘기했었는데요, 가능하다면 다시 만나고 싶습니다. 편하게 975-2310으로 연락 부탁드립니다.

| 고득점 TIP | **전화 녹음 메시지**로 가끔씩 꼭 출제되는 유형이다. **인물의 이름과 전화를 건 목적을 강조**한다. exhibition, exhibit, quality 등의 단어에 주의하고, **열거하는 부분의 억양**에 신경을 써서 읽는다. |

| 어휘 | **exhibition** 전시회   **exhibit** 전시품   **manufacture** 제조/생산하다, 만들다   **horn** 경적   **rear** 뒤쪽   **vehicle** 차량   **get back in touch with** ~와 다시 연락하다 |

Question 3 Describe a Picture

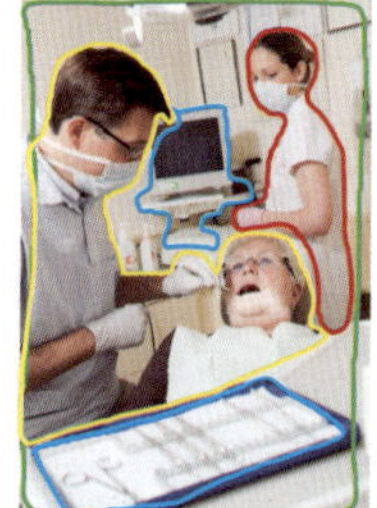

|고득점|
| T I P | **치과**에서 찍힌 사진이므로 **dental**이 들어간 표현들을 많이 사용할 수 있다(~ office/chair/tools/bib). **의사, 환자** 등 각 인물들의 **특정 의상**과 '**입을 벌린 채, 바라보다, 누워있다**' 등 자주 나오는 **동작 묘사**에 유의한다.

🎧 01-09-03

초·중급 Model Answer

This picture appears to be in a dental office. The first thing I notice is a woman lying on a dental chair with her mouth open. She is wearing glasses and a white dental bib. She looks nervous. On the left, there is a man holding dental tools and looking at her. It seems that he is a dentist. He is wearing a striped shirt, a mask and surgical gloves. Behind them there is a woman wearing a mask and medical smock. She is looking at the woman on the chair. In the foreground, there are some dental tools and in the background I can see a monitor and some papers on the wall.

이 사진은 치과에서 찍은 사진 같습니다. 처음에 보이는 것은 입을 벌린 채 치과 의자에 누워 있는 한 여성입니다. 그녀는 안경을 쓰고 있고 흰 치과용 턱받이를 하고 있습니다. 그녀는 긴장한 듯이 보입니다. 왼쪽에는 한 남성이 치과 기구를 들고 그녀를 바라보고 있습니다. 그는 치과 의사인 것 같습니다. 그는 줄무늬 셔츠를 입고 마스크와 수술용 장갑을 착용하고 있습니다. 그들 뒤에는 마스크를 쓰고 의료용 스목을 입고 있는 한 여성이 있습니다. 그녀는 의자에 있는 여성을 바라보고 있습니다. 사진의 앞쪽에는 치과 기구가 몇 개 있고 배경에는 모니터와 벽에 문서들이 보입니다.

고급 Model Answer

This picture appears to have been taken in a dental office. The first thing I notice is a woman in a dental chair with her mouth open. She has blond hair and is wearing glasses as well as a white dental bib. It seems that she is having some kind of dental work done but she isn't enjoying it. To her right, a person who appears to be a dentist is sitting and holding dental tools in each hand. He is wearing a blue and white striped smock or uniform, surgical gloves and glasses as well as a mask. In front of the woman what looks like a tray full of dental tools is beside the dentist. Behind them, there is a woman standing and wearing a mask, white medical smock and surgical gloves as well. She seems to be a dental assistant. In the background, I can see a desktop computer and some papers on the wall.

이 사진은 치과에서 찍은 사진 같습니다. 처음으로 보이는 것은 입을 벌린 채 치과 의자에 있는 여성입니다. 그녀의 머리는 금발이며 흰 치과용 턱받이와 안경을 착용하고 있습니다. 그녀는 어떤 치과 시술을 받고 있는 것으로 보이는데 그리 좋아하고 있는 것 같지는 않습니다.

그녀의 오른쪽에는 치과 의사처럼 보이는 한 사람이 앉아있고 양 손에 치과 기구를 들고 있습니다. 그는 청색과 흰색의 줄무늬 스목 혹은 유니폼을 입고 있고, 수술용 장갑 및 마스크, 그리고 안경을 착용하고 있습니다. 여성 앞에는 치과 기구로 가득한 쟁반이 치과 의사 옆에 있습니다. 그들 뒤에는 마스크와 흰색 의료용 스목 그리고 수술용 장갑을 착용하고 서 있는 여성이 있습니다. 그녀는 치과 보조 진료원인 것으로 보입니다. 배경에는 데스크톱 컴퓨터가 보이고 벽에 문서들이 있습니다.

|어 휘| **dental office** 치과　**bib** 턱받이　**nervous** 불안해하는　**dentist** 치과의사　**surgical** 외과의, 수술의　**medical** 의료의　**smock** 작업복　**as well as** ~뿐만 아니라　**tray** 쟁반, 납작한 상자　**assistant** 보조원

Questions 4-6 Respond to Questions

호주의 한 마케팅 회사가 당신의 나라에서 설문 조사를 하고 있다고 가정해 보세요. 당신은 '다른 사람들과 차를 함께 타는 것'에 관한 전화 인터뷰에 응하기로 동의했습니다.

Question 4
 01-09-04

Q. How often do you share a ride to work or school with other people?

당신은 출근 또는 등교하면서 다른 사람들과 얼마나 자주 차를 함께 탑니까?

초·중급 Model Answer

A. I usually share a ride to school 5 days a week. My friend picks me up near my house and we ride to school together.

저는 보통 1주일에 5번 학교까지 차를 함께 탑니다. 친구가 저희 집 근처로 와서 저를 데리고 함께 학교까지 타고 갑니다.

고급 Model Answer

A. I usually share a ride to school about 5 days a week but sometimes I take public transportation. A friend of mine comes right by my house on his way to school and I ride with him.

저는 보통 1주일에 5번 학교까지 함께 차를 타는데, 가끔은 대중교통을 이용합니다. 제 친구가 학교 가는 길에 저희 집 바로 앞에 들르고 저는 그와 함께 차를 탑니다.

고득점 TIP │ How often~ 질문에 대해서는 **횟수 표현**으로 답한다. **once/twice/three times a week(a month), everyday** 등 다양한 방법으로 말할 수 있다.

Question 5
01-09-05

Q. Besides commuting to work or school, when would you consider sharing a ride with other people? 출근 또는 등교하는 것 외에, 언제 다른 사람들과 함께 차를 타는 것을 고려하겠습니까?

초·중급 Model Answer

A. I would consider sharing a ride with someone any time I am going someplace. I share rides to church on Sunday sometimes.

언제 어디를 가든 누군가와 함께 차를 타는 것을 고려할 것입니다. 저는 가끔 일요일에 교회에 갈 때 함께 차를 탑니다.

고급 Model Answer

A. I would consider sharing a ride anytime I could get one. I don't mind the subway and busses but sharing a ride with a friend is always better.

저는 언제든지 가능하다면 차를 함께 타는 것을 고려할 것입니다. 저는 지하철이든 버스든 상관없지만 친구와 함께 차를 타는 것은 항상 더 좋습니다.

Question 6

🎧 01-09-06

Q. Which of the following is the most beneficial when sharing a ride?

당신은 차를 함께 탈 때 다음 중 어떤 사항이 가장 큰 이점이라고 생각합니까?

Convenience 편의성

Saving money 비용 절약

Protecting the environment 환경 보호

초·중급 Model Answer

A. The most beneficial part of sharing a ride is the convenience. In my case, I like the way I can just go to a place near my house and get a ride with my friend. I also think it's convenient because I don't have to wait in lines at the bus or subway station and I always have a seat in my friend's car.

차를 함께 타는 것의 가장 유익한 점은 편의성입니다. 제 경우에는, 그냥 집 근처에 있는 장소로 가서 제 친구와 함께 차를 탈 수 있다는 점이 좋습니다. 또한, 버스정류장 또는 지하철역에서 줄을 서서 기다릴 필요가 없고, 언제든지 제 친구의 차에 자리가 있어서 편리하다고 생각합니다.

고급 Model Answer

A. The most beneficial part of sharing a ride is without a doubt the convenience. I enjoy knowing that my friend will meet me near my house and we will ride in a comfortable vehicle. Additionally, I get to miss out on all the lines and waiting for the subway and bus with the added bonus of knowing I will have a seat.

차를 함께 타는 것에 대해 가장 유익한 부분은 두말할 나위 없이 편의성입니다. 친구가 제 집 근처에서 저를 만나고 우리가 함께 편안한 차를 타고 갈 것이라는 사실이 좋습니다. 추가로, 지하철과 버스를 타기 위해 줄을 서서 기다리지 않아도 되고 덤으로 항상 앉을 자리가 있습니다.

| 어 휘 | **ride** 타기 **pick up** ~를 (차에) 태우러 가다 **public transportation** 대중교통
on one's way to ~로 가는 길에 **commute** 통근(통학)하다 **beneficial** 유익한 **convenience** 편의성
doubt 의심 **vehicle** 차량 **miss out on** ~를 놓치다

Trinity Lake Festival

10th Anniversary
Sat. Aug. 14

Noon – 1 P.M.	Lunch on the beach: · $10 plate - hamburger, two vegetable rolls and two of our famous biscuits! · $5 plate - hotdog, one vegetable roll and one biscuit! · Plus - salads, fruits, drinks available separately!
1 P.M. – 3 P.M.	Boat show on Trinity Lake ($10 per person to ride)
3 P.M. – 5 P.M.	Horseback riding ($10 per person - 2 hour ride)
4 P.M. – 6 P.M.	Trinity Nature Walk / Petting Zoo ($2 per person for guided tour). Check out our unique plants and feed animals!

Trinity 호수 축제

10주년 기념일
8월 14일 토요일

정오~오후1시	해변에서의 점심 식사 · 10달러 식사 – 햄버거, 채소롤 2개 그리고 인기 비스킷 2개! · 5달러 식사 – 핫도그, 채소롤 1개 그리고 비스킷 1개! · 추가 – 샐러드, 과일, 음료 별도 구입 가능!
오후 1시~3시	Trinity 호수 보트 쇼 (탑승 1인 당 10달러)
오후 3시~5시	승마체험 (1인당 10달러 – 2시간 체험)
오후 4시~6시	Trinity 자연 산책로 / 동물원(동물을 직접 만져볼 수 있는) (1인당 2달러, 가이드 동반) 저희의 독특한 식물들을 만나보고, 동물들에게 먹이도 줄 수 있습니다.

Hello, my name is Kevin Jones and I'm planning to visit your festival but I need more information. Can I ask you a few questions?

안녕하세요, 제 이름은 Kevin Jones이고 그곳 축제에 방문할 계획인데 추가 정보가 필요합니다. 몇 가지 질문을 해도 될까요?

Question 7
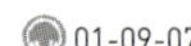 01-09-07

Q. Last year my kids loved the boat rides. Will we be able to get boat rides on the Trinity?

작년에 제 아이들이 보드 타는 것을 아주 좋아했습니다. 그곳 Trinity에서 보드를 탈 수 있을까요?

초·중급 Model Answer

A. Yes, you will be able to ride on a boat during the boat show from 1 P.M. to 3 P.M. at a cost of $10 per passenger.

네, 오후 1시부터 3시까지 Boat Show(보트 쇼)가 열리는 동안 보트를 타실 수 있습니다. 비용은 1명당 10달러입니다.

고급 Model Answer

A. Yes, that's right! On Saturday August 14th during our 10th Anniversary, you can hop on a boat for the boat show from 1 P.M. to 3 P.M. for $10 a head.

네, 맞습니다! 8월 14일 토요일 저희 10주년 행사 때 오후 1시부터 3시까지 Boat Show(보트 쇼)가 열리는 동안 보트를 타실 수 있습니다. 비용은 승객 1명당 10달러입니다.

고득점 TIP **boat rides**가 **key word**이다. **you**를 **주어**로 해서 **쉬운 문장을 완벽하게** 만들도록 노력한다. **시간** 및 **가격 표현**에 주의한다.

Question 8
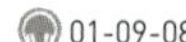 01-09-08

Q. My kids are crazy about plants and animals right now. Do you have any kid friendly events that are centered around that?

제 아이들이 요즈음 식물과 동물에 빠져 있습니다. 동식물과 관련해 아이들이 즐길 수 있는 행사가 있을까요?

초·중급 Model Answer

A. Yes, they can check out our unique plants and feed animals at the Trinity Nature Walk and Petting Zoo. It costs $2 per person for the guided tour.

네, 그들은 Trinity 자연 산책로와 동물원에서 저희의 독특한 식물들을 만날 수 있고, 동물들에게 먹이를 줄 수도 있습니다. 비용은 1인당 2달러이며 안내원이 있는 투어입니다.

A. Yes, we have a wonderful Trinity Nature Walk and Petting Zoo available from 4 P.M. to 6 P.M., where your children can check out our unique plants and feed animals.

그렇습니다. 오후 4시부터 6시까지 저희의 근사한 Trinity 자연 산책로와 동물원을 이용하실 수 있으며, 귀하의 아이들이 저희의 독특한 식물들을 만날 수 있고 동물들에게 먹이를 줄 수도 있습니다.

| 고득점 TIP | Do you~와 같이 **조동사**로 **질문**할 경우 우선 **처음에는 Yes/No**로 답한다. **plants and animals**를 잘 듣고 표에 연관된 내용인 **Trinity Nature Walk/Petting Zoo**에 대해서 문장으로 답한다.

Question 9

01-09-09

Q. Sorry but my children are on a special diet and we are hoping to join the Lunch on the Beach. Can you give me the details of what food you will have there?

죄송한데요, 제 아이들이 식단을 관리하는 중인데 해변에서의 점심 식사에 참여하고 싶습니다. 어떠한 음식이 제공되는지 알려주실 수 있나요?

A. Lunch will be served from noon to 1 P.M. We will have a $10 plate with a hamburger, two vegetable rolls and two of our famous biscuits and a $5 plate with a hotdog, one vegetable roll and one biscuit. We will also have salads, fruits and drinks available separately.

점심은 정오부터 오후 1시까지 제공됩니다. 햄버거 한 개, 채소롤 두 개와 저희의 유명한 비스킷 두 개가 포함된 10달러짜리 식사가 있고 핫도그 한 개, 채소롤 한 개 그리고 비스킷 한 개가 포함된 5달러짜리 식사가 있습니다. 또한 샐러드, 과일 그리고 음료도 별도로 구입 가능합니다.

A. We will be serving up lunch from noon to 1 P.M. We will have two plates to choose from: our $10 plate will have a hamburger, two vegetable rolls and two of our famous biscuits and our $5 plate will have a hotdog, one vegetable roll and one biscuit. Additionally, we will also have salads, fruits and drinks available for purchase separately.

정오부터 오후 1시까지 점심이 제공됩니다. 2가지 식사 중에서 선택하실 수 있습니다: 저희 10달러 식사에는 햄버거 한 개, 채소롤 두 개 그리고 저희의 유명한 비스킷 두 개가 포함되며, 저희 5달러 식사에는 핫도그 한 개, 채소롤 한 개, 그리고 비스킷 한 개가 포함됩니다. 추가로, 별도로 구입 가능한 샐러드, 과일 그리고 음료도 있습니다.

| 고득점 TIP | **메뉴와 가격**에 대해 언급할 때는 **we will (also) have**와 같이 쉬운 표현으로 시작할 수 있다. **dollar**와 같은 **단위는 단수로** 읽는다.
ex) a $10 plate → a 10 **dollar** plate

| 어휘 | **trinity** 삼위일체, 3인조　**anniversary** 기념일　**separately** 별도로　**pet** 어루만지다　**hop** (차량에) 타다　**centered** (어떤 것을) 주된 대상으로 한　**be on a diet** 다이어트 중이다

Actual Test 09

Question 10 Propose a solution

Hello, this is Jenny Sams. As you know, our Special Woman's line of clothing has been a huge success but I was told that we're going to change many of the models by next month. However, there may be some problems. I've been thinking of some ways to tell our customers about this change, but I'm having a very difficult time figuring out how to promote this new concept about the new models of the Special Woman's line. I'm calling you since you're the manager of our marketing department. I hope you can come up with some ideas on this matter. Again, this is Jenny Sams, and my number is 777-4321. I'll be waiting for your call. Thanks.

안녕하세요, Jenny Sams입니다. 아시다시피, 우리의 Special Woman 의류 제품라인은 큰 성공이었지만 다음 달까지 많은 모델을 바꿀 것이라는 소식을 들었습니다. 그러나 몇 가지 문제가 있습니다. 고객들에게 이러한 변경에 대해 알리기 위한 몇 가지 방법을 생각해봤는데, Special Woman 제품라인의 새로운 모델에 대한 새로운 콘셉트를 어떻게 홍보할 것인지 생각해내는 것이 매우 어렵습니다. 당신이 마케팅 부서의 매니저이기 때문에 이렇게 전화를 드립니다. 이 사항에 대해 몇 가지 아이디어를 생각해낼 수 있기를 바랍니다. 다시 말씀드리면, 저는 Jenny Sams이고 제 번호는 777-4321입니다. 전화 기다리겠습니다. 감사합니다.

Question 10

01-09-10

초·중급 Model Answer

Hello, Ms. Sams. This is Julia from marketing. I'm returning your call about your request. I got your message saying that we will change many models of the Special Woman's line and you're asking me how to promote this to our customers. First of all, thank you for calling me. I would be glad to help. Why don't we give out some discount coupons to customers? They can use the coupon when they buy new models. Or, we can hold a fashion show on the street. I think it can be a good way to promote our new clothing line. If you're interested please call me again to discuss this further. Thank you.

Sams 씨, 안녕하세요. 마케팅 부서의 Julia입니다. 요청하신 사안에 대해 답신 전화 드립니다. 우리가 Special Woman 제품라인의 많은 모델을 변경할 것이고, 이를 고객들에게 어떻게 홍보해야 하는지에 대해 제게 문의하셨습니다. 우선, 전화해 주셔서 감사합니다. 기꺼이 도와드리겠습니다. 고객들에게 할인 쿠폰을 나누어 주는 것은 어떻습니까? 그들이 새 모델을 구매할 때 쿠폰을 사용할 수 있습니다. 아니면, 길거리에서 패션쇼를 열 수도 있습니다. 우리의 새로운 상품라인을 홍보하기 위한 좋은 방법이라 생각합니다. 관심이 있으시면, 더욱 자세히 논의하기 위해 다시 전화 부탁드립니다. 감사합니다.

고급 Model Answer

Hello, Jenny. This is Julia the marketing manager. I am very sorry I missed your call about the upcoming changes being made. I got your message and understand that our Special Woman's line of clothing has been a great success but we will change many models by next month and you are asking me how to promote the new concept to our customers. First of all, thank you for calling me. I would be glad to help. How about giving out some discount coupons which can attract people to come by our stores and purchase the new models? Additionally, why don't we launch a fashion show with the new models of our Special Woman's line? I can contact some modeling agencies which have business relationships with us. I hope this helps. If you're interested please call me again to discuss this further. My extension is 234. Thanks.

Jenny 씨, 안녕하세요. 마케팅 매니저인 Julia입니다. 앞으로 있을 변경 사항들에 관한 당신의 전화를 받지 못해서 죄송합니다. 우리의 Special Woman 제품라인은 큰 성공을 거두었지만, 다음 달까지 많은 모델을 변경할 것이고 어떻게 새로운 콘셉트를 고객들에게 홍보할 것인지 저에게 문의하는 당신의 메시지를 받았습니다. 우선, 제게 전화해 주셔서 감사합니다. 기꺼이 도와 드리겠습니다. 사람들로 하여금 우리 매장을 방문해 새로운 모델을 구매하도록 할인 쿠폰을 나누어 주는 것은 어떻습니까? 추가로, Special Woman 제품라인의 새로운 모델로 패션쇼를 개최하는 것은 어떨까요? 우리와 사업 관계에 있는 몇몇 모델 에이전시에 연락을 해볼 수 있습니다. 도움이 되었기를 바랍니다. 관심이 있으시면, 더욱 자세히 논의하기 위해 다시 전화 부탁드립니다. 내선 번호는 234입니다. 감사합니다.

| 고득점 TIP | '제품이나 서비스의 변화에 대해 어떻게 홍보할 것인가?' 하는 문제로, 홍보 방법 혹은 고객수 증가를 위한 아이디어를 묻는 상황도 빈번히 출제된다. 일반적으로 매장의 종류와 관계없이 **할인 쿠폰**을 나누어 주는 방법을 사용할 수 있으며, 이 문제의 경우 의류 회사이므로 **패션쇼**를 개최해서 고객의 눈길을 끌 수도 있다.

| 어휘 | **figure out** 알아내다 **promote** 홍보하다 **come up with** 찾아내다 **give out** 나누어 주다
upcoming 다가오는 **attract** 끌어들이다 **launch** 시작하다 **extension** 내선(번호)

Actual Test 09

Question 11 Express an Opinion

As a business owner, you would prefer to hire talented employees. In order to attract talented employees, which of the following options would be better? Use specific reasons or examples to support your opinion.

- Give a private office
- Give a lot of vacation days

사업주로서, 당신은 유능한 직원들을 채용하는 것을 선호할 것입니다. 유능한 직원들을 끌어 들이기 위해 다음 방안들 중 어떤 것이 더 낫다고 생각하십니까? 당신의 의견을 뒷받침할 구체적인 근거나 사례를 제시하세요.
- 개인 사무실 제공
- 많은 휴가를 제공

Question 11

01-09-11

초·중급 Model Answer

I think it's better to give a lot of vacation days for the following reasons. First of all, it can make employees feel refreshed and reduce stress. This allows them to have better ideas and work harder. So, it will increase the work efficiency. Second, giving a private office can be a good solution but it can cause some problems communicating with other coworkers. In my case, sometimes it's hard for me to approach the boss and have an informal meeting with him because he has a private office. For these reasons, I would prefer to give a lot of vacation days.

다음과 같은 이유로 휴가를 많이 제공하는 것이 더 좋다고 생각합니다. 무엇보다, 직원들이 기분 전환을 하고 스트레스를 줄일 수 있습니다. 이로 인해 그들은 더 좋은 아이디어를 생각해 내고 더욱 열심히 일하게 됩니다. 따라서, 업무 효율성을 증가시킬 것입니다. 둘째로, 개인 사무실을 제공하는 것은 좋은 해결책일 수 있지만 다른 동료들과 의사소통을 하는 데 문제를 야기할 수도 있습니다. 제 경우에는, 가끔씩 상사에게 다가가서 비공식적인 만남을 갖는 것이 어려운데, 그 상사가 개인 사무실을 갖고 있기 때문입니다. 이러한 이유로, 저는 휴가를 많이 주는 것을 선호합니다.

고급 Model Answer

If I were a business owner and I had to choose between these two options, I would choose to give more vacation days. There are a couple of reasons for me to say this. First of all, most of the people who are talented and know what they are doing are older and have families. They want to spend more time with their families and I want them to work hard when they are here so it's a win-win situation. Secondly, the talented people I seek are always looking at ways to make the company better and some of their best ideas come only after they are well rested. As a result, once an employee comes back from a nice break they can give more to the company. For these reasons, I would allow more vacation days.

제가 사업주이고 이 두 방안들 중에서 한 가지를 선택해야 한다면 휴가를 더 많이 주는 것을 선택할 것입니다. 제가 이렇게 주장하는 데는 몇 가지 이유가 있습니다. 우선, 대부분의 유능하고 일을 잘 아는 사람은 나이가 많고 가족이 있습니다. 그들은 가족들과 더 많은 시간을 보내고 싶어하고 저는 그들이 직장에 있을 때 열심히 일하기를 바라기 때문에 모두에게 유리한 해결책이 될 수 있습니다. 둘째로, 제가 찾는 유능한 사람들은 항상 회사를 발전시키기 위한 방법을 모색하고 있고 그들의 최고의 아이디어 중 어떤 것들은 그들이 편안히 휴식을 취한 후에야 나올 수 있습니다. 결과적으로, 직원이 휴식을 잘 취한 후 돌아왔을 때 회사에 보다 더 기여할 수 있습니다. 이러한 이유로, 저는 휴가를 더 많이 줄 것입니다.

고득점 TIP '**스트레스를 줄일 수 있다, 업무 효율을 높일 수 있다**'와 같은 아이디어는 다수의 문제에 쉽게 적용할 수 있고 이 문제에서도 휴가와 연관지어 생각해 볼수 있다. 또는 **회사의 입장에서 직원과 win-win 할 수 있는 방안**을 생각해보는 것도 좋은 접근방법이다.

|어 휘| **talented** 재능 있는   **refreshed** 상쾌한   **efficiency** 효율   **approach** 다가가다
informal 격식에 얽매이지 않는   **win-win** 모두에게 유리한   **seek** 찾다

Actual Test 10

Questions 1-2 Read a Text Aloud

Question 1

01-10-01

May I **have** your **attention** please? ↗ // Will **all priority** passengers / for **Royal Line flight 1901** ↗ / please **proceed to** gate 58. ↘ // **Royal Line flight 1901** ↗ / will **begin general boarding** / in **10 minutes**. ↘ // **Priority passengers** are those / who will **require extra time** and **assistance**, ↗ / those **traveling** with **small children**, ↗ / **active duty service members** ↗ / or **members** of the **Royal Air Alliance**. ↘

안내 말씀 드리겠습니다. Royal Line 1901 항공편 우선 탑승객들은 모두 58번 게이트로 가시기 바랍니다. Royal Line 1901항공편 일반 탑승은 10분 후에 시작하겠습니다. 우선 탑승객들은 추가 시간과 도움이 필요하신 분들, 어린 아이들과 함께 여행하시는 분들, 현역 군인 또는 Royal Air Alliance 회원 분들입니다.

고득점 TIP **공항의 탑승 관련 공지글**이다. **항공편 번호**, **게이트**와 같은 주요 정보를 천천히 강조해서 읽고, 항공편 번호는 한 자리씩 끊어 읽는 것이 좋다. priority, royal 발음에 주의하고, **마지막 문장의 호흡이 길기 때문에 끊어 읽기**와 **억양**에 주의한다.

어휘 **attention** 주목   **priority** 우선   **passenger** 승객   **proceed** 진행하다   **assistance** 도움
active duty 현역(근무)

Question 2

01-10-02

If **you** are **thinking** about **Rome**, ↗ / think **no further** / than the **Coliseum Bed** and **Breakfast**. ↘ // **Located** just **behind** Termini Station, ↗ / we are **central** to **everything** / you would **want** to **see** and **enjoy** ↗ / while **you** are **here**. ↘ // Termini Station has all the **bus**, ↗ / **train** ↗ / and **tourist transportation** / **right** at the **front door**. ↘ // In addition, ↗ / **our rooms** are **near** / **all** the **best** night life. ↘ // **Check** us out **online** ↗ / at **ColiseumB&B.com.** ↘

Rome으로 가실 생각이시라면 Coliseum Bed and Breakfast가 최상의 선택입니다. Termini역 바로 뒤에 위치하고 있으며, 여기에 머무시는 동안 보고 즐기고 싶어할 만한 모든 것들의 중심에 있습니다. Termini역에서는 모든 버스, 열차 및 관광객 교통수단들을 바로 앞에서 이용하실 수 있습니다. 추가로, 저희 업소 근처에서 모든 밤의 문화를 즐기실 수 있습니다. 온라인에서 ColiseumB&B.com을 확인하세요.

고득점 TIP **숙박업소를 광고하는 글**이다. **광고 대상**, **장점** 및 특히 no, everything, all, best, check 등 광고에서 자주 등장하는 어휘들을 강조해서 읽는다. r, l 이 들어간 어휘들의 발음에 주의한다.

어휘 **coliseum** 대경기장   **termini** terminus의 복수   **terminus** (기차, 버스 등) 종점   **front door** 정문, 현관

 **Question 3** Describe a Picture

■ 도입 ■ 중심 ■ 주변 ■ 마무리

고득점 TIP 등장 인물이 4~5명일 때 답변시간 안에 묘사를 끝내기가 가장 어렵다. **인물들 전체나 그 안에서의 소그룹에 대한 공통점을 먼저 최대한 묘사**한다. 이 사진에서는 앞의 4명의 공통점을 말하고, 각 인물 중 특징적인 내용을 덧붙인 후에 스크린의 인물을 묘사한다.

Question 3

🎧 01-10-03

초·중급 Model Answer

This picture appears to be in a conference room. The first thing I notice is 4 people. They are sitting around a big table, holding pens and looking at a TV in the middle. All of them are wearing black suits. The woman on the left is pointing to the TV with her hand. I can see a speaker on the TV. She is also wearing a suit and smiling with her hands gathered together. On the table, notepads are placed in front of each person. It seems that everyone is concentrating on the meeting.

이 사진은 회의실에서 찍힌 것 같습니다. 처음에 눈에 띄는 것은 네 명의 사람들입니다. 그들은 큰 테이블에 둘러 앉아 있고 펜을 들고 있으며 중간에 있는 텔레비전을 보고 있습니다. 모두 검은색 정장을 입고 있습니다. 왼쪽에 있는 여성은 손으로 TV를 가리키고 있습니다. TV에 발표자가 보입니다. 그녀 또한 정장을 입고 있으며 손을 모은 채 미소를 짓고 있습니다. 테이블 위에는 각 사람 앞에 메모장이 있습니다. 모두 회의에 집중하고 있는 것으로 보입니다.

고급 Model Answer

This picture appears to be in a conference room. The first thing I notice is four people sitting at a conference room table. They are all looking at a monitor while they are holding pens with notepads open in front of them. All of them are wearing dark suits with two women sitting closest to the monitor while the two men are in the foreground of the picture. The woman on the left is making a gesture with her hand toward the monitor. I can see another woman on the monitor; she is wearing a check suit with a white shirt and she has her hands clasped. It seems like everyone is very focused on the meeting.

이 사진은 회의실인 것으로 보입니다. 처음에 눈에 띄는 것은 회의실 테이블에 앉아있는 네 명의 사람입니다. 그들은 모두 펜을 들고 있고 앞에 메모장을 펼친 채 모니터를 보고 있습니다. 모두 어두운 색 정장을 입고 있고, 두 명의 여성은 모니터와 가장 가까이에 앉아 있으며 두 명의 남자들은 사진 앞부분에 있습니다. 왼쪽에 있는 여성은 모니터를 향해 손짓을 하고 있습니다. 모니터에 다른 한 명의 여성이 보입니다. 그녀는 흰색 셔츠에 체크무늬 정장을 입고 있으며 양손을 깍지 끼고 있습니다. 모두 회의에 매우 집중하고 있는 것처럼 보입니다.

|어 휘| **point to** ~을 가리키다 **gather** 모으다 **notepad** 메모지 **concentrate** 집중하다
make a gesture 손짓하다 **clasp** 움켜쥐다

Actual Test 10

 **Questions 4-6** Respond to Questions

Imagine that an American marketing firm is conducting research in your country. You have agreed to participate in a telephone interview about libraries.

미국의 한 마케팅 회사가 당신의 나라에서 설문 조사를 하고 있다고 가정해 보세요. 당신은 '도서관'에 관한 전화 인터뷰에 응하기로 동의했습니다.

Question 4
01-10-04

Q. What services do you use when you go to a library? 당신은 도서관에서 어떤 서비스를 이용하나요?

[초·중급 Model Answer]

A. I get books and sometimes I sit and read. I also take my books from home and go there to read the books as it is really quiet there.

저는 책을 찾아서 가끔씩 앉아서 읽습니다. 또한 도서관은 매우 조용하기 때문에 집에서 제 책을 가져가서 읽기도 합니다.

[고급 Model Answer]

A. I like to go to the library to check out books and at times I will go there to just sit and read. Additionally, I enjoy going there to study and meet friends that are in study groups with me.

저는 책을 대여하기 위해 도서관에 가는 것을 좋아하고 가끔은 그냥 앉아서 책을 읽기 위해 갑니다. 뿐만 아니라, 그곳에 가서 공부하는 것과 저와 같은 스터디 그룹에 있는 친구들을 만나는 것을 좋아합니다.

고득점 TIP | **복수형**으로 질문했으므로 간단하게라도 **두 가지 이상 대답**하는 것이 좋다. **service**라는 말을 어렵게 생각할 필요 없이 '**책을 읽고 대여하거나 친구들과 공부한다**'는 등의 쉬운 답변을 한다.

Question 5
01-10-05

Q. What services could the library offer to be more helpful?

도서관이 어떤 서비스를 제공한다면 더 도움이 되겠습니까?

[초·중급 Model Answer]

A. I think libraries could offer more online services. If I could get information from the library by email it would be very good.

제 생각에는 도서관이 온라인 서비스를 더 제공할 수 있을 것 같습니다. 이메일을 통해 도서관에서 정보를 받을 수 있다면 매우 좋을 것 같습니다.

[고급 Model Answer]

A. In my opinion, libraries need to be more up to date with how people get information. By this I mean that the library could get more research and material available through online options like email or instant messenger.

제 생각에는 사람들이 정보를 얻는 방법과 관련해 도서관이 보다 최신화될 필요가 있습니다. 제 말은, 도서관이 이메일 또는 메신저 등 온라인 수단을 통해 더 많은 연구 내용 혹은 자료를 이용할 수 있도록 만들면 좋겠다는 뜻입니다.

'서비스 개선'에 관한 질문에 대해서 아이디어가 바로 떠오르지 않는다면 '**온라인 서비스**' 라는 개념으로 접근할 수 있다. 도서관, 박물관, 학교 등 그 **서비스 주체에 관계없이 답변이 가능**하다.

Question 6

01-10-06

Q. Which of the following three things do you think is the most in need of change with regard to the library? 다음 세 가지 중 도서관과 관련해 변화가 가장 필요한 것이 무엇이라고 생각합니까?
- hours of operation 운영 시간
- computer systems 컴퓨터 시스템
- materials available 가용 자료

초·중급 Model Answer

A. I think the hours of operation are the most in need of change with regard to the library. In general, libraries are open from 9 A.M. to 6 P.M. In my case, as an office worker, I can't use the library after work and that is very inconvenient. Also, if I could use the library on weekends, it would be great.

제 생각에 도서관과 관련해 가장 변경할 필요가 있는 것은 운영 시간입니다. 보통 도서관은 오전 9시에서 오후 6시까지 운영합니다. 제 경우에는 회사원이기 때문에 퇴근 후에 도서관을 이용할 수 없어서 매우 불편합니다. 또한, 주말에 도서관을 이용할 수 있다면 매우 좋을 것 같습니다.

고급 Model Answer

A. The most needed change in the library comes from the need to modernize their computer systems. I feel that the library really needs to develop ways to make information more accessible through their website. If a library could offer more information and services online through downloads or just to view online, it would increase the number of people using the library.

도서관에 있어 가장 변경이 필요한 것은 컴퓨터 시스템을 현대화하는 것입니다. 도서관은 웹사이트를 통해 정보에 대한 접근성을 높이기 위한 방법을 개발할 필요가 절실하다고 생각합니다. 도서관이 다운로드 또는 단순한 온라인 보기를 통해 보다 많은 정보 및 서비스를 온라인 상에서 제공하게 된다면, 도서관 이용자 수를 증가시킬 것입니다.

평소에 **건의하고 싶었던 사항**이 있으면 그대로 말해도 좋고, 불만 사항이 없거나 표현하기가 어렵다면 보기 중에서 **말하기 쉬운 쪽**을 택한다. **운영 시간을 늘려달라**는 식의 쉬운 접근도 가능하며, **5번 문제와 연계해 컴퓨터 시스템** 쪽으로 방향을 정하는 것도 좋은 방법이다.

|어 휘| **check a book out** 책을 대출하다 **at times** 가끔은 **up to date** 최신의 **available** 이용할 수 있는
with regard to ～와 관련하여 **hours of operation** 운영 시간 **in general** 보통 **modernize** 현대화하다
accessible 이용 가능한

Actual Test 10

 **Questions 7-9** Respond to Questions Using Information Provided

---

JM Corp.   *Second draft*
Orientation for New Employees

09:00 - 09:30	Opening speech – Dexter Lee, vice president
09:30 – 11:00	Presentation on How to adapt to JM Corp. – John Forrest
~~11:00 – 12:00~~	~~Salary Policies~~ **rescheduled - change from first draft**
12:00 – 13:00	Lunch break
13:00 – 14:00	Tour of the Headquarters building
14:00 – 15:00	Discussion – Jessica Simpson
15:00 – 16:00	Meeting with your team managers

* Coffee, water and snacks will be available throughout the day.

JM사   **두 번째 안**

신입사원을 위한 오리엔테이션

09:00~09:30	개회사 – Dexter Lee, 부사장
09:30~11:00	JM사 적응 방안에 대한 발표 – John Forrest
~~11:00~12:00~~	~~임금정책~~ **일정 변경됨 – 초안에서 변경됨**
12:00~13:00	점심 식사
13:00~14:00	본사 건물 투어
14:00~15:00	토의 – Jessica Simpson
15:00~16:00	팀장과의 만남

* 커피, 물, 다과는 하루 종일 제공됨.

Hello. This is Pamela, the manager of the Human Resources Department. Since you are in charge of the orientation for new employees, I think you can give me some detailed information on my inquiries about it.

안녕하세요, 인사과 매니저 Pamela입니다. 당신은 신입사원 오리엔테이션을 담당하고 있으니, 이에 관한 제 문의 사항에 대해 자세한 정보를 제공해줄 수 있으리라 생각합니다.

Question 7

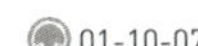

Q. What time will we get started and who will give the opening speech?

일정은 몇 시에 시작하며, 개회사를 누가 합니까?

초·중급 Model Answer

A. The orientation for new employees will start at 9 o'clock and Dexter Lee the Vice President will give the opening speech.

신입사원 오리엔테이션은 9시 정각에 시작될 예정이며 Dexter Lee 부사장님께서 개회사를 하실 것입니다.

고급 Model Answer

A. We will kick off the orientation for new employees at 9 A.M. with a speech from our Vice President Dexter Lee. Coffee, water and snacks will be available throughout the day.

우리는 Dexter Lee 부사장님의 개회사와 함께 오전 9시에 신입사원 오리엔테이션을 시작할 것입니다. 커피, 물, 다과는 하루 종일 제공될 것입니다.

고득점 TIP **육하원칙** 문제는 7, 8, 9번 중 한 번 이상 꼭 출제된다. **what time/started/who/opening speech**와 같은 **핵심내용**을 잘 듣고 **동사** 및 **전치사** 표현에 주의하면서 답한다.

Question 8

Q. Are there any changes between the first and second drafts?

초안과 두 번째 안 사이에 변경된 부분이 있습니까?

초·중급 Model Answer

A. Yes, there was a talk on salary polices from 11 A.M. to 12 P.M. but it has been rescheduled. We have not set the time for this session yet.

네, 오전 11시부터 오후 12시까지 임금 정책에 대한 논의가 계획되어 있었으나 일정이 변경되었습니다. 아직 본 세션의 시간을 정하지 않았습니다.

Actual Test 10

A. Yes, we had a session on salary policies that was scheduled between 11 and 12 and it had to be rescheduled. However, we are not sure what time we will be having that now.

네, 임금 정책에 관한 세션이 11시부터 12시까지 계획되어 있었고, 일정이 변경되어야 했습니다. 그러나 그 일정이 언제 진행될 것인지 현재까지는 확실히 정해지지 않았습니다.

고득점 TIP **변경된 부분을 물어보는 문제**는 새로운 유형에 속한다. 하지만 보통은 표에 두드러지게 표시가 되어 있으므로 충분히 **문제를 미리 예측**할 수 있다. **be rescheduled**와 같은 **수동 표현** 및 **시간 표현**에 주의한다.

Questions 9   🎧 01-10-09

Q. Could you tell me all of the sessions after lunch? 점심 이후에 있는 모든 세션들에 대해 말씀해 주시겠습니까?

A. Yes, we have three sessions after lunch. First, there will be a tour of the headquarters building from 1 to 2 P.M. Next, a discussion with Jessica Simpson is scheduled from 2 to 3 P.M. Finally, new employees will meet their team managers from 3 to 4 P.M.

네, 점심 이후에는 세 가지 세션이 있습니다. 우선, 오후 1시부터 2시까지 본사 건물 투어가 있습니다. 다음으로는, Jessica Simpson과의 토의가 오후 2시부터 3시까지 예정되어 있습니다. 마지막으로, 신입사원들은 오후 3시부터 4시까지 그들의 팀장들을 만나게 될 것입니다.

A. Sure, we have three sessions after lunch. We will start with a tour of the headquarters building that will be from 1 to 2 P.M. The tour will be followed by a discussion with Jessica Simpson from 2 to 3 P.M. We will finish out the day with one final session from 3 to 4 P.M. where the new employees will meet their team managers.

물론입니다. 점심 이후에는 세 가지 세션이 있습니다. 본사 건물 투어로 시작되며 이는 오후 1시부터 2시까지 진행될 것입니다. 투어에 이어서 오후 2시부터 3시까지 Jessica Simpson과의 토의가 있을 것입니다. 오후 3시부터 4시까지의 마지막 세션으로 일정이 마무리 되는데, 본 세션에는 신입 사원들이 팀장들을 만나게 될 것입니다.

고득점 TIP **after lunch**라고 했으므로 **점심 식사 이후의 프로그램**에 대해 모두 언급한다. '**첫째, 그 다음에는, 마지막으로**'와 같은 표현을 사용해서 짜임새 있게 말할 수 있다. **there will be, we will, the employees will** 등과 같이 **다양한 표현**을 사용해서 **문장을 시작**할 수 있다.

| 어 휘 | **Corp.(corporation)** 기업   **draft** 원고, 초안   **opening speech** 개회사   **vice president** 부사장
adapt 적응하다   **policy** 정책   **headquarters** 본부   **throughout** ~동안 내내
Human Resources Department 인사과   **in charge of** ~을 담당해서   **inquiry** 질문   **kick off** 시작하다

 **Question 10** Propose a solution

Hello, this is Lisa from Student Affairs. I am calling to try to get your input and wisdom on the graduation ceremony for this year. As you may recall last year, we had a lot of problems with the ceremony primarily due to the large number of unanticipated visitors who came to it. The good news is that this is a sign that we are growing and our student numbers show that. The bad news is that we don't have any space large enough to accommodate the type of crowd like we had last year or could have this year. I would appreciate any suggestions that you might come up with and I would value any input that you would lend in this situation. I have heard that in years past you were the go to person as far as graduation planning and as such I really would appreciate your advice. Once again, this is Lisa from Student Affairs and I can be reached at extension 754. Thank you very much for your time.

안녕하세요, 학생과의 Lisa라고 합니다. 올해 졸업식과 관련하여 귀하의 조언과 지혜를 얻기 위해 전화 드립니다. 작년을 기억하시겠지만, 졸업식 때 많은 문제가 있었는데 주로 예상치 못한 많은 방문자들로 인한 것이었습니다. 좋은 소식은, 이는 우리가 성장하고 있다는 신호이고 저희 학생 수가 이를 보여주고 있습니다. 나쁜 소식은 작년에 왔었던 사람들 혹은 이번에 올 수 있는 사람들의 수만큼을 수용할 수 있는 충분히 넓은 공간이 없다는 것입니다. 생각하시는 제안 사항이 있을 경우 무엇이든 말씀해 주신다면 감사하겠으며, 현 상황에서 어떠한 조언을 주신다 해도 소중히 여기겠습니다. 과거에 졸업식을 계획하는데 있어서 전문가셨다는 얘기를 들었습니다. 그래서 이렇게 부탁드리오니 조언을 해주신다면 매우 감사하겠습니다. 다시 한 번 말씀드리면, 저는 학생과의 Lisa이고 내선 754번으로 연락 주시면 됩니다. 시간 내주셔서 감사합니다.

 01-10-10

초·중급 Model Answer

Hello, Lisa. This is William. I'm returning your call about your request. I got your message saying that you are expecting a lot of people at the graduation ceremony this year but we don't have any space for it. So, you're asking me to deal with this problem. Well, as you know, there is a large gymnasium next to our school. I think, there won't be any sports games because it's the off season these days. I will contact them as soon as possible and let you know whether it is available on our graduation day. If you have any questions please call me anytime. Thanks.

안녕하세요, Lisa. 저는 William입니다. 요청하신 사안에 대해 답신 전화 드립니다. 올해 졸업식 때 많은 방문자를 예상하고 있지만 이를 위한 공간이 없다는 메시지를 받았습니다. 그래서 이 문제를 해결해달라고 제게 요청하셨습니다. 아시다시피, 학교 옆에 큰 체육관이 있습니다. 요즘 비수기여서 스포츠 경기가 없을 것 같습니다. 최대한 빨리 그들에게 연락해보고 졸업식 날에 사용이 가능한지 알려 드리겠습니다. 문의 사항이 있으시면 언제든지 연락 바랍니다. 감사합니다.

Actual Test 10

Hello, Lisa, this is William from Academic Affairs. I am sorry I missed your call. I got your message and understand that you are trying to plan the graduation ceremony for this year but you're worried because last year was a bit of a challenge and kind of a problem with the lack of space and the size of the crowds. Well, I think it's possible to hold the graduation ceremony at the main stadium. Or, as you know, there is a large gymnasium beside our school and it might be available these days because it's the off season so there won't be any sports games going on. Maybe the gymnasium is better because it's too cold outside. I'll let you know whether we can use the place as soon as I contact them. I hope the graduation day can be a memorable event for all graduates and their families. Talk to you soon. Thanks.

안녕하세요, Lisa. 교무처의 William입니다. 전화를 못 받아서 죄송합니다. 올해 졸업식을 계획하고 있지만 작년에 수용 공간 부족과 인원 수에 대한 문제로 곤란을 겪었기 때문에 걱정이 된다는 메시지를 받았고, 이 점에 대해 이해가 갑니다. 글쎄요, 제 생각에는 주경기장에서 졸업식을 개최하는 것이 가능할 것 같습니다. 아니면, 아시다시피. 학교 옆에 큰 체육관이 있는데 요즘 비수기여서 진행되는 스포츠 경기가 없을 것이기 때문에 사용 가능할 수도 있습니다. 야외는 너무 춥기 때문에 체육관이 나을 수도 있습니다. 연락을 취해 본 후에 우리가 그 장소를 사용할 수 있을지에 대해 바로 알려 드리겠습니다. 졸업식 날이 모든 졸업생들과 그들의 가족들에게 기억에 남는 행사가 되기를 바랍니다. 조만간 또 통화합시다. 감사합니다.

고득점 TIP 졸업식 장소가 협소할 것 같아 조언을 구하는 문제이다. '장소가 부족하다'는 상황을 하나의 유형으로 구분할 수 있을 정도로 다수의 문제가 출제되었다. (임시 직원을 위한 사무실 공간 부족, 병원의 환자 대기실 부족 등) **보통은 '근처에 다른 공간을 활용할 수 있다'는 식으로 쉽게 답변**할 수 있다. (이웃 부서의 빈 책상들, 회의실 등) 이 문제에서는 근처의 체육관을 사용할 수 있을 것이라고 답변했다.

| 어 휘 | **Student Affairs** 학생과 **input** 조언 **graduation ceremony** 졸업식 **recall** 상기하다 **primarily** 주로 **due to** ~에 기인하는 **unanticipated** 예상치 못한 **accommodate** 수용하다 **value** 소중히 여기다 **lend** (도움 등을) 주다 **go to person** 기댈 수 있는 사람 **as far as** ~에 관한 한 **extension** 내선 **deal with** 처리하다 **gymnasium** 체육관 **off season** 비수기 **Academic Affairs** 교무처 **bit** 조금 **main stadium** 주경기장 **going on** 진행되고 있는 **memorable** 기억할 만한 **graduate** 대학 졸업생

 **Question 11** Express an Opinion

Which of the following jobs contributed to the world the most? Give specific reasons or examples to support your opinion.
· lawyer
· doctor
· farmer

다음 중 세상에 가장 크게 기여하는 직업은 무엇입니까? 당신의 의견을 뒷받침할 구체적인 근거나 사례를 제시하세요.
· 변호사
· 의사
· 농부

[초·중급 Model Answer]

In my opinion, the farmer contributed the most to the world. There are some reasons to support my opinion. First, the farmer is actually the oldest job. The first man had to eat and at some point he got some fruits or vegetables from the ground. This is what farming is and so farming is the profession that has contributed the most to the world. Second, without the farmer nothing else would exist. The farmer is the one that provides what we need daily to survive. As a result, everything else is dependent on what the farmer produces. For these reasons, I think the farmer has contributed the most to the world.

저는 농부가 세상에 가장 크게 기여한다고 생각합니다. 이러한 제 주장을 뒷받침할 몇 가지 이유가 있습니다. 첫째, 농부는 사실상 가장 오래된 직업입니다. 첫 인류 역시 먹어야 했고, 어느 순간 땅에서 몇몇 열매와 채소를 얻기 시작했습니다. 이것이 바로 농사이고, 그렇기 때문에 농사를 짓는 것이야말로 세상에 가장 크게 기여하는 직업이라고 생각합니다. 둘째로, 농부가 없다면 다른 그 어떤 것도 존재할 수 없기 때문입니다. 농부는 우리가 매일 생존하기 위해 필요한 것을 제공해줍니다. 결과적으로, 다른 모든 것들이 농부가 생산하는 것에 의존하고 있는 것입니다. 이러한 이유들로 인해, 저는 농부가 세상에 가장 크게 기여한다고 생각합니다.

[고급 Model Answer]

From what I can see, the farmer is by far the clear choice for the one who has contributed the most to the world. Here are a couple of reasons why I say this. First, farming is actually the oldest profession. At some point, early man had to eat and so he picked a piece of fruit or he got some root out of the ground. This is called harvesting and it is an essential part of a farmer's job. Second, everything else that lives is dependent on the farmer. Everything that lives has to have food and that comes from the farmer. If it wasn't for the farmer planting, watering and harvesting the crops, no other job would exist, as people wouldn't be able to exist. For these reasons, I think it's obvious that the farmer has contributed the most to the world.

제가 본 바로는, 농부야말로 세상에 가장 크게 기여하는 사람이 누구인가 하는 질문에 대한 가장 명확한 답이라고 생각합니다. 여기 제가 왜 그렇게 생각하는지에 대한 몇 가지 이유가 있습니다. 첫째, 농사를 짓는 것은 사실 가장 오래 전부터 있어왔던 직업입니다. 어느 순간 첫 인류도 먹을 것이 필요했고, 그래서 열매를 주워 먹거나 땅에서 뿌리를 캐서 먹었습니다. 이것이 바로 수확이고, 농부의 일에 있어서 필수적인 부분입니다. 둘째로, 살아있는 다른 모든 것들은 농부에게 의존하고 있습니다. 모든 생명체는 음식을 취해야 하고, 이는 농부로부터 나옵니다. 농부가 농작물을 심고, 물을 주고, 수확하지 않는다면 인간이 존재할 수 없기 때문에 다른 어떤 직업도 존재할 수 없었을 것입니다. 이러한 이유들 때문에, 저는 농부가 세상에 가장 크게 기여해왔다는 것이 명백하다고 생각합니다.

| 고득점 TIP | **세 가지 중**에서 선택하는 경우, **가장 포괄적인 개념을** 고르면 **답변하기가 수월**할 때가 많다. 이 문제에서도 농부가 가장 오래된 직업이고, 농부가 없다면 그 어떤 것도 존재할 수 없다는 논리로 접근할 수 있다. |

| 어 휘 | **contribute** 기여하다　**profession** 직업　**exist** 존재하다　**dependent on** ~에 의존하는　**by far** 훨씬
harvest 수확(하다)　**essential** 필수적인　**crop** 농작(물)　**obvious** 분명한 |

Actual Test 11

Questions 1-2 Read a Text Aloud

Question 1

01-11-01

Atlanta's Museum of **Photography** ↗ / is **proud** to **announce** a **new exhibition** / of **World War 2 photographs**. ↘ // This **exhibit** contains photos / from **French**, ↗ / **Spanish**, ↗ / Italian and **Polish photographers** / who **risked** life and **limb** ↗ / in order to **document** this **amazing** time / in **history**. ↘ // For **more information** ↗ / **call** 789-2745. ↘

애틀랜타 주 사진 박물관은 새로 열리는 2차 세계 대전 사진 전시회를 발표하게 되어 자랑스럽게 생각합니다. 본 전시회에서는 역사에 이 놀라운 시기를 기록하기 위해 생명의 위험을 무릅쓴 프랑스, 스페인, 이탈리아와 폴란드 사진작가들의 사진을 만나실 수 있습니다. 추가 정보가 필요하시면 789-2745로 연락 바랍니다.

고득점 TIP 사진 박물관의 전시회 **안내문**이다. **전시회 내용**과 **작가들의 국적** 등 **주요 내용**을 **강조**해서 읽는다. **열거하는 부분의 억양**에 주의하고, **전화번호는 한 자리씩** 끊어서 읽는다. exhibition, exhibit의 발음 및 강세에 주의한다.

어휘 **proud** 자랑스러운   **announce** 발표하다   **exhibition** 전시회   **exhibit** 전시품(회)
risk life and limb 목숨을 걸 정도로 위험을 무릅쓰다   **document** 기록하다

Question 2

01-11-02

Hello ↗ / and **welcome** to the **KPBP** / hourly **traffic update**. ↘ // The **new asphalt** on **635** / is causing a **delay** ↗ / **all the way** to the 36 **kilometer** / mark **east bound**. ↘ // In **addition**, ↗ / we have the **regular backup** / on the **toll way**. ↘ // That's at the **Jupiter** on **ramp** ↗ / where **Iron Corp.** and **TWR Inc.** / **all leave work** to head **home** / at the same **time**. ↘ // **Other** than **that** ↗ / it **looks** like / the **problems on 183** / have been **eliminated** ↗ / so **enjoy** the **ride home**. ↘

안녕하세요, KPBP 매시간 교통 상황 업데이트에 오신 것을 환영합니다. 635에 있는 새 아스팔트 때문에 동쪽 방향 36km까지 정체 상태입니다. 또한, 유료 고속도로에서 정기적으로 상황을 전달해드리고 있습니다. Iron Corp.와 TWR Inc. 직원들이 동시간에 퇴근하면서 Jupiter 진입로 구간이 막히고 있습니다. 이 외에는 183에 있었던 문제가 해결된 것처럼 보이니, 집으로 가시는 길이 즐거울 것 같습니다.

고득점 TIP **교통방송**이다. **고속도로 이름**이나 **방향** 등 운전자에게 중요한 정보들을 **강조**해서 읽는다. Corp. 와 Inc. 는 각각 Corporation, Incorporated 로 읽는 것이 좋다.

어휘 **traffic** 교통(량)   **bound** ~로 향하는   **toll way** 유료 도로   **on-ramp** 진입로   **Corp.(corporation)** 기업
Inc.(incorporated) 주식회사   **eliminate** 제거하다

Question 3 Describe a Picture

| 고득점 TIP | 상점의 **계산대 사진**도 종종 출제되는 편이다. **사람들을 먼저 묘사**하고 계산대 및 배경 묘사를 한다. 물건이 많을 경우 두세 개만 묘사하고 **많은 물건들**이라는 식으로 말할 수 있다. |

01-11-03

초·중급 Model Answer

This looks like a store checkout stand. The first thing I see is two customers and one man at the checkout stand. The two customers are women who are standing on the left and smiling. The first one is wearing a pink shirt and has brown hair. Behind her, there is another woman wearing a blue shirt. The man who looks like a worker is on the right behind a cash register. He is wearing a blue shirt and an apron. Between the man and the first woman, there are a bunch of things that it looks like the woman is buying. In the background, I can see an aisle with more things to buy. This picture reminds me of my grocery shopping last week.

상점의 계산대인 것 같습니다. 처음 눈에 띄는 것은 두 고객과 계산대에 있는 한 남자입니다. 두 고객은 여성이며 좌측에 서서 웃고 있습니다. 첫 번째 여성은 핑크색 옷을 입고 있으며 머리는 갈색입니다. 그녀의 뒤에는 파란색 셔츠를 입고 있는 또 다른 여성이 있습니다. 직원으로 보이는 남성은 우측 계산대 뒤에 있습니다. 그는 파란색 셔츠와 앞치마를 입고 있습니다. 남성과 첫 번째 여성 사이에는 여성이 구매하고 있는 것으로 보이는 많은 물건이 있습니다. 배경에는, 통로가 있는데 구매할 수 있는 물건들이 더 보입니다. 이 사진을 보니 지난주에 장을 보러 갔던 것이 생각납니다.

고급 Model Answer

This picture appears to be in a supermarket at the checkout stand. The first thing I notice is two customers and one person working the checkout stand. The two customers are on the left, both are women, with the first one wearing a pink sweater and the second one wearing a blue sweater. On the right is the store employee who is a man wearing an apron and ringing the first lady up. Between them on the counter, there are a lot of groceries on the conveyor belt and a computer cash register. In the background, I can see a large refrigerated section and some other goods stacked up. It seems like all the customers are happy with shopping at this store.

이 사진은 슈퍼마켓의 계산대로 보입니다. 가장 먼저 눈에 띄는 것은 두 명의 고객과 계산대에서 일하고 있는 한 사람입니다. 두 고객은 좌측에 있고 둘 다 여성입니다. 첫 번째 여성은 핑크 스웨터를 입고 있으며 두 번째 여성은 파란색 스웨터를 입고 있습니다. 우측에는 앞치마를 두르고 첫 번째 여성의 물건을 계산하고 있는 상점의 남자 직원이 있습니다. 그들 사이에 있는 계산대에는, 컨베이어 벨트에 많은 식료품이 있고 컴퓨터 금전 등록기가 있습니다. 배경에는 큰 냉장부와 쌓여 있는 다른 물품들이 보입니다. 모든 고객들이 이 상점에서 장 보는 것에 만족해하고 있는 것으로 보입니다.

어 휘	**checkout stand** 계산대　　**apron** 앞치마　　**a bunch of** 다수의　　**aisle** 통로　　**groceries** 식료품 및 잡화
	ring up (금전 등록기에 상품 가격을) 입력하다　　**cash register** 금전 등록기　　**refrigerated** 냉장한
	stacked up 쌓여 있는

 **Questions 4-6** Respond to Questions

Imagine that a Canadian marketing firm is conducting research in your country. You have agreed to participate in a telephone interview about traditions around gift giving.

캐나다의 한 마케팅 회사가 당신의 나라에서 설문 조사를 하고 있다고 가정해 보세요. 당신은 '선물을 주는 관례'에 관한 전화 인터뷰에 응하기로 동의했습니다.

Question 4

01-11-04

Q. When was the last time you gave a gift to any of your friends or family?

귀하의 친구들 혹은 가족들에게 마지막으로 선물을 준 것은 언제입니까?

초·중급 **Model Answer**

A. It was on my father's birthday last week. The whole family got together for a special meal and then my father opened his presents.

지난주 저희 아버지의 생신 때였습니다. 온 가족이 모여 특별한 식사를 하고, 아버지께서 선물들을 열어보셨습니다.

고급 **Model Answer**

A. The last time I gave a present to anyone was my friend's birthday last month. Several of my friends and I got together to take him out. We had a great dinner, went to a bar and had a birthday cake with presents for him at the bar.

제가 마지막으로 누군가에게 선물을 준 것은 지난달 제 친구의 생일 때였습니다. 다른 몇몇 친구들과 함께 그 친구를 데리고 나갔습니다. 근사한 저녁 식사를 하고, 바에 가서 케이크를 먹고 그에게 선물을 전달했습니다.

고득점 **TIP** **과거시제**로 답하고 **예를 들어 쉽게** 말한다. 실제로 언제 선물을 주었는지 생각이 안 나더라도 **4번 문제는 무조건 긍정적으로** 답변하는 것이 좋다.

Question 5

01-11-05

Q. Are there special days when you are more apt to give a gift to your friends or perhaps a family member? 친구들 혹은 가족들에게 유난히 더 선물을 하고 싶은 특별한 날이 있습니까?

초·중급 **Model Answer**

A. Birthdays, Christmas and Chuseok which is Korean Thanksgiving are all special days for gifts. I might also give a gift for a graduation, wedding or other special celebration for a friend or family member.

생일, 크리스마스, 그리고 한국의 추수 감사절인 추석이 모두 선물을 주고 받는 특별한 날들입니다. 또한 졸업, 결혼 혹은 다른 특별한 행사가 있는 경우에도 친구들이나 가족들에게 선물을 주기도 합니다.

A. A few of those days would include birthdays, Christmas as well as Chuseok and Seollal which are both Korean holidays. In addition graduations, weddings and a baby's first 100 days could all mean gifts to the friend or family member.

그런 날 중에 몇 가지를 꼽자면 한국의 명절인 추석과 설날 이외에도 생일, 크리스마스가 있습니다. 또한 졸업, 결혼 그리고 백일과 같은 날에도 모두 친구들 혹은 가족들에게 선물을 줄 수 있습니다.

고득점 TIP '쉽게 쉽게'. Part 3는 준비시간이 없으므로 **쉬운 단어와 문법으로 편안하게 말한다.** 생일, 크리스마스, 추석 등 쉬운 예를 들어 설명할 수 있다.

Question 6　　　　　01-11-06

Q. What are some key deciding factors for you when considering what gift you will give your friends and family members? 친구들 혹은 가족들에게 줄 선물을 결정할 때 가장 중요하게 고려하는 요소들은 무엇입니까?

A. Some key deciding factors for me when considering a gift for a friend or family member are what event they are celebrating and how close I am to them. I think that for some events there are better gifts to give than for other events. In addition, I may not give a gift for some family members that I am not that close to.

제가 친구나 가족을 위한 선물을 결정할 때 가장 중요하게 고려하는 요소로는 무엇을 축하하는 행사인가 그리고 내가 그들과 얼만큼 친밀한가 하는 것입니다. 제 생각에 어떤 행사에는 다른 행사 때보다 선물하기에 더 적합한 것들이 있는 것 같습니다. 또한, 그다지 가깝지 않은 친척들에게는 선물을 잘 주지 않습니다.

A. Some key points that weigh in on my decision for gifts to give a friend or family member are the type of occasion as well as how close I am to the person. The occasion or situation has a lot to do with what gift is appropriate. For example, I wouldn't buy the same thing for a 21st birthday that I would for a 100 day celebration. The other factor is that I have some friends and family members that I am obviously closer to than others so that has an impact on what I buy.

친구나 가족을 위한 선물을 결정하는 데에 영향을 끼치는 주요 요소들은 제가 그 사람과 얼만큼 가까운가 하는 것과 그 행사의 종류입니다. 행사의 종류나 상황은 그에 따른 적합한 선물이 무엇인가와 많은 관련이 있습니다. 예를 들어, 누군가의 21번째 생일에 백일 때 줄 선물과 같은 것을 준비하지는 않을 것입니다. 또 다른 요소로 제겐 다른 사람들보다 분명히 더 가까운 친구나 가족이 있는데 이러한 점은 어떤 선물을 고를지에 영향을 줍니다.

고득점 TIP 선물의 가격을 고려 요소로 해서 쉽게 말할 수도 있지만, 여기에서는 **'무엇을 축하하는 행사인가, 그리고 나와 얼만큼 친밀한가'** (what event they are celebrating and how close I am to them)를 고려 요소로 꼽았다.

어휘 **get together** 모이다　**apt** ~하는 경향이 있는　**weigh** 영향을 주다　**occasion** 행사
have a lot to do with ~와 많은 관련이 있다　**appropriate** 적절한　**obviously** 분명히　**impact** 영향을 주다

Actual Test 11

Food & Style Magazine

Rough draft meeting – Monday Dec. 3

Topic	Author	Status
"'All In' Annual Chili Cook Off - Chance to win a new F-150!"	Jack Bowers	In progress - need photos and rules
"10 Foods for Good Luck"	Crystal Smith	To be edited - too long Interview on Tues. Dec. 4
"Soused mackerel with pickled vegetables"	Jackie Pans	Need more photos Taking photos on Wed. Dec. 5
"The Best Red Wines from Johnson Mountain Winery"	Rob Teaman	To be edited - too long

Final Deadline – Fri. Dec. 7

음식 & 스타일 잡지

대략적인 초안을 바탕으로 한 미팅 – 12월 3일 월요일

제목	저자	현황
"올해의 고추 요리 경연 대회에 도전하기 – 새로운 F-150을 획득할 기회!"	Jack Bowers	진행 중 – 사진 및 규칙 필요
"행운을 위한 10가지 음식"	Crystal Smith	편집 예정 – 분량이 너무 많음 12월 4일 화요일에 인터뷰
"김치를 곁들인 절인 고등어"	Jackie Pans	사진이 더 필요함 12월 5일 수요일에 사진 촬영
"Johnson Mountain 와이너리 최고의 적포도주"	Rob Teaman	편집 예정 – 분량이 너무 많음

최종 마감 시간 – 12월 7일 금요일

Hello, this this is Ivan. I wasn't able to get to the meeting on this month's edition but I know you had to finalize some things. Can you please bring me up to speed on where we are with a few things?

안녕하세요, 저는 Ivan입니다. 제가 이번 달 호와 관련한 미팅에 참석할 수가 없었는데요, 당신이 마무리 지어야 할 일들이 몇 가지 있다는 것을 알고 있습니다. 현 상황에 좀 더 속도를 낼 수 있도록 질문 몇 개만 해도 될까요?

Question 7
01-11-07

Q. Where are we with the article written by Jackie?

Jackie가 쓴 기사는 어떻게 되어 가는 중인가요?

초·중급 Model Answer

A. The article written by Jackie is titled "Soused mackerel with pickled vegetables". It is currently in need of more photos.

Jackie가 쓴 기사의 제목은 "김치를 곁들인 절인 고등어"입니다. 현재 사진이 더 필요한 상황입니다.

고급 Model Answer

A. Sure, the article written by Jackie is titled, "Soused mackerel with pickled vegetables." The current status of the article is in progress as the photos for it are scheduled for this Wednesday December 5th.

네, Jackie가 쓴 기사의 제목은 "김치를 곁들인 절인 고등어"입니다. 이 기사는 현재 작업 중이며 사진 촬영이 12월 5일 수요일에 예정되어 있습니다.

고득점 TIP 고유명사, 특히 **사람 이름**은 이렇게 문제에서 바로 언급될 수 있으므로 중요하다. **준비 시간에** 사람 이름들을 **미리 발음해보고 그 위치까지 최대한 기억**해 둔다.

Question 8
01-11-08

Q. Did I hear correctly that Jack Bowers is ready to go to print with his article?

Jane Bowers는 본인의 기사를 인쇄할 준비가 되었다고 들었는데. 맞습니까?

초·중급 Model Answer

A. No, Jack's article titled, "'All In' Annual Chili Cook Off - Chance to win a new F-150" is still in progress as well. He needs photos as well as rules to finish the article.

아닙니다. "올해의 고추 요리 경연 대회에 도전하기 – 새로운 F-150을 획득할 기회!"라는 제목의 Jack의 기사 또한 여전히 진행 중에 있습니다. 그는 기사를 끝내기 위한 규칙과 더불어 사진도 필요합니다.

고급 Model Answer

A. No, Jack's piece is still a work in progress. His article, "'All In' Annual Chili Cook Off - Chance to win a new F-150" is in need of photos as well as the rules to the contest in order to be complete.

아닙니다. Jack의 기사는 아직 진행 중에 있습니다. 그의 기사 제목은 "올해의 고추 요리 경연 대회에 도전하기 – 새로운 F-150을 획득할 기회."이고, 마감을 하기 위해서는 경연에 대한 규칙 및 사진이 필요한 상황입니다.

고득점 TIP '잘못된 정보를 바탕으로 질문'하는 경우이다. 아니라는 답변 후 필요한 정보에 대해 언급한다. 표에 있는 **주요 표현**들을 사용해 **완벽한 문장**을 만들어야 한다.

Question 9 🎧 01-11-09

Q. I have a lot of catching up to do before the final deadline. Could you tell me which articles need to be shortened and what is the final deadline?

저는 최종 마감 전에 만회해야 할 일들이 많이 있습니다. 어떤 기사들에 대해 그 양을 줄여야 하는지, 그리고 최종 마감 기한은 언제인지 알려주실 수 있나요?

초·중급 Model Answer

A. Yes, two articles currently need to be shortened. The first is "10 Foods for Good Luck" by Crystal Smith. It needs to be edited but also is waiting for an interview on Tuesday December 4th. The second one is "The Best Red Wines from Johnson Mountain Winery" by Rob Teaman and that is only waiting on editing because it is too long. The final deadline will be Friday December 7th.

네, 현재 두 개 기사의 양을 줄여야 합니다. 첫 번째는 Crystal Smith 의 "행운을 위한 10가지 음식"입니다. 편집이 필요하고, 또한 12월 4일 화요일에 인터뷰가 예정되어 있습니다. 두 번째 기사는 Rob Teaman의 "Johnson Mountain 와이너리 최고의 적포도주" 인데, 너무 길어서 편집만 하면 됩니다. 최종 마감 기한은 12월 7일 금요일입니다.

고급 Model Answer

A. Sure, there are currently two articles that need to be edited for length. The first one is "10 Foods for Good Luck" by Crystal Smith. This article is also in need of an interview which as of this moment is scheduled for Tuesday December 4th. The second article which is waiting only for editing due to length is "The Best Red Wines from Johnson Mountain Winery" by Rob Teaman. The final deadline for this edition is Friday December 7th.

물론입니다. 현재 분량 때문에 편집이 필요한 기사가 두 개 있습니다. 첫 번째는 Crystal Smith 의 "행운을 위한 10가지 음식"입니다. 이 기사를 위해 아직까지는 12월 4일 화요일에 예정되어 있는 인터뷰를 진행해야 합니다. 분량 때문에 편집만 하면 되는 두 번째 기사는 Rob Teaman의 "Johnson Mountain 와이너리 최고의 적포도주"입니다. 이번 호의 최종 마감 기한은 12월 7일 금요일입니다.

고득점 TIP **내용을 줄여야 할 부분**과, **마감 기한**에 대해서 말해야 한다. **9번 문제**는 이렇게 **표의 여러 부분을 언급**해야 할 때가 많다. 시간이 30초로 충분한 편이므로 **첫째, 둘째** 등의 표현을 사용해서 천천히 답변한다.

어휘 **rough** 대략적인　**draft** 초안　**cook off** 요리 경연 대회　**soused** 소금과 식초를 넣은 물에 절인
mackerel 고등어　**pickled vegetables** 김치　**winery** 포도주 양조장　**status** 현황　**in progress** 진행 중인
edit 편집하다　**deadline** 마감 기한　**edition** 간행물의 판(호)　**finalize** 마무리 짓다　**currently** 현재
complete 완료된　**catch up** 따라잡다　**shorten** 짧게 하다

 **Question 10** Propose a solution

Hi, this is Ellie and I am the owner of Ellie's House of Hair. I was calling to see if you could help us get more involved with the local college campuses. My thought is that lots of students will need a haircut sooner or later so I would like to find ways to get the word out about my shop. Just to let you know a couple of new hair shops have opened near our shop so we have a little competition now and I am not too sure I know how to compete with other hair shops. Could you give me some detailed information on how to make our hair shop more appealing to college students? Once again, my name is Ellie and please feel free to call me on my mobile phone at 281-890-6783. Thank you.

안녕하세요, 저는 Ellie's House of Hair(미용실)를 운영하고 있는 Ellie입니다. 지방 대학 캠퍼스 학생들에게 좀 더 다가갈 수 있도록 도움을 좀 구할 수 있을까 해서 전화 드렸습니다. 제 생각에는 조만간 많은 학생들이 머리 손질을 받아야 할 것이기 때문에 제 미용실에 대한 입소문을 퍼뜨릴 방법을 찾고 싶습니다. 상황을 알려드리자면 저희 미용실 근처에 새로 개장한 미용실이 몇 개 있어서 현재 작은 경쟁을 하고 있고, 저는 다른 미용실들과 어떻게 경쟁해야 할지에 대해 제가 잘 알고 있는 것인지 확신이 없습니다. 저희 미용실을 대학생들에게 어떻게 더 어필할 수 있을지에 대한 상세한 정보를 좀 주실 수 있나요? 다시 한 번 말씀 드리면, 저는 Ellie이고, 제 휴대 전화 번호 281-890-6783으로 부담 없이 전화주세요. 감사합니다.

01-11-10

초·중급 Model Answer

Hello Ellie, this is Joey at the newspaper ad department. I am sorry I missed your call. I understand that you are the owner of Ellie's House of Hair and you are trying to find ways to get more customers from the universities in town, especially with all the events that will be going on. I also understand that you should compete with some other shops. We could put an advertisement in the paper. We could also print some posters for you that you could place up all around the universities. If you're interested, please call me again to discuss this further. My number is 281-374-8231. Thank you.

안녕하세요 Ellie 씨, 저는 신문사 광고 부서의 Joey입니다. 당신의 전화를 받지 못해서 죄송합니다. 당신이 Ellie's House of Hair를 운영하고 있고 당신 도시의 대학교에서 더 많은 손님들을 모으기 위한 방법을 찾고 있다는 말을 들었습니다. 특히 앞으로 있을 모든 행사와 관련해서요. 또한 당신은 다른 몇몇 미용실들과 경쟁을 해야 한다는 것도 이해합니다. 저희가 신문에 광고를 게재해 드릴 수 있습니다. 또한 당신을 위해 학교 주변 많은 곳에 붙일 수 있는 포스터를 인쇄해 드릴 수 있습니다. 관심이 있으시면, 이 사안에 대해서 더 의논해 볼 수 있도록 다시 연락 바랍니다. 제 번호는 281-374-8231입니다. 감사합니다.

고급 Model Answer

Hello Ellie, this is Joey from the newspaper ad department. I apologize for missing your call, I was on another line. From your message I understand that you are the owner of Ellie's House of Hair and you are trying to find ways to gain more market share from the universities in town, especially in light of the events they have coming up. It sounds like you have some competition for that market and you aren't sure about how to deal with that. I feel very confident that we can

Actual Test 11

make your shop stand out. Have you ever considered running a coupon ad in the newspaper? Our paper is the number one paper on campus so we can give you a lot of exposure. Give me a call on my mobile phone and let's talk about it. My number is 281-374-8231. Thank you.

안녕하세요 Ellie 씨, 저는 신문사 광고 부서의 Joey입니다. 통화 중이었던 관계로 당신의 전화를 받지 못해서 죄송합니다. 메시지를 듣고 당신이 Ellie's House of Hair를 운영하고 있으며 도시의 대학교 상권에서 시장 점유율을 더 높이기 위한 방법을 강구하고 있다는 것을 알았습니다. 특히 요즈음의 행사들과 관련해서요. 당신은 그 시장과 관련해 작은 경쟁을 하고 있고 어떻게 해야 할지 확신이 없다고 하셨던 것 같습니다. 자신 있게 말씀 드립니다. 당신의 미용실이 부각될 수 있도록 저희가 도와드릴 수 있습니다. 혹시 신문에 쿠폰 광고를 게재하는 것에 대해 고려해 보신 적이 있나요? 저희 신문은 대학교 내에서 제일가는 신문이므로 당신의 미용실을 많이 노출할 수 있습니다. 제 휴대 전화로 연락 주시길 바라며 상세하게 논의를 해봅시다. 제 번호는 281-374-8231입니다. 감사합니다.

고득점 TIP　　**미용실의 경쟁 및 홍보 방안**에 대해서 도움을 요청하는 내용이다. 이렇게 **점포의 종류에 관계없이 경쟁 방법에 대해 묻는 문제**가 많이 출제되었다. 일반적으로 **광고 게재 및 포스터 제작** 등의 방안을 생각해 볼 수 있다. 전화를 받는 이가 누구인지 확실하지 않으므로 처음부터 신문사 광고부서라는 식으로 시작하는 것도 좋은 방법이 될 수 있다.

어휘　　**get involved** 관여하다　　**sooner or later** 조만간　　**get the word out** 말을 퍼트리다
compete with ∼와 경쟁하다　　**appealing** 매력적인　　**ad(advertisement)** 광고　　**apologize** 사과하다
market share 시장 점유율　　**in light of** ∼을 고려하여　　**stand out** 두드러지다　　**run** (기사 등) 싣다
exposure 노출

 **Question 11** Express an Opinion

Do you prefer to work in a big company or in a small company? Why? Use specific reasons or examples to support your opinion.

당신은 큰 기업과 작은 기업 중 어느 곳에서 일하는 것을 선호합니까? 그 이유는? 당신의 의견을 뒷받침할 구체적인 근거나 사례를 제시하세요.

Question 11 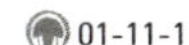 01-11-11

초·중급 Model Answer

I prefer to work for a big company. Here are a few reasons why. First, in a big company there are more chances to move up. More managers will be needed as the company grows and as a result I have more places where I could be moved up at. Second, in a big company there are better benefits. Many big companies give cars and large bonuses to their best people. For these reasons, I think a big company is better.

저는 큰 기업에서 일하는 것을 선호합니다. 다음과 같은 몇 가지 이유가 있습니다. 우선, 큰 기업에서는 승진할 기회가 더 많이 있습니다. 회사가 성장하면서 더 많은 관리자가 필요할 것이고 결과적으로 제가 승진할 수 있는 자리도 더 많을 것입니다. 둘째로, 큰 기업은 더 많은 혜택을 제공합니다. 규모가 큰 많은 기업들이 능력 있는 직원들에게 차량이나 높은 보너스를 제공합니다. 이러한 이유들 때문에, 저는 큰 기업이 더 낫다고 생각합니다.

고급 Model Answer

I would rather work for a large company. Here are a couple of reasons. First, larger companies have offices overseas and that means more opportunities to grow and possible live abroad. The chance to live overseas carries many added benefits with it, for example paid housing and great schools for the children. Second, larger companies have a better bonus structure and usually a better benefits package than smaller companies. A large company typically has better finances and more money to spend on keeping the employees happy. These are a couple of reasons why I would go with a larger firm over a small mom and pop style organization.

저는 큰 기업에서 근무하고 싶습니다. 다음과 같은 몇 가지 이유가 있습니다. 우선, 규모가 더 큰 기업들은 해외 지사들을 보유하고 있고 이는 곧 성장할 수 있는 더 많은 기회와 해외에서 살 수 있는 더 많은 가능성을 의미합니다. 해외 지사 생활을 하게 되면 그에 따른 많은 부가적인 혜택이 따라오는데, 예를 들어 집세나 아이들을 위한 훌륭한 학교 등입니다. 둘째로, 큰 기업에서는 작은 기업에 비해 보너스 체계나 직원들에 대한 복리 후생 제도가 더 잘 갖추어져 있습니다. 큰 기업은 일반적으로 자금 사정이 더 좋고 직원들의 행복을 위해 사용할 수 있는 예산이 더 많습니다. 이러한 점들이 바로 제가 소규모 영세 조직이 아닌 큰 기업에서 일하고 싶어 하는 몇 가지 이유들입니다.

고득점 TIP 이처럼 **대기업과 중소기업** 혹은 **큰 조직과 작은 조직** 중 선택을 하는 문제도 여러 번 출제되었다. 준비 시간이 짧으므로 **빨리 답할 수 있는 쉬운 쪽을 선택**한다. **대기업**을 택할 경우 **복지, 급여, 해외 근무, 승진 기회** 등에 대해 언급할 수 있다.

어휘 **move up** 승진하다　**as a result** 결과적으로　**benefit** 혜택　**would rather** 차라리 ～하겠다　**overseas, abroad** 해외에　**added** 추가된　**structure** 구조　**typically** 일반적으로　**mom and pop** 가족 경영의, 영세한

Actual Test 12

Questions 1-2 Read a Text Aloud

> ★ **Bold** ⇨ 강조 어휘   ★ 녹색 ⇨ 빈출 어휘, 발음과 강세에 주의해야 할 어휘
> ★ 밑줄 ⇨ 연음   ★ / ⇨ 끊어읽기   ★ ↗ ↘ ⇨ 올려읽기, 내려읽기

Question 1

01-12-01

Attention, ↗ / **Bed** and **Bath Avenue** **Shoppers.** ↘ // We would like to **remind you** ↗ / that until **further notice** / **all Pebo Laru bathmats** / have an **additional 35%** off. ↘ // That's **right** / all the **colorful,** ↗ / **soft** ↗ / and **stylish bathmats** by **Pebo Laru** / that **you** love ↗ / are now **35%** off! ↘ // Your **discount** will be **applied** / at the **cash register** ↗ / for a **limited time** only! ↘

Bed and Bath Avenue 쇼핑객들에게 안내 말씀 드립니다. 추후 통지가 있을 때까지 Pebo Laru 욕실용 매트를 추가적으로 35% 할인해 드린다는 것을 다시 한 번 알려 드립니다. 맞습니다. 여러분께 사랑받고 있는 Pebo Laru의 알록달록하고 부드럽고 멋있는 욕실용 매트 모두가 지금 35% 할인 중입니다! 한정된 시간 동안만 계산대에서 할인이 적용됩니다!

| 고득점 TIP | 광고글이므로 **품목, 할인폭, 수식하는 표현**들을 강조해서 읽는다. 자주 등장하는 [b], [v], [p], [r] 발음에 주의하고 **긴 문장**들의 경우 **끊어 읽기**에 더 신경 써서 읽는다. |

| 어휘 | **avenue** 거리, ~가   **remind** 상기시키다   **bathmats** 욕실용 매트   **additional** 추가의 **cash register** 금전 등록기 |

Question 2

01-12-02

Hello / and **thank you** ↗ / for **coming** to the **product launch** ↗ / of this **exciting new innovative battery.** ↘ // This **battery** can be **recharged** / by **solar,** ↗ / **wind** ↗ / and **hydro power.** ↘ // The light on the **right** of the **battery** ↗ / gives a **constant indication** / for **what** is **needed** ↗ / and the **light** / will exhibit a **progressively brighter red light** ↗ / to **show** the **need** / to be **recharged.** ↘

안녕하십니까. 이 흥분되고 새롭고 획기적인 배터리의 제품 출시 기념행사에 와주셔서 감사합니다. 본 배터리는 태양력, 풍력 및 수력으로 충전될 수 있습니다. 배터리 우측에 있는 불빛은 무엇이 필요한지에 대해 항시 표시해주며, 충전이 필요하다는 것을 보여주기 위해 불빛은 점차적으로 더욱 밝고 붉은 빛을 나타낼 것입니다.

| 고득점 TIP | 신상품의 출시를 알리는 글이다. [l], [r] 발음이 자주 나오므로 주의해서 읽는다. **열거하는 부분의 억양**과, **긴 주어 및 접속사 부분의 끊어 읽기**에 주의한다. |

| 어휘 | **product launch** 제품 출시(행사)   **innovative** 획기적인   **recharge** (재)충전하다   **hydro power** 수력 **constant** 끊임없는   **indication** 조심   **exhibit** 보이다   **progressively** 점진적으로 |

Question 3 Describe a Picture

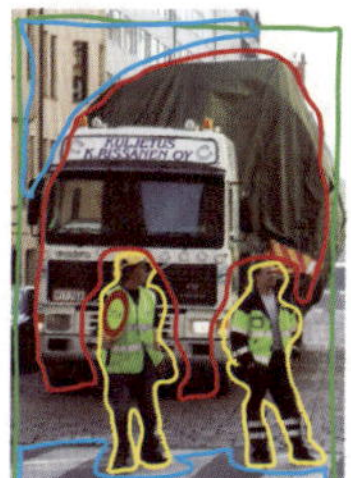

━ 도입 ━ 중심 ━ 주변 ━ 마무리

|고득점|
|T I P|
거리 및 횡단보도 사진도 꾸준히 등장한다. **두 명의 공통점을 먼저 언급**하고 각 인물의 특징을 설명한다.
'**안전보호장비, ~을 들고 있다, 주머니에 손을 넣고 있다**' 등과 같이 자주 나오는 표현에 주의한다.

Question 3   01-12-03

초·중급 Model Answer

This picture appears to be on a city road. The first thing I notice is two men standing on the crosswalk. They are wearing light green safety gear and looking to the right. The man on the left is wearing a yellow helmet and holding a sign saying "stop". The other man on the right has his hands in his pockets. Behind them, there is a big white truck with a big load covered with a green canopy. It seems that there is some road construction nearby.

이 사진은 도시의 도로에서 찍힌 것 같습니다. 처음 눈에 띄는 것은 횡단보도에 서 있는 두 남성입니다. 그들은 옅은 녹색 안전 장비를 착용하고 있으며 우측을 바라보고 있습니다. 왼쪽에 있는 남성은 노란색 헬멧을 쓰고 있고 "STOP"이라고 적혀 있는 표지판을 들고 있습니다. 오른쪽에 있는 다른 남성은 주머니에 손을 넣고 있습니다. 그들 뒤에는 큰 흰색 트럭이 있는데, 화물이 가득 실려 있고 녹색 덮개로 덮여 있습니다. 근처에 도로 공사가 진행되고 있는 것 같습니다.

고급 Model Answer

This picture appears to be on a city street. The first thing I notice is two men standing in the middle of a crosswalk in the street. Both men are wearing bright green reflective safety gear and looking to the right. The man on the left has a yellow hard hat on and his reflective gear is a vest. Additionally, he is holding a stop sign. The man on the right is wearing a reflective safety coat and has some stripes on the bottom of his pants. In addition, he has his hands in his pockets. Behind these two men is a large white truck with an oversized load covered by a green tarp. It seems that this is a residential area because of the buildings in the background.

이 사진은 도시의 거리에서 찍힌 것 같습니다. 처음 눈에 띄는 것은 거리의 횡단보도 중간에 서 있는 두 남성입니다. 두 남성 모두 빛을 반사하는 밝은 녹색의 안전 장비를 착용하고 있으며 우측을 바라보고 있습니다. 왼쪽에 있는 남성은 노란색 안전모를 쓰고 있고 그의 빛을 반사하는 보호 장비는 조끼입니다. 또한 그는 STOP 표지판을 들고 있습니다. 오른쪽에 있는 남성은 빛을 반사하는 보호용 코트를 입고 있으며 바지 밑부분에는 약간의 줄무늬가 있습니다. 추가로 그는 주머니에 손을 넣고 있습니다. 이 두 남성 뒤에는 큰 흰색 트럭이 있는데, 녹색 방수포로 덮인 화물이 가득 실려 있습니다. 배경에 있는 건물들을 보니 이 지역은 주택가인 것 같습니다.

|어 휘| **crosswalk** 횡단보도   **safety gear** 안전 장비   **load** 화물   **canopy** 덮개   **nearby** 근처에
reflective 빛을 반사하는   **tarp** 방수포   **residential** 주택지의

Actual Test 12

Questions 4-6 Respond to Questions

Imagine that an American marketing firm is conducting research in your country. You have agreed to participate in a telephone interview about American food.

미국의 한 마케팅 회사가 당신의 나라에서 설문 조사를 하고 있다고 가정해 보세요. 당신은 '미국 음식'에 관한 전화 인터뷰에 응하기로 동의했습니다.

Question 4

 01-12-04

Q. How often do you cook at home and have you ever cooked American food?

얼마나 자주 집에서 직접 요리를 합니까? 미국 음식을 요리해 본 적이 있습니까?

초·중급 Model Answer

A. I usually cook at home five or six times a week. I have cooked American food before and once I had a cook out at an American friend's house.

저는 보통 일주일에 대여섯 번은 집에서 요리를 합니다. 예전에 미국 음식을 요리해 본 적이 있고, 한번은 미국인 친구 집을 방문해 야외에서 요리를 해먹기도 했습니다.

고급 Model Answer

A. I usually cook at home five or six times a week because it's less expensive. I have cooked American food before several times and I once went to a real barbeque cook out at an American friend's house.

저는 보통 일주일에 대여섯 번은 집에서 요리를 합니다. 왜냐하면 더 저렴하기 때문입니다. 전에 미국 음식을 몇 번 요리해 본 적이 있고, 한번은 미국인 친구의 집에서 실제로 야외 바비큐 파티를 하기도 했습니다.

고득점 TIP 두 가지 질문에 대해 **모두 답변**을 해야 한다. **Have you ever~** 처럼 **경험을 물어보는 경우**, 특히 **4번 문제**에서는 **그러한 경험이 있다**고 해야 5번, 6번의 **관련 질문**에 답하기가 수월하다.

Question 5

 01-12-05

Q. What kinds of American food do you think are better to eat at a restaurant than to cook at home?

집에서 직접 해먹는 것보다 레스토랑에서 사먹는 것이 더 낫다고 생각하는 미국 음식에는 무엇이 있습니까?

초·중급 Model Answer

A. I think it is better to eat hamburgers and fries at the restaurant because it is fast and easy. I eat hamburgers and fries at fast food restaurants once a week.

햄버거와 감자튀김은 레스토랑에서 사먹는 것이 더 빠르고 쉽기 때문에 더 낫다고 생각합니다. 저는 일주일에 한 번씩 패스트푸드 레스토랑에서 햄버거와 감자튀김을 먹습니다.

A. Burger and fries are always better at a restaurant because it takes so long to prepare everything at home. Spaghetti on the other hand is something I am picky about the taste so I do that at home.

햄버거와 감자튀김은 레스토랑에서 먹는 것이 항상 더 낫습니다. 왜냐하면 집에서 요리하기 위해 이것저것 준비하느라 너무 오랜 시간이 걸리기 때문입니다. 반면에 스파게티는 제가 그 맛에 민감한 음식이기 때문에 집에서 직접 해먹습니다.

고득점 TIP **일반적으로 생각해내기 쉬운 햄버거와 감자튀김으로** 답했다. 집에서 만들어 먹기에는 조금 번거로운 음식들이다.

Question 6

🎧 01-12-06

Q. Do you think you are a good cook with American food? Why? Would cooking classes help?

본인이 미국 음식을 잘 한다고 생각합니까? 그 이유는 무엇입니까? 요리 학원이 도움이 될 것이라고 생각합니까?

A. I don't think I am a good cook with American food. Many of my friends who have tasted my American cooking say it is not cooked right. Some say it needs more cooking and some say it needs less. I would like to take cooking classes if I could as I think that would be very helpful for me.

제가 미국 음식을 잘 만든다고는 생각하지 않습니다. 제가 요리한 미국 음식을 맛 본 많은 친구들이 요리법이 잘못되었다는 말을 했습니다. 어떤 친구들은 조금 더 요리할 필요가 있다고 하고, 또 다른 친구들은 조금 덜 요리해야 한다고 합니다. 요리 수업은 저에겐 매우 도움이 될 것 같아 가능하다면 수강하고 싶습니다.

A. I am not a very good cook when it comes to American food. Most of my friends and family that have tasted my cooking say it's either overcooked or undercooked. Cooking classes might be just what the doctor ordered as I would enjoy learning a new skill and additionally I would like to learn how to use more spices.

미국 음식에 관해서 제가 그다지 훌륭한 요리사는 아닌 것 같습니다. 제 음식을 맛 본 대부분의 친구들이나 가족들은 너무 많이 혹은 지나치게 덜 요리되었다고 말합니다. 요리 수업은 저에게 아주 안성맞춤일 것 같습니다. 왜냐하면 저는 새로운 기술을 배우는 것을 즐기고, 또한 더 많은 양념을 사용하는 방법을 배우고 싶기 때문입니다.

고득점 TIP **5번, 6번 문제는 꼭 긍정적으로만 답할 필요는 없다.** 잘 못한다고 할 경우 그 근거가 되는 주위의 반응을 말할 수도 있고, 요리 학원이 도움이 될 것이라는 식으로 해당 질문에 대해서도 자연스럽게 답변을 연결할 수 있다.

어휘 **cook** 요리하다, 요리사　**expensive** 비싼　**prepare** 준비하다　**on the other hand** 반면에　**picky** 까다로운
taste 맛(보다)　**when it comes to** ~에 관한 한　**either** (둘 중) 어느 하나
just what the doctor ordered 정확히 필요한

 **Questions 7-9** Respond to Questions Using Information Provided

Travel Itinerary – Keith Grace

The annual conference for IT Professionals
Marriot Conference Center, Main Hall
Marriot Hotel
100 Marriot Drive
Boston, MA

	▸ **Friday May 13**
11 A.M.-3:30 P.M.	Delta Flight 156 Atlanta to Boston Change planes in Memphis (Shuttle bus to the Hotel)
6:30 P.M.	Welcome dinner @ The Marriot Restaurant and social mixer to follow
	▸ **Saturday May 14**
9 A.M.-3 P.M.	Conference and meetings
5:00 P.M.	Dinner with sub-committee
	▸ **Sunday May 15**
9 A.M.-11 A.M.	Delta Flight 155 Boston to Atlanta (Direct flight)

여행 일정표 - Keith Grace

IT 전문가 연례 회의
Marriot 회의장, 대강당
Marriot 호텔
100 Marriot Drive
Boston, MA

	▸ **5월 13일, 금요일**
오전 11시 ~ 오후 3시 30분	Delta 156 편 Atlanta 출발 Boston 도착 Memphis 경유 (셔틀버스로 호텔 이동)
오후 6시 30분	Marriot 레스토랑에서 환영 만찬 후 파티
	▸ **5월 14일, 토요일**
오전 9시 ~ 오후 3시	회의
오후 5시	분과 위원회 만찬
	▸ **5월 15일, 일요일**
오전 9시 ~ 오전 11시	Delta 155 편 Boston 출발 Atlanta 도착 (직항)

Hello, this is Grace Keith. I'm going to travel to Boston for the annual IT conference but I haven't got the travel itinerary yet. Would you please give me some details on it?

안녕하세요, Grace Keith입니다. 연례 IT 회의를 위해 Boston으로 여행을 할 예정인데 아직 여행 일정표를 받지 못했습니다. 그것에 대한 자세한 내용을 좀 알 수 있을까요?

Q. Where will the conference be held? 회의는 어디서 개최되나요?

초·중급 Model Answer

A. The annual conference for IT Professionals this year will be held at the Marriot Conference Center in the Main Hall of the Marriot Hotel in Boston.

올해 IT 전문가 연례 회의는 Boston에 있는 Marriot 호텔의 Marriot 회의장 대강당에서 개최됩니다.

고급 Model Answer

A. The conference this year will be held at the Marriot Conference Center in the Main Hall of the Marriot Hotel in Boston. The conference and meetings will be on Saturday the 14th with the dinner and social mixer on Friday the 13th.

올해 IT 전문가 회의는 Boston에 있는 Marriot 호텔의 Marriot 회의장 대강당에서 개최됩니다. 회의는 14일 토요일에 개최되며 만찬 및 파티는 13일 금요일에 예정되어 있습니다.

고득점 TIP 7번에서는 **전체 행사의 장소나 시간을 물어보는 경우**가 많다. 답변 시 **전치사 표현**에 주의하고, 질문에는 없더라도 날짜와 같은 간단한 내용은 덧붙이는 것이 좋다.

Q. I have some personal affairs on Saturday afternoon. Is there any free time on Saturday afternoon? 토요일 오후에 사적인 용무가 좀 있습니다. 토요일 오후에 자유 시간이 있나요?

초·중급 Model Answer

A. Yes, there is some free time on Saturday afternoon. The conference and meetings will end at 3 P.M. and you will have a dinner with your sub-committee at 5 P.M.

네, 토요일 오후에 약간의 자유 시간이 주어집니다. 회의는 오후 3시에 끝날 예정이며 오후 5시에 분과 위원회 만찬에 참석하시면 됩니다.

고급 Model Answer

A. Yes, you will have two hours free time between the end of the conference and the dinner with your sub-committee. The conference will end at 3 P.M. on Saturday and the dinner is at 5 P.M.

네, 회의가 끝난 후 분과 위원회 만찬까지 2시간의 자유 시간이 있습니다. 회의는 토요일 오후 3시에 끝나며 만찬은 오후 5시입니다.

고득점 TIP **Saturday afternoon, free time** 이라는 **keyword**를 듣고 답할 수 있다. **be동사로 질문**했으므로 **첫 대답은 yes/no로** 답하는 것이 좋다.

01-12-09

Q. Could you tell me the flight schedule? 비행 일정 좀 알려주실 수 있나요?

초·중급 Model Answer

A. Sure, you will leave Atlanta at 11 A.M. on Friday the 13th on Delta flight 156 for Boston. You will arrive in Boston at 3:30 P.M. and you will have a shuttle bus to The Marriott Hotel. Your return flight will be on Sunday the 15th on Delta flight 155. It will leave Boston at 9 A.M. You should arrive back in Atlanta around 11 A.M.

물론입니다. 당신은 13일 금요일 오전 11시에 Delta 156편으로 Atlanta에서 Boston을 향해 출발할 것입니다. 그 후 오후 3시 30분에 Boston에 도착할 것이며, Marriot 호텔까지 셔틀버스를 타고 가시면 됩니다. 돌아오는 항공편은 Delta 155편으로 15일 일요일 비행기입니다. Boston에서 오전 9시에 출발합니다. 오전 11시경에 Atlanta에 도착할 것입니다.

고급 Model Answer

A. Sure, no problem, your flight out is leaving Atlanta at 11 A.M. on Friday the 13th. You will be on Delta flight 156 and you will change planes in Memphis. You should be in Boston around 3:30 P.M. where you can catch a shuttle bus to The Marriot. Your flight home will be on Sunday the 15th. You will be returning on Delta flight 155 which is a direct flight leaving Boston at 9 A.M. and you should be back in Atlanta around 11 A.M.

물론입니다. 당신은 13일 금요일 오전 11시에 Atlanta를 출발합니다. Delta 156편이며 Memphis를 경유할 것입니다. 오후 3시 30분에 Boston에 도착 예정이며, Marriot 호텔까지 셔틀버스를 타고 가실 수 있습니다. 돌아오는 항공편은 15일 일요일에 있습니다. 직항 Delta 155편으로 오전 9시에 Boston을 출발해서 오전 11시경에 Atlanta에 도착할 것입니다.

고득점 TIP flight schedule이라고 했으므로 **출발/경유/도착지 위주**로 표현한다. **leave, arrive** 등의 **동사**와 **전치사** 표현에 주의하고, **비행기 번호는 한 자리씩 끊어서** 읽는다.

어휘 **itinerary** 여행 일정표　**annual** 매년의　**professional** 전문가　**sub-committee** 분과 위원회
direct flight 직항편　**personal affairs** 사적인 일

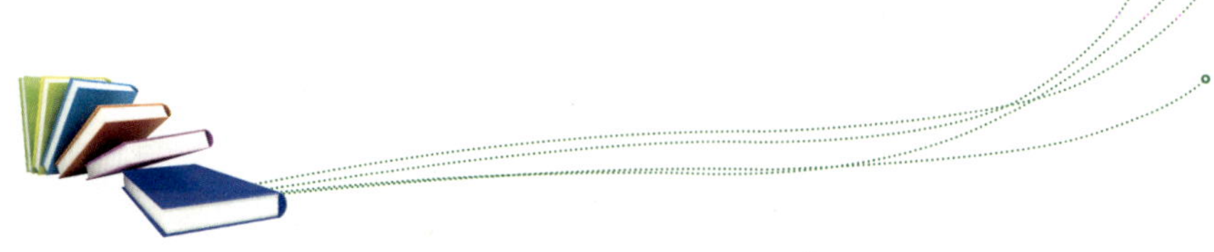

Question 10 Propose a solution

Hello, this is John Williams at the Westlake Community Center. As you know our community center has been providing a variety of services to the community for the past 20 years. We have held everything from educational programs to sports events to conventions and the people of the community have really enjoyed what we have done through the years. Next week the community center is planning on holding an appreciation party for the people who have made us so popular. I really want to do this right and as a result I am calling you to get some advice since you have been working in event promotions for the last 8 years. I would really appreciate and treasure your advice. Once again this is John Williams at Westlake Community Center.

안녕하세요, 저는 Westlake 시민 문화회관에서 근무하는 John Williams라고 합니다. 아시다시피, 저희 회관은 지난 20년동안 지역 사회에 다양한 서비스를 제공하고 있습니다. 저희는 교육적인 프로그램에서부터 스포츠 행사나 컨벤션 등 모든 행사를 개최해왔고, 지역 주민들도 저희가 지난 수년 동안 해온 행사들을 진심으로 즐겨주셨습니다. 다음 주에 저희 회관에서는 저희를 여기까지 올 수 있도록 만들어 주신 분들을 위해 감사 연회를 열고자 합니다. 이번 일을 정말 차질 없이 진행하고 싶어서 조언을 좀 구하고자 이렇게 연락을 드립니다. 왜냐하면 당신은 지난 8년 동안 행사 홍보 및 기획 분야에 종사하고 계시기 때문입니다. 조언을 해주신다면 진심으로 감사하겠습니다. 다시 한번 말씀 드리면 저는 Westlake 시민 문화회관의 John Williams입니다.

01-12-10

초·중급 Model Answer

Hello, John this is Tom from Alpha Dog Promotions. I am sorry I missed your call about your upcoming celebration. As I understand it, you are basically having an appreciation party next week and you would like some ideas of how to make it special. First, let me say thank you for asking for my advice. I would like to suggest that you have something that everyone gets for free when they come that will remind them of the Westlake Community Center every day. A calendar would be something many people use and see all the time. I can connect you with some companies that provide give away material if you would like. Feel free to call me back anytime or email me at: tom@alphadogpromotions.com

안녕하세요 John, 저는 Alpha Dog Promotions의 Tom입니다. 곧 있을 당신의 기념 행사에 관한 전화를 받지 못해서 죄송합니다. 제가 이해한 바로는, 당신은 기본적으로 다음 주에 감사 연회를 열 계획이며 그 연회를 특별하게 만들 수 있는 아이디어를 원하시는 것 같습니다. 우선은 제게 의견을 요청해 주신 것에 대해 감사드립니다. Westlake 시민 문화회관을 매일 기억할 수 있도록 사람들이 방문했을 때 모두에게 무료로 무엇인가를 배포하는 것을 제안하고 싶습니다. 예를 들어, 달력은 많은 사람들이 항상 사용하고 바라보는 것입니다. 원하신다면 기념품을 제작하는 몇몇 업체들을 소개해 드릴 수 있습니다. 부담 갖지 마시고 언제든지 다시 연락 주세요. 아니면 tom@alphadogpromotions.com으로 이메일을 보내주시기 바랍니다.

Hello, John this is Tom with Alpha Dog Promotions. I apologize for not being able to get your call about your upcoming celebration. If I understand you right, you are throwing a big appreciation party for the community and you would like some input from us on how to make it memorable. First, let me say that I really am grateful for everything you do for the community and I am honored to help. Have you considered giving something to everyone that comes? We have a number of connections with promotional product companies that make personalized pens and that sort of thing. In addition to that you might consider having balloons for the kids which is always a winner. Please feel free to call me again or contact me through email at tom@alphadogpromotions.com for more thoughts and assistance.

안녕하세요 John, 저는 Alpha Dog Promotions의 Tom입니다. 곧 있을 당신의 기념 행사에 관한 전화를 받지 못해서 죄송합니다. 제가 맞게 이해했다면, 당신은 지역 사회를 위해 큰 감사 연회를 열 예정이고 그것을 기억에 남을 만한 행사로 만들 수 있는 방법에 대해 저희에게 조언을 구하시는 것 같습니다. 우선은, 당신이 지역 사회를 위해서 하시는 모든 일에 대해 진심으로 감사하다는 말씀을 전하고 싶고 제가 도움을 드릴 수 있게 되어서 영광으로 생각합니다. 오시는 모든 분들에게 무엇인가를 선물해 주는 것을 고려해 보셨는지요? 저희는 방문객 본인의 이름을 새겨 넣을 수 있는 펜을 비롯해 다른 여러 종류의 판촉물을 제작하는 다수의 회사들과 친분이 있어 쉽게 연결해 드릴 수 있습니다. 더불어서 아이들에게 항상 좋은 선물이 되는 풍선을 준비하는 것도 고려해볼 수 있을 것입니다. 좀 더 많은 의견이나 도움이 필요하시면 부담 갖지 마시고 다시 연락 주시거나 tom@alphadogpromotions.com으로 이메일을 보내주시기 바랍니다.

|고득점 T I P| 감사연회를 열기 위해서 **조언**을 구하는 문제이다. 마지막 부분에서 언급한 것처럼 행사를 기획하는 **전문가 입장**에서 대답한다. **펜, 달력**과 같은 **사은품**이나 아이들을 위한 **풍선** 등을 생각해 볼 수 있다.

|어 휘| **community center** 지역 문화회관 **a variety of** 다양한 **convention** (대규모) 협의회
appreciation 감사 **treasure** 귀하게 여기다 **upcoming** 곧 있을 **for free** 무료로 **remind** 상기시키다
apologize 사과하다 **throw a party** 파티를 열다 **input** 조언 **memorable** 기억할 만한
grateful 감사하는 **personalize** (개인 소유물) 표시를 하다 **balloon** 풍선 **assistance** 도움

Question 11 Express an Opinion

Do you agree with this statement? 'In order for a business to succeed it needs to have a continual flow of new customers as well as dedicated regular customers.' Give specific reasons or examples to support your opinion.

당신은 다음 의견에 동의하십니까? '사업이 성공하기 위해서는 충성스러운 고정 고객뿐만 아니라 끊임없는 신규 고객의 유입 또한 필요하다.' 당신의 의견을 뒷받침할 구체적인 근거나 사례를 제시하세요.

Questions 11　　　　　　　　　　　　　　　　　　　　　　　01-12-11

초·중급 Model Answer

I agree that in order for a business to succeed it needs to have a continual flow of new customers as well as dedicated regular customers. I have several reasons why I agree with this opinion. First, a business has to grow and in order to grow it must have new customers who will buy from them. This shows that the business is developing and growing in its reputation. Secondly, the business must have dedicated regular customers because this shows that the business is good and takes care of its customers. If no one wants to return to the business everyone will think that they are no good. For these reasons, I go along with this statement.

저는 사업이 성공하기 위해서는 충성스러운 고정 고객뿐만 아니라 끊임없는 신규 고객의 유입 또한 필요하다는 의견에 동의합니다. 제가 이 의견에 동의하는 몇 가지 이유가 있습니다. 첫째, 사업은 성장을 해야 하고 성장을 하기 위해서는 제품을 구매할 신규 고객들을 반드시 확보해야 합니다. 이는 사업이 평판대로 발전하고 성장하고 있다는 것을 보여줍니다. 둘째로, 사업에 있어서 충성스러운 고정 고객들도 반드시 필요합니다. 왜냐하면 이것은 사업이 잘 되고 있고, 고객들에게 많은 관심을 쏟고 있다는 것을 보여주기 때문입니다. 만약 아무도 재구매를 하고 싶어 하지 않는다면, 모든 사람들은 해당 기업이 좋지 않다고 생각할 것입니다. 이러한 이유들 때문에, 저는 이 의견에 동의합니다.

고급 Model Answer

I agree with this opinion. Businesses need to have both the new customers who develop and grow the company as well as the dedicated return customers which are the backbone of the business. I have several reasons why I believe this opinion is correct. First, a business must be expanding and that means new customers and new markets. If the business doesn't have new blood coming in the door, it will not grow past its current reach. Secondly, the regular customers create a sense of stability and security for the company. The customer that comes back is saying that the business must have something of value or they wouldn't be coming back. For the above reasons, I go along with this statement and I feel like it is the cornerstone of a successful business.

저는 이 의견에 동의합니다. 기업은 사업의 중추적인 역할을 하는 충성스러운 재구매 고객뿐만 아니라 사업을 발전시키고 성장시킬 수 있는 신규 고객 모두 필요합니다. 제가 이 의견이 옳다고 생각하는 데에는 몇 가지 이유가 있습니다. 첫째, 사업은 꼭 확장되어야 하고 이는 곧 신규 고객과 신규 시장을 의미합니다. 새로 들어오는 신규 고객이 없다면 그 사업은 현재의 도달점 이상으로 성장할 수 없을 것입니다. 둘째로, 고정 고객은 기업으로 하여금 안정감을 느낄 수 있도록 합니다. 재구매를 하는 고객이 있다는 것은 그 사업이 가치 있는 무엇인가를 분명히 보유하고 있다는 것을 의미하고, 그렇지 않다면 고객들은 다시 오지 않을 것입니다. 위와 같은 이유들로 저는 이 의견에 동의하며, 이러한 점은 성공적인 기업의 초석이라고 생각합니다.

고득점 TIP | 기업에 있어서 충성스러운 **기존 고객**들처럼 **신규 고객**도 중요한가를 묻는 문제이다. **양 쪽 고객들의 필요성을 각각 언급**하면 자연스럽게 두 가지 근거를 제시할 수 있다

| 어 휘 | **in order to** ~하기 위하여　**continual** 끊임없는　**flow** 흐름　**as well as** ~에 더하여　**dedicated** 헌신적인
reputation 평판　**go along with** ~에 동의하다　**backbone** 중추　**expand** 확장되다
new blood 새로운 인물　**stability** 안정성　**security** 보장, 안심　**cornerstone** 초석

TOEIC SPEAKING Actual Test

모범답안 · 해설

★ 최신 출제 경향 분석,
　최신 기출 변형 모의고사 15회 수록

★ 중급자는 만점, 초보자는 레벨 6 공략 가능하도록
　초·중급, 고급 답변 2개씩 수록

★ 100% 실전 활용 가능한 고득점 TIP 제공

Read a
text aloud
Describe a
Picture
Respond to
Questions

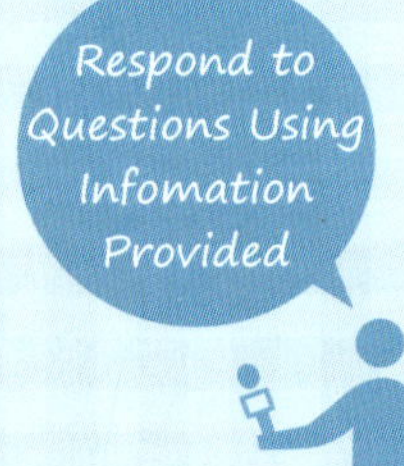

Respond to Questions Using Infomation Provided

Propose a Solution

Express an Opinion